Shady lives with her partner, Scott, in the Illawarra and teaches creative writing at the University of Wollongong. Before that she was a journalist with John Fairfax Holdings. Her short stories and articles have appeared in *Best Australian Stories 2006*, *Antipodes*, *Southerly*, *Overland*, the *Illawarra Mercury*, the *Sydney Morning Herald* and the *Melbourne Age*.

SHE PLAYED ELVIS

A pilgrimage to Graceland

Shady Cosgrove

ALLEN&UNWIN

First published in Australia in 2009

Allen & Unwin
83 Alexander Street
Crows Nest NSW 2065
Australia
Phone: (61 2) 8425 0100
Fax: (61 2) 9906 2218
Email: info@allenandunwin.com
Web: www.allenandunwin.com

Cataloguing-in-Publication details are available
from the National Library of Australia
www.librariesaustralia.nla.gov.au

ISBN 978 1 74175 724 8

Set in 11.5/14 pt Garamond Premier Pro by Bookhouse, Sydney
Printed and bound in Australia by Griffin Press

10 9 8 7 6 5 4 3 2 1

CONTENTS

'Before Elvis, there was nothing.'

—John Lennon

'Elvis Presley's death deprives our country of a part of itself. He was unique, irreplaceable.'

—US President Jimmy Carter, 1977

'I've a reason to believe we all will be received in Graceland.'

—Paul Simon

THAT'S ALL RIGHT

I'm with my family when Elvis offers the first sign.

We're sitting at the dining table after three bottles of wine and a salmon barbecue. My little sister and brother have gone to bed and my mother is wiping her plate with a crust of sourdough. She stops and beams at me. It'll soon be time for her to start telling me how much she loves me, which is nice to hear but there's something overindulgent about our family displays.

'I am so thankful you're visiting . . .' She announces each syllable, pausing between words for effect.

I glance at the ceiling. The room tilts slightly and my gaze catches on the stained-glass lamp—it's like I can feel the smooth red-orange-yellow sections just by looking at them.

Next to me on the piano bench, my boyfriend Scott nudges me in the back. He loves my melodramatic family who need to discuss every feeling in relentless detail but I step on his foot and concentrate on staring back at my mother. It's a little hard for me to focus without laughing: she's just dyed her crew-cut bright pink.

'It's nice to be here, Mom.' Even with how much I've missed her, the 'mom' is ironic—I've always called her by her given name, Irene—but I *am* glad to be here. I've missed Vashon Island. It's where I grew up—a short ferry ride from Seattle, tucked in the northwest corner of the United States. On the other side of the world, in Australia, my life has been hesitant, wondering: have I chosen the right home?

Irene turns to my stepfather, Jim, who's piling the empty plates at the end of the table, scraping each one with slow ceremony. He has strong hands and thin legs. He used to be a carpenter before he joined our family and began working with my mother on the tiles.

'Aren't you glad to have them here?' Irene asks him, pushing up her sleeves. The cuffs of her lavender cashmere sweater are streaked with glaze.

'Couldn't be happier.' Jim raises his eyebrows at Scott like the two are contestants in a game show on handling emotional women. He eases to his feet and takes the stack to the kitchen counter, sidestepping a pile of laundry on the floor.

With only the wilted tub of ice-cream and our glasses left, the table looks too bare. In a house that's never clean and rarely tidy, every other surface is cluttered—books and CDs are stacked on top of the piano, newspapers splayed open on the couch.

Jim looks back at us from the sink. His blue eyes seem even more intense with his summer tan but his hair is finally beginning to thin. Approaching fifty, he's eight years younger than my mother and for a while the gap appeared much bigger. 'So how you getting to Memphis?'

I top up my glass for this one and Scott pats my leg under the table. In five days, we'll be leaving on a pilgrimage to Graceland. Considering my fondness for plans and lists, you'd think I'd know how we're getting there but it's been hard committing to any one plan because Scott and I are on a tight budget and with each possibility there's this ever-elusive hope that something cheaper will come up. At this point, all I have is a desire to understand my home, and a willing travel partner.

'It's a long way,' Jim says. Behind him, the kitchen is grouted with bright pieces of colour and it's like the walls are dancing without music. Most of the designs are my mother's—a pair of red shoes with stars on them, a beach scene through an open window—but they've been cut into a series of square and rectangular mosaics.

'What about the hatchback that was listed?' Jim continues.

'Too expensive.'

Focusing on the table, I reach for the ice-cream. The block has melted but we don't have Ben & Jerry's in Australia so I dig deep anyway, scooping out the chocolate-covered peanut-butter pretzels. The alcohol has overridden any will for restraint.

'I've saved the classifieds,' Irene says. Then, scooting over to the stereo cabinet like this will solve everything, 'How about some Elvis?'

A five-disc tray pops open in front of her and she sets a CD inside. The twangy guitar jumps out of the speakers and Elvis starts singing 'That's All Right' like life is so good he can only laugh.

Irene is now tapping her foot with an exaggerated knee lift and stepping back and forth, which only emphasises her floral bicycle shorts. I glance at Scott, embarrassed and proud of her, but he's clapping along and grinning. His smile takes up his whole big face and it's obvious I'm the most uptight person in the room.

'It'll work out. Come on,' she says.

I stand, pushing a chair out of the way, and unhook a papier-mâché frog that hangs from the ceiling at forehead level. We shift the table and roll back one of my mother's rag rugs. The sense of ritual is heightened by the life-sized Virgin Mary over the fireplace. Her gown and halo are pieced together with bright jagged bits of tile—fierce dark blues, festive reds. Behind her, the speckled black glaze gives the impression she's suspended in space. Despite the fact that my mother's been working on her for five years, our family isn't Catholic, it's non-denominational—or perhaps 'pro-denominational' better describes it. There are over fifty representations of the Virgin around the house: paintings, tiles, icons. Concrete statues of the Buddha meditate in the upper garden. A many-armed Kali watches over Irene as she glazes downstairs. Our favourite family hymns are from the south of the United States and centre on praying down at the riverside, though we don't go to church. Irene never baptised us as kids but we can belt out 'Wayfaring Stranger' like we're packing for a journey to Jordan.

Irene's hands are slippery as we swing dance in the open living room. She only stands as tall as my chin and the rule is that whoever's tallest leads, but she gets too excited for the steady beat, urging us faster and faster. I backtrack us through a move my older sister showed us on my last visit to the States. 'No, you go under here.'

Jim hands Scott another beer and my boyfriend nods back, his large frame part of the gesture. They're preparing for the group hug that will soon seem like such a great idea to my mother.

Irene follows through my arms but our hands don't meet up; we let go and try again. Jim claps anyway and my arrival home feels prodigal, fated. Across the living room, the mirrors that line the Virgin glint movement back to us. Someone's lit the candles.

When the song's over, Irene retreats to the stereo and pushes the track number back. In the slight pause, she picks up the CD cover. 'Hey, look at this.'

Elvis starts up again and she turns down the volume, handing me the case. At first I think she's showing me the mismatched liner notes—someone's stored the wrong disc in it. But then, on the inside sleeve of the cover, Elvis is standing in front of a Greyhound. The lettering is shaded, carved into the bus behind him.

Her smooth palm grabs mine. 'It's a sign. It's *all right* to take the Greyhound.'

I can imagine the camera panning in, the photograph of Elvis in sharp focus for this revelatory moment. I haven't ridden the bus in years, since college, when the experience left me with head lice, but my mother's staring into my eyes as though she's channelling the power of the King. Maybe it's the wine but her voice is uncharacteristically forceful. 'You're supposed to take the Greyhound.'

Even in our haze, there's an underlying logic to the plan. America may be a road trip country but we don't have to travel by car. As transportation goes, the car is nothing more than a self-contained, overpriced box speeding along the freeway. The Greyhound fits within budget and offers a shared path across the United States. It'll be inevitable that I meet my country: isn't that exactly what I want?

Jim spritzes open his beer. 'I don't know, it's a long way to Memphis.' Jim's not renowned for travelling. He doesn't even like to venture off-island to Seattle.

'Of course it's a long way, that's the point,' my mother says. Her face is flushed the same shade as her hair. She grips my hand and I squeeze it back.

Outside through the balcony doors, the night sky pales towards the tree line; Seattle must be awake tonight. With the breeze, the room smells of cypress needles, sweat and incense.

Jim shakes his head slowly. 'If Scott and Shady found a picture of Elvis in front of a limousine, could they hire a chauffeur?'

Scott sets his beer down on the table in allegiance with my mother. 'It's too late. Elvis has spoken.' My boyfriend's having a laugh at me and my family—he believes in the power of cheap bus tickets rather than the spiritual voice of Elvis—but our decision is made.

Elvis has always been a central figure in our family music canon but my love for him came in 1986 with the release of Paul Simon's *Graceland*. I was twelve years old and the title track stirred a spooky longing within me. I played it over and over on my birthday ghetto blaster, keeping track of the spinning numbers in the tape counter so I could stop rewinding it in exactly the right spot.

Even though it was about a road trip, the introductory bass line reminded me of a mystery train ambling across America. The song was a story of pilgrimage, a man travelling to Graceland with his nine-year-old son, the child from his first marriage. I was only pre-adolescent but that casual detail seemed so heartbreaking—maybe because I was a child from a first marriage, maybe because the song itself was about suffering heartbreak. The words echoed loss; the singer had been left by his wife, but there was also a sense of hope and that hope lived at Graceland— all you had to do was get there. Simon mentioned pilgrims and families as though we were all searching for our family trees, searching for ourselves amid ancestral ghosts. The song exudes a loneliness, but not an entirely unpleasant loneliness. Even now when the last notes fade, I'm nostalgic for the singer's experience— like a series of snapshots, I imagine the glove box filled with cassette tapes and his son riffling through them, or the dusty sunshine at a gas station as the driver fills the tank.

After discovering Paul Simon, I rediscovered Elvis. His albums had always been in my mother's music collections. When our family danced together after dinner, his upbeat early numbers always featured right after dessert and his slower ballads signalled we'd soon be disbanding for bed. But after hearing Paul Simon, I began to listen to Elvis by myself, turning the volume down low even on the rocking numbers, as though there was some secret to his music I didn't want to share. I borrowed my mother's cassettes without telling her and even purchased my own with saved allowances—first the hit singles, then the country ballads and the gospel numbers. The *Sun Sessions* was played so often the shiny tape broke. It took a surgical procedure to repair it—using my sister's miniature screwdriver I opened the case and pieced the black ribbon together with Scotch tape. I trimmed it to feed easily through the player and the album kept going with only a slight glitch in the second chorus of 'Blue Moon of Kentucky'.

The idea of a pilgrimage had come to me from Heather, an old friend from college. We had the kind of friendship that was punctuated with bursts of email—long gaps in communication and then a stream of frenetic messages popping up in each other's inboxes.

In 2002, I wrote: *I'm flying out of Australia on May 30th. Scott and I are going to travel my country. I need something from my homeland. What, exactly? I don't know. But it's like that old Paul Simon song—I need to be received.*

She replied: *If you really want to see the United States, come back for Elvis. It's the twenty-fifth anniversary of his death—August 16. You can't miss that. Maybe you need to be received at Graceland.*

Before I finished reading the rest of Heather's email, my journey to Graceland became inevitable and busking a devoted extension.

If I was going to honour the King, I had to do it completely. I had to commit myself in some kind of public way. I'm not a professional musician but there was something humbling about performing in spite of that—what mattered was the songs, not the person singing them. I would be a conduit, giving voice to Elvis's legacy and influence and in some minuscule way that might add to his music's power.

I could justify the quest easily with my love for the King and those early cassettes, but there was a deeper purpose to my mission. I wanted to follow Paul Simon in recognition of his homage and this sense was so strong it surprised me, especially as his song was about negotiating loss. On the plane, I wondered if I was facing the immigrant's loss, the heartbreak of leaving a homeland. If so, a pilgrimage to Graceland made sense—academics have argued that Elvis acts as a symbolic American and a catalyst for the ways Americans think of themselves. The connection between Elvis and the United States was cemented when US President Jimmy Carter said Elvis's death deprived the country of a part of itself. I could think of no one more iconic than Elvis if I wanted to understand my country of birth.

The idea of being received was also connected to one of acceptance. I'd lived in Australia almost continuously since 1994 when I arrived at the University of Wollongong as an exchange

student. I returned to Vassar College in New York State to finish
my undergraduate degree the following year but came back to
the 'Gong as soon as finances would allow. I also had stints in
Sydney (waitressing) and Canberra (undertaking a PhD). As an
American living in Australia, I am more American than I ever
had to be in the United States. On Vashon most people share a
nationality but in Australia, when I open my mouth, I'm branded
a foreigner. Before Scott and I left Wollongong on this journey,
the new woman at the post office asked how my holiday was, and
when did I have to go 'home' to the States. She was trying to be
friendly but it reinforced a sense of not-belonging, that I'm a
puzzle piece stubbornly committed to the wrong space.

Sometimes it's more blatant—in the pub, a drunk guy at the
next table started yelling at me because he heard my accent and
hated American imperialism. I didn't feel like explaining that I'm
also wary of a global monoculture and for that reason support
local businesses—I only consume American chain products when
in the United States (and Starbucks, which I love, is a Seattle-only
treat because that's the city where it first began). The man's breath
was sour with beer, his long blond hair pulled back in a ponytail. I turned away, tired of being an American ambassador—
demonstrating to the rest of the world that Americans *can* be
critically engaged with the world and their government—and
didn't point out he was wearing a *Seinfeld* t-shirt.

One thing was certain: my discomfort with cultural imperialism
wasn't going to be assuaged by visiting Graceland. Elvis (via his
relationship with the quick-talking manager Colonel Tom Parker)
was arguably a pioneer of cultural capitalism—his image and
music are recognised worldwide and his house is a monument to
this 'success'. In that way, Elvis actually represented exactly what
made me uncomfortable with the United States. My ambivalence
reminded me of an Alex Gregory cartoon that appeared in the
New Yorker. Studded handwriting advertises 'Graceland Tours'
and beneath it are two ticket windows: 'Ironic' and 'Non-ironic'.
I wanted to take both tours. Part of me was drawn to Elvis and

his home; part of me wanted to gape in horror at the hub of Americana and stare down the throat of kitsch.

To some extent, my fascination with America came from growing up on its fringes. Vashon was a food-stamp, hippie enclave. Class roll included names like Sunshine, Leaf, Kwab, Rosebud and Unity. The demographic was well below middle class and most parents smoked pot. The euphemism in my family was 'air quality testing' when visitors went out on the balcony to smoke a joint. My best friend in third grade, Coba, had no running water for the toilet, only a drop latrine out back. Trailers and tired, beat-up cars littered most of the yards but even so, the term 'white trash' had little resonance, in part because of the rich green water and rocky beaches. The island's stoic, certain evergreens brokered the area between the shore and the town. With such regal beauty, the place—the land itself—demanded a respect deeper than socioeconomic class.

Twenty years later, a few people still live in teepees and trailers but with Microsoft came soaring Seattle real estate prices. Funky old pick-ups have been replaced with tank-force SUVs. Many old-time residents who didn't get in before the land rush opted for the Washington coast or northern Oregon. Even so, the island still attracts artists and oddballs. Most people don't lock their doors and the ageing reggae group still plays annual Halloween gigs at the Blue Heron Arts Center.

Every time I return to Vashon, I'm caught between talking high-speed with my mother or Jim—whoever picked us up from the airport—and focusing on how beautiful the island is. It towers with deep shades of foliage, the kind that only exists in places where it rains nine months of the year and trees are valued. But inevitably I start noticing the little changes: a cleared field, another shopfront. Most telling are the new driveways—their houses are rarely visible but brightly painted mailboxes mark their presence. The fifteen-minute boat ride to West Seattle has attracted commuters, lengthening the ferry queues. Despite this, Vashon isn't crowded yet. The only traffic signals are three flashing red lights positioned along the island's highway spine.

As a kid, I thought Vashon was huge but in fact it only measures about nineteen kilometres long and ten kilometres wide. On the eastern side, another island—Maury—connects to Vashon. It used to be separated by water but early town planners filled in the gap with gravel, to the dismay of present-day naturalists: this land-bridge has affected the tidal passage and salmon runs. Occasional cars at the post office and supermarket wear bumper stickers that read 'Free Maury Island'. I now understand why a conventional bridge would be better, that the gravel landfill has wreaked havoc on the marine environment, but growing up with hippies for parents inspired its own brand of cynicism. On summer nights when I was home from college, I used to drink red wine at the beach with my friend Meghan and make fun of the Free Maury activists. It was like they were a symbol of our home—a place where women (including my mother) posed naked in a large peace sign to protest the Iraq war and residents marched through the streets when there was talk of building a bridge between Vashon and the mainland. It seemed people on Vashon had to politicise everything, even the fish.

'Never mind world hunger, we've got to make sure those salmon have a place to breed,' I said one night to Meghan as we sat beside a dwindling bonfire, gazing across the harbour towards Maury's black-green trees.

She passed me the bottle, still wrapped in a paper bag, and cupped her hands to form a megaphone. 'What do we want?' she called out.

'A free Maury Island.' I stressed the syllables as though we were part of a demonstration. This was an ongoing joke between us—we turned local issues into protest chants partly to make fun of local issues and partly to make fun of protest chants.

'When do we want it?'

'Now!'

With a population that fluctuates between 11,000 (winter) and 15,000 (summer), Vashon has its own high school: my graduating class had eighty students—the majority I'd known since kindergarten. Islanders are forced acquaintances in part because we only have one movie theatre, one main post office and two supermarkets. In high school, this proximity was a mixed blessing: when my first boyfriend introduced me to his mother before the homecoming dance, I already knew her—she was my school bus driver. I'd never acted up on the school bus but had watched, complicit, when kids shouted and swore. Smiling at the camera in my skin-tight black knit dress, I wondered how much she remembered, and vowed to be forever kind to bus drivers.

The sense that the past is living around us is especially apparent in the ferry queue. The last time my mother picked Scott and me up from the Sea-Tac airport and pulled onto the dock, my high school band teacher was sitting in the car ahead of us and the boy who auditioned opposite me in *The Crucible* was walking along the white pylon fence, suddenly in man-form. I can't help myself—I love this familiarity. I always get out, careful not to open the door into the car nudged beside ours, and walk casually to the passenger area at the edge of the pier. Sometimes I stand outside the square building, looking back at West Seattle; sometimes I pretend I have to use the restroom inside.

The ferry demands an even greater awareness of time. Any new model Saab speeding down the empty dock, hoping the boom gate might lift, hasn't been on Vashon long. When that red and white arm drops, the ferry may as well have pulled away, so most cars and houses are littered with schedules. The drive to the dock and crossing time are factored into any estimated time of arrival. But even the most fastidious planner, who's checked the blue and pink print on the schedule taped to the phone, can't rely on the patron saint of ferries—one might be broken or delayed, waiting for an ambulance. Over the years, a number of children have been born en route to Seattle. One was even named after his vessel: Quinault, or Quin for short.

The morning that Scott and I leave Vashon, I check the ferry schedule three times. We arrive with ten minutes to spare and Jim drives us along the dock, passing the long string of vehicles waiting to board the next car ferry. The large boats are like green and white whales that migrate the short path between Vashon and West Seattle but we're taking the passenger-only to downtown. The small, pointed craft is already waiting; water churns white and frothy at its base.

'It's okay. The gate hasn't opened yet,' Jim says, shifting Ruby into second gear. Ruby is a red Ford Geo four-door—the only new car my family has ever owned. When my mother drove her out of the car lot, she sandpapered the glossy magenta finish and covered her with glitter and epoxy. Sparkling music notes, tiny saxophones, satiny hearts and glistening stars: it looks as if the car has been rolled in permanent confetti. At first, driving in Ruby was like manoeuvring a giant disco ball: people would honk and stare on the freeways and at gas stations. But my mother's inspirations aren't always maintained and no one has re-glittered Ruby in three or four years. The sequins are now faded and crusty, and the tiny tinsel pieces have collected dirt. When Jim eases onto the ferry dock, only a few people wait outside the terminal for the off-peak 9.40 am and because it's Vashon, no one pays attention to our eccentric car.

Jim pulls into the bus-loading zone—all the other spaces are taken. The cars begin unloading from the ferry behind us: their tyres hitting the steel grates—thud-thud, thud-thud. Above the boat, the sky is an impossible, Australian blue. Impossible because we're in the American Pacific Northwest, a place known for its prodigious rainfall and forest-studded islands. Back towards Vashon, the water is darker than the sky, greener, as though mimicking the trees along the pebbled shore rather than the hue overhead. I've spent so much time in Australia missing this place that leaving it now seems ridiculous.

Jim and Scott have already unloaded the black guitar hard case and the red backpack from the trunk. The gate to the passenger ferry eases open. I'm still sitting in the front seat. A small Buddha with a fat belly has been glued to the front dash. A red button that says 'Panic' has been added next to the steering column. I don't want to get out of the car.

Scott peers in the window. 'You coming?' His face is too clean from shaving this morning.

A small group of people, maybe five or six, have started walking along the jetty to the boat.

'Be safe,' Jim says. Somehow, I'm out of the car and hugging him. When I pull away, Scott has already hoisted his backpack into place. I pick up the guitar case.

'Take care of her, Scotty.' Jim steps forward and the two men hug—a brief pact. Scott is trying to seem comfortable with this intimacy for my benefit but his solid frame looks awkward in Jim's embrace.

Late commuters and city day-trippers hurry along the dock. Scott and I follow across the metal bridge, onto the snug craft. We climb upstairs and settle into a booth with a fake-wood laminate table that's slightly too high. I prop my elbows on it and watch Scott lift his backpack so it's next to him, boxing him into his seat. With both of our things packed into it, the pack is large and square, at least fifteen years old. Scott's name and childhood address have been stained into the canvas with permanent ink. Sitting next to him, the red piece looks like a family relation.

Outside the window, a few timber houses are tucked into the shore. Many of the waterfront properties are accessible only by steep walking trails from the island's bluffs or by the rocky beach at low tide. The pier is still, except for Ruby streaming along. She disappears around the bend and because of all the blackberry bushes and fir trees, it seems she has been swallowed by a lonely shade of green.

The ferry is easing out and I'm suddenly anxious. For the past eight years I've been caught between two versions of the United

States. The one I grew up with—the one I remember—and the one I've witnessed as an expat in Australia. Through television sitcoms and newspaper accounts in the South Pacific, the United States doesn't come across as the redeeming and interesting place I remember. This trip is supposed to be about understanding where I'm from. But *this* is it, I think. This small hippie island hidden from the rest of the States: this is my home.

I turn to Scott, projecting my worry onto him. 'Why are you taking this trip?'

He eyes me off—it's obvious he thinks I'm getting beady and intense. 'Someone has to carry your bags.'

This is Scott's mantra. He's been to the States before and there are other countries he'd like to visit but he decided early on that we should take this trip together. When I booked the tickets, I asked if he was serious about coming and he nodded, telling me he had a strong back.

Behind the receding island, Mount Rainier is perched on the horizon. I'm uncomfortable with how grand it is—it's like an image of a mountain rather than an actual landmark. The white peak and grey base belong on a postcard. The island nestled beneath the towering monument is too pristine, the water too reflective.

I'm waiting for Scott to say something. I want him to explain me back to myself so I can become another version of Shady, one that's kooky and carefree, one that can ignore last-minute nerves and embrace our eccentric adventure—but he knows me well enough to keep quiet. Nothing will reassure me and I'd only argue with anything he put forward.

'The difference between you and me,' he once said, 'is that when I see my demons walking past the window, I let them keep walking. You invite them in for a cup of tea.'

Watching the island shrink into the distance, I imagine a windowsill with long purple curtains and a series of thick shadows passing by outside—self-doubt, fear of the unknown, trepidation at singing in public. In this scene, the tea kettle is behind me, locked in the cupboard with a link chain and a combination lock that has a round black dial.

Our boat hits a wave from the larger ferry and a spray of water drenches the window. Even though I'm not entirely certain I understand, Elvis and this ritual of pilgrimage seem important. Certainly he's played a strong role in my family but there's something deeper: as if by journeying to his house I'm journeying to some interior heart of America and, by association, myself.

HEARTBREAK HOTEL

After a smooth journey to Seattle, Scott and I disembark at pier fifty. Downtown was built on a steep hill that towers over the waterfront so we climb a set of stairs to Pike Place Market. I've chosen this path to the bus station to show off the warren of shops that sell everything from beads and antiques to magic tricks. The premises are stacked on top of each other, built into the city escarpment. We pause to rest, incense wafting from an open doorway, and then continue along the wooden walkways that are bowed and worn from footsteps.

'What about here?' Scott asks when we reach an outdoor landing about three-quarters of the way up. Though it's empty now, I know it as a hallowed busking area. I'd come here in eighth grade with my best friend and listen shyly before buying indie music posters inside—Morrissey, Robert Smith.

'No.'

'If you're going to busk . . .'

'I know, but not here.' It's a place for musicians with street cred and I don't have enough experience yet—I'd play outside the dirty restrooms before venturing anything in this spot.

Scott shakes his head and we emerge on Pike Street, shifting past the crowd at the fish-throwing stall where the glass displays are packed with crushed ice and posed seafood. The man behind the register calls out a customer's order and his assistant yells back, tossing him a full-grown salmon from the other end of the stall; it whips through the air past delighted onlookers.

Scott watches my city with shy affection—it's the same expression he wears at our family dinner table, like he's waiting to say thank you. I'm secretly glad he's charmed and pull him along by the arm, past the sculpted copper pig. 'Don't be such a tourist.'

'I am a tourist.' He squeezes my waist and I knock his hand aside. He squeezes it again and I pinch him back through the folds of his shirt. Scott wears his clothes a size too large so the fabric drapes off his wide shoulders. It's not much of a fashion statement but as he says, 'It's not like we live in Milan.'

Crossing the cobbled alleyway, we wait at the intersection near The Crumpet Shop. The strip club over the road flashes at us: girls girls girls! After the light turns, we continue on.

'Here?' he asks a few minutes later. We're in front of the Westlake Starbucks, the corner of Fourth and Pike, halfway between the ferry dock and the bus station. The glass mall is in front of us, on the left—a tall building with windows for walls and long, low concrete steps. My mother sells her ceramics at one of the galleries inside. As a kid I'd run in with tile orders, the heavy squares wrapped in cardboard and tissue paper, while my first stepfather, Garry, waited right here, double-parked in our old pick-up truck. This familiarity bolsters my courage. 'Okay.'

No one else is busking. I rest the guitar case on its side and open it. It's this one act—the unlatching of the case—that proves most difficult. Eventually, I'll be quicker and the guitar will be hanging from its leather strap before the next person walks by, but this first time I'm too cautious; the transition from pedestrian to performer is laboured. Despite my unease, it's a graceful instrument with two tones of mahogany and a curved outline that seems overtly feminine. A pick-up has been embedded in the top panel but I'm playing it straight, without amplification.

'What about your sign?' Scott steps back, appraising.

I reach down and set the magenta-purple sign before me. It details my journey in fourteen-point white writing: 'My name is Shady Cosgrove. I am on a pilgrimage, playing and singing my way to Graceland in honour of the 25th anniversary of Elvis Presley's death on August 16th.' The earnest manifesto continues, outlining how this journey is a return to my homeland and I'm trying to live entirely on donations. The wording is so melodramatic it could be ironic, a joke at my expense, but it's not—I can be dreadfully serious even when doing the most ridiculous things.

Scott nods towards me with confidence and moves to the Starbucks entrance like he's waiting for someone. There's a signpost behind me and I lean against it for comfort. My fingers begin stuttering through 'Heartbreak Hotel'. I give myself sixteen bars of introduction—the same chord progression on repeat. Eighth notes trickle over each other in my folksy-blues rendition.

A group of truant schoolgirls chortles past. I feel exposed, like my skin is brittle and allergic to the sun. Reminding myself to breathe, I give myself a pep talk, but I'm nervous. The actual performing is harder than I thought; it feels like I'm undressing on the street.

A moment later two women click by, talking. Their pace is quick, hungry, and I envy their lunch break routine.

The song runs at half speed. The slower tempo infuses it with a gentle melancholy but my voice is curiously strong against the streaming guitar.

A man who's all stomach and glasses shuffles up, pausing in front of me. I finish the first verse with relief and then launch into the chorus. He reaches for his pocket and throws a handful of change at the guitar case.

'Thanks,' I say, like an accomplished street performer, but then I come in too late on the next verse and have to repeat it.

That's the only donation in the first twenty minutes. Sixty cents. Back in Sydney, I'd practised busking. In the tiled tunnel beneath Central Station, I'd set up with a friend and we made eighty dollars in two and a half hours. Australians may indeed be a more generous people, though I suspect part of the discrepancy lies in their one- and two-dollar coins. If someone empties their pockets in Sydney, the gold change can easily add up to eight or nine bucks.

My fingers move from 'Heartbreak Hotel' to 'Hound Dog'. And then, because those are the only two Elvis songs I can perform with confidence, I repeat the set. I do know more—I took guitar lessons before leaving Australia—but they're not ready. My two-number set proves more than ample: people walking by have a listening span of about twenty seconds.

After my second round, a hotted up low-rider pauses in front of me at the lights, its engine gunning over my voice. Custom-painted pea green, the car's been polished so fiercely it glints with my reflection, my whole frame visible along the passenger door—thin boot-cut jeans, short brown hair, arms stiffly in position around the guitar.

When it revs off, I turn around, scanning the Westlake entrance. The city has cleaned up in the past eight years. The colourful trash from the grunge era has been swept away to reveal a concrete skeleton. The mall gleams; even from this distance I can see the polished chrome door handles. I remember when the Westlake Mall was erected. I remember when they called Seattle a village in a city.

A man in a blue pinstriped suit walks by. A mother pushing a pram.

Scott is watching me from the coffee shop and grins—the only man who would pretend to be stood up so I'd have moral support playing to my city. I'm home and not-home at the same time, I realise. In fact, I may never and always be home here again.

My left hand slides into position for 'Heartbreak Hotel'.

In early 1997, Scott and I met in a sharehouse in Wollongong, Australia, a city-town about an hour and a half south of Sydney.

The Kembla Street dwelling had seven bedrooms with at least six of them filled at any given time. According to legend, the building had once been either a brothel or a Buddhist monastery, but as far back as anyone could remember it'd been more of a long-term hostel, with most residents enrolled at the local university. Rent was $35 a week and this included electricity, local phone calls and all the milk and tea you could drink. Black and white fuzzy seventies wallpaper coated the living room, inspiring most visitors to pet our walls. Postcards from previous residents covered the kitchen—hundreds of vivid rectangles taped along the wall, leaving a bare area only for the light switch. Someone had painted the bathroom bright red.

Though Scott had lived at the Kembla Street residence for four years when I moved in, he spent most of his time in his room. Every now and then he'd leave his door open—inside, the walls were painted a sickly green and clothes were piled out of a metal filing cabinet set up across from his unmade bed.

We were tentative friends for a year and a half until I drank too many whiskey sours and lurched at him late one night after I'd moved out of the house. None of our housemates—and certainly neither of us—thought it would last. Even our interests weren't compatible: Scott had read six books in his entire life and his passion was sport. I worked part-time as a journalist, had just enrolled in a PhD in women's studies and had never seen a professional game, of any kind, in my entire life. Add to that Scott's habit of playing devil's advocate for the sake of riling people, especially feminists. After a house video night, he once firmly declared that Demi Moore deserved everything she got in *The Scarlet Letter*.

'It's Hester Prynne,' I said immediately, but he'd already eased back on the sagging sofa to watch the verbal explosions like a kid setting off fireworks in the lounge room.

After we began going out, Scott only started arguments he was committed to, because I'd carry them on for days. Eventually, he signed up for a library card and joined my book club while I began to follow rugby league, arguably the most violent and dangerous code of football. Our first full season together saw the St George Illawarra Dragons make it to the grand final against Melbourne; it was a game that seemed more like combat, with Jamie Ainscough and that infamous penalty try. The following year we bought a flat together and four years into our relationship, he took leave from his job for this pilgrimage.

Scott has a round face with disproportionately large cheeks and crinkly eyes: a late thirties, tanned Saint Nicholas. His frame is sturdy from years of playing local rugby league—because the teams don't wear padding or helmets, their bodies are literally their shields. This filled me with awe and horror, especially because Scott was in the front row, which meant he was responsible for moving the ball down the field by running straight into the opponents (also called a hit-up, I soon learned). This resilience is reflected in his nature, though he's generally quieter in his approach than you'd think from watching him on the field. He left school at fifteen for an apprenticeship in carpentry and now works in plumbing, maintaining the region's water infrastructure. Frequently he's on call for emergency work.

When we first started dating, Scott took me wombat-spotting in water catchment areas and showed me a bowerbird's nest he'd found near a pumping station. I thought he'd set up the blue straws and bottle caps as an elaborate joke, but then I saw a bowerbird swoop down with a blue plastic wrapper in its beak. When Scott worked stand-by, I'd visit him on the job in the middle of the night. The whole road would be cordoned off, lights flashing, backhoes scooping into the ground. During the 1998 Wollongong floods, he worked twenty-four hours straight, helping people who were stranded and clearing the city's waterways.

With true Aussie spirit, he worries about the underdog. Which, in his line of work, involves trees. When a water main breaks, crews access it with backhoes. Often greenery has grown in the way of the piping and it's quicker to pull out the shrubs but if he can do it safely, Scott works around the roots. So far, he's saved twenty-eight trees and counting.

In his job and football career, Scott worked entirely with men. He's now retired from sport but still carries himself with an archetypal, on-field masculinity. When we first met, this presence intrigued me; I'd never known a man so capable in his body. Even the way he sat at the kitchen table and filled in the crossword was physical and protective—his arms resting on the laminate, the newspaper folded back in front of him. Of course I sexualised this (the crossword as erotic symbol) but I was drawn to his stable nature as much as his muscular frame. I'm not the only one who feels more secure in his presence. As my mother said years later when we were visiting: 'I feel safer sleeping at night because I know Scott's here.'

I forget that Scott's shy. The first time my mother picked us up from the airport in Ruby, he sat in the front seat, eyes focused on the Virgin Mary postcard tucked into the ashtray. The car was packed with women—my mother, my sister, my cousin—all clamouring over each other. I kept willing Scott to look up, to make eye contact with Irene. I knew they'd get along. Scott's the best storyteller I've ever met and in my family, that talent is revered. But he'll only open up if he feels comfortable and so a lot of people overlook him and miss out. My family was patient—the combination of accent and low volume meant they couldn't comprehend a thing he was saying and for the first week I had to translate. When they could understand him, they decided they had a celebrity in their midst. My mother started telling people in the post office that Scott had charmed crocodiles and tussled with sharks. Scott was just big enough that people believed her and he'd corroborate her story with tales of hoop snakes and drop bears.

When we meet new people, I introduce him as Scotty. Sometimes I think that by knowing me, he's on more familiar terms with the world. He's never said as much (in fact, he could just be a masochist with a penchant for difficult women) but I think it's a reciprocal arrangement that we have. I ask him why he likes me, sometimes two or three times a day, but he's not prone to articulation.

'I like to sleep near you,' he once said.

'What does that mean? Your favourite moments with someone are when she's unconscious?'

'That's just how it is.'

Before Scott and after college, my uncle sold me the Martin guitar at cost when a law-student boyfriend left me. It had been perfect for writing intense three-chord hate songs full of the angst and bad poetry that accompany particularly banal break-ups. The first guitar Elvis bought for himself was a twelve-year-old 1942 Martin that cost $175. I couldn't play mine well but compensated by treating it well—buffing the finish and removing the strings to clean the fret board on a weekly basis. Whoever'd played it before had worn a large belt buckle that left scars in the wood—long, thin stripes against the red mahogany. The neck was thick, forcing my short fingers to stretch for difficult chords, but the full sound that echoed from its belly gave anyone who picked it up the benefit of the doubt.

I'd played off and on for years and in the two months before leaving Australia I took lessons from Lindsay, a skittish man with long auburn hair. In his mid-thirties, he seemed more like a student: slightly undernourished and rumpled. He never wore shoes and that, in combination with his cut-off shorts, emphasised how thin his ankles were. He'd cock one foot up on the opposite knee and tweak my guitar into foreign tunings.

His teaching studio had been converted from a sunroom; heavy sheets covered the windows, blocking out the stubborn Australian sun. Whenever I entered, it took a few moments for my eyes to adjust from the glare outside. Shelves lined the walls, filled with music books that were organised into categories. The floor was ordered likewise with instrument cases. Two chairs were marooned in front of matching music stands in the middle of the room.

I'd sit down, eyes focused on the notebook before me. Lindsay would nod, the signal for me to start with my chord progressions.

'No, the shift is to F,' he'd say, manipulating my hand into place.

When Elvis recorded 'Heartbreak Hotel', he sang over its sadness with bravado and sex appeal, especially the opening words. But the song, written by Mae Axton and Tommy Durden in 1955, was inspired by a newspaper article about a man who killed himself; he left a note that said 'I walk a lonely street'.

I tried to play the original sorrow back into the song by taking it slow. Following Elvis's tune at half-speed turned it into a lullaby for heartbreak, an attempt to soothe the ache to sleep. My voice was thin, as though the song was reflecting the hollow walls of the Heartbreak residence. If he was in a good mood, Lindsay joined in on his own guitar, filling the space behind my melody with a gentle rhythm.

Lindsay's studio fronted onto the verandah so I could hear the next student climb the steps and sit on the outside bench just before my hour-long lessons wrapped up. Most were teenagers, only arriving for half-hour slots. I'd convinced Lindsay to take me double-time twice a week. As a student I tried hard, but I wasn't a fast learner and would need all the help I could get.

'You'll have time to practise through everything between lessons?' he'd asked.

'This is the stuff I'll need to know.'

He hesitated and it was only later I realised he might have assumed my passion was not limited to Elvis. This miscommunication wasn't helped by my feverish enthusiasm—at home I practised two hours a day, drilling my fingers with picking exercises.

One afternoon I stormed into his studio; I'd been possessed, trying to nut out a difficult passage until well past midnight and could finally roll through it seamlessly.

'Lindsay, I finally got it. I got it.' My voice overfilled the compact room.

'That's great, Shady.'

'I can get through all the chords. And I can fingerpick without stopping . . .'

Lindsay took a deep breath and I reminded myself not to act so stereotypically American. It's not just an accent that implies heritage, but decibels.

I opened my case and pulled the instrument out, setting it on my knee. My face was still flushed as my left hand paced through the chords. When I made a mistake, he didn't shift my fingers into place but demonstrated on his own guitar for me to imitate, as though setting some new boundary. In front of this new distance, a blush squirmed down my neck, leaving a rash in its wake. Almost an hour later, when the sound of someone's shoes tripped up the verandah stairs, we both looked up in relief.

But with an aural voyeur perched outside, my skills dropped yet again. The exuberance I'd been trying to contain in my voice bubbled into the song, disrupting it. Each chord demanded sudden attention—the semiconscious ease of what I was doing had disappeared. Just as the notes would follow faithfully, I'd hit a wrong string and the glaring sound would reverberate through the small room.

What was I thinking, busking across the United States? I'd finished my PhD and given notice at the newspaper. The airplane tickets were already purchased but I couldn't even get through one song.

'Let's take it back to standard before we finish,' Lindsay said, looking down at his watch. I wound the strings back and strummed with manic eagerness in some effort to compensate for my poor playing.

In the final weeks of our lessons, we moved on to 'Hound Dog' and Lindsay began to sit further and further from me.

In part I was so excited at my guitar lessons because I was learning how to play my family history. The women in my family have always communicated through mix tapes and CDs, choosing songs and arranging them in ordered playlists. Whole periods of our lives are documented this way and Elvis has featured throughout—'Heartbreak Hotel' for break-ups, 'Mean Woman Blues' for confidence, 'Little Sister' when my older sister Serena studied in France for a year and I felt impossibly far away from her. Just the fact that it had 'sister' in the title was enough for me. I made a mix tape on which it featured right next to Michelle Shocked's 'Don't You Mess Around With My Little Sister', as though the two were in some kind of communication.

During my sophomore year of college, when my mother was pursuing my second stepfather, Jim, she left more than fifteen cassette tapes on the dash of his blue van. He was a carpenter who'd been working on the remodelling of our house. Unaware she had a massive crush on him, he brought dahlias from his father's garden for the housewarming party. My mother took them downstairs and ate them so they'd be 'close to her heart'.

'You did what?' I asked over the phone.

'I ate them.'

'Are dahlias poisonous? Are you going to die?'

'I hope not.'

She also stole rocks from his driveway and wore them in a locket around her neck. As the romance began to burgeon, so too did the cassettes. And meanwhile, I was making my own mixes for a tall lacrosse player who lived in my dorm. Irene had more luck than I did—my crush wasn't an Elvis fan and favoured women with large breasts.

Elvis wasn't the only one to feature in our family soundtrack. We listened to Jimmy Cliff's *The Harder They Come* album when my mother separated from my biological father. I was only six months old but Serena remembers the songs 'Sitting in Limbo' and 'You Can Get It If You Really Want It'. The orange and purple psychedelic cover still sits in the family record stack.

Dire Straits were also central to our family history. When I was in sixth grade, my mother fell in love with Mark Knopfler. He inspired her ceramic work during that time—on one tile panel too large for Irene to carry by herself I remember an image of the Expresso love train passing distant couples down by the waterline. After corresponding with Mark's press secretary, my mother was invited backstage on the Seattle leg of his tour that year where he kissed her on the cheek.

That was around the time my Aunt Molly and mother swapped kids and I went to live in Florida for a year while my older cousin came to Vashon. He was in his late teens, at loggerheads with his parents. I was eleven years old and afraid of public school ('socially awkward' is putting it kindly). I'd gone to Pegasus, a cooperatively run hippie school on Vashon with things like yoga and tree appreciation on the class syllabus. But I was about to graduate fifth grade and petrified of going back to Vashon Elementary. Florida sounded exotic and thrilling, and I couldn't wait to go. While I was there, my mother visited and sent mix tapes. My favourite began with Dire Straits's 'So Far Away' and continued on to George Thorogood's 'I Drink Alone', which I misheard as 'I Drink Cologne'. I played it nonstop, wondering who on earth would name a perfume 'Buddy Weiser'.

In my earliest music memory, I'm three or four years old— Serena and Irene are crooning 'House Carpenter' with Joan Baez as we wait for the car to warm up. We're side by side in a massive gas-guzzler; the mismatched blue door is held closed with a bungee cord. I'm listening to my sister, thinking she's going to be a folk star because she sounds just like Joan Baez. After that, the memories slip together—Serena swinging me around the living room to

Bob Dylan's 'Leopard-Skin Pillbox Hat' and 'Rainy Day Women #12 and 35'. I was still young, maybe four or five years old, shouting out that everyone should get stoned with no idea what that meant. What I did know at the time was that Elvis would be playing soon and 'Blue Suede Shoes' and 'Heartbreak Hotel' were my favourites.

In Seattle, after thirty minutes of busking at Westlake, I've still only earned sixty cents—two quarters and a dime. Scott's now leaning against a 'No Parking' sign. He lifts his hand, motioning upwards for me to sing louder on 'Hound Dog'.

In preparation for this trip, I've been researching Elvis so I know 'Hound Dog' was originally recorded by Big Mama Thornton in 1953 and Elvis was inspired to sing it when he heard Freddy Bell and the Bellboys perform it in Las Vegas. His cheerful voice seems to contradict the lyrics, which are from a woman's perspective, scolding a cheating man.

I try singing it deep and angry like every man who walks by has been sleeping around on me but this strategy, surprisingly enough, doesn't bring any tips so I take it a bit slower.

In the middle of the chorus I dig my hand into my jeans pocket and drop all of my change into the yellow velour lining of the case. My hand is back on the guitar neck, positioned in G, but a woman walking by is witness to my self-donation and shakes her head.

After she's gone, the next three people look in my case and contribute. A woman tosses some coins in without making eye contact but the two men behind her read my sign and contribute one-dollar bills. Apparently the saying 'you need money to make money' is true.

Ten minutes later, an old man approaches. He walks like he's struggling for balance but he has a polished air. His shoes are patent leather and he wears his shirt and pants like they belong to a suit with tails. Pausing in front of me, he reaches into his back trouser pocket for his wallet. I wonder if he's a millionaire or a record producer with a passion for late fifties rock-and-roll—maybe we'll work together to bring Elvis back to the masses.

He leans down to read my sign, his whole body tilting with the effort. Folding his wallet back into his pocket, he swears. 'That's the most ridiculous thing I've ever read. You need a job.'

As he stomps away, I round back on the chorus for a third time. My mouth forms the words, trailing along the melody, and suddenly I'm aware how public this corner is. I want to put the guitar away but back at the 'No Parking' sign Scott is laughing, his large shoulders shaking into the metal post behind him, and I know I'm taking myself too seriously. His voice echoes inside my head: 'Have you ever seen a grumpier American in your life? Guess it makes sense: imagine looking in the mirror and seeing his melon every day.'

Just then, a man with dark curly hair stops. He's dressed casually in shorts and a poncho but his briefcase is curiously formal. I pause, flexing my hand, which is sore from the chord changes.

He reads over my sign. 'So, Elvis, eh?'

I let the guitar rest on my hip, the strap taut. 'Yeah.'

'Why?' Poncho Man looks up and slides his sunglasses back on his forehead. His eyes are dark brown.

'I don't know. Elvis is such a packed cultural symbol.'

Poncho Man has a round face but his body is surprisingly thin.

'It's political.' I sound more certain than I am. 'Music isn't about stereo systems and recording equipment. You don't need to be a superstar to write good songs.' The irony that I'm singing Elvis (a superstar who didn't write most of his songs) isn't lost on me but he keeps nodding his head.

'Anyone harassed you?'

'Truthfully? I haven't been doing this very long.'

My visitor looks up the sidewalk as though he's just realised he's on a city street. 'You know, I'm going to bring my drum out here. Why not? Music belongs everywhere.'

People are walking past us, watching. As though he's part of the act, he reaches into his briefcase with a dramatic motion and pulls out an eight-by-ten photograph. 'I don't have a lot of money right now but take this: it's one of my prints.' He places it in my case—the shape on the page resembles a hieroglyph of a dancing woman playing a strange horn. 'Artists have to stick together. Can you do "Heartbreak Hotel" again?'

My fingers feel shy and humble after his gift. I have to concentrate for the chord change to B7. Halfway through, he nods: the pedestrian light has changed on the corner and he's going to catch it.

'Say hi to the King for me.'

As he scurries to the crosswalk, heading towards the water, Scott comes over. He waits until I finish the song.

'What happened there?'

'Gave me a photograph.'

'Not bad. You done?'

I nod. I have too much pride to stop of my own accord but my left hand is numb. When I was emailing my college friend Heather, Elvis offered a structure to our journey and playing his songs on the street seemed a natural progression. After all, it'd sound great to say: 'I played my way to Graceland.' But the actuality of street performance isn't what I'd expected—in the United States, the line between busker and beggar isn't a wide one.

Scott scans the guitar case. 'Doesn't look like we'll make it far on your earnings.'

In the last hour, I've made just over six dollars. 'Good thing we have traveller's cheques,' I say.

Scott glances across the street where a row of beggars has formed. 'A lot of homeless people here. Too much competition.' Eight or nine people, all with cups before them, are leaning against the windowed glass of a department store. I want to argue with him, as though to defend the United States, but it's true.

'Come on,' Scott says. 'Let's get going.'

Stashed away from downtown on Eighth Avenue, the Greyhound depot is crowded—all the benches are filled and the line of customers extends well beyond the thin roped area. With three open cubicles at the counter for people to be served, only two are staffed. Fluorescent lighting covers everything with the hue of urine. In front of us, a man with pale skin and an eighties headband moves from foot to foot like he's boxing. 'Hurry it up, will you?' he calls out. Every time the line advances, he looks back at Scott and me as though we might try to cut in front of him.

I swallow audibly. Scott just watches me, grinning.

On the far side of the room, a mean-thin woman with two kids swears at the lockers. Along the wall behind her, people are sitting on their luggage, reluctant witnesses.

When Scott and I finally make our way to the front, we each lay out five hundred and sixty dollars cash. Dominic—according to his nametag—serves us. He's even more solid than Scott with bright teeth that seem like a counter-charm to the station: good things will come to us.

'Here are your luggage tickets and you'll need to sign these.' He turns the passes over. 'You're fine to go anywhere in the continental US until August twelfth.'

The receipt is resolute; the money has been paid. I sign my name with a flamboyant 'S'—my passport signature.

Dominic hands us two copies of the Greyhound North America route map, the travel paths marked in bright colours— blue, red, green and orange.

'Look at all the places we can go,' Scott says.

We have two months.

MEMORIES

The Greyhound seats are plush and the guitar fits in the overhead compartment easily. As the bus swings out of the station I poke Scott in the arm and then turn around, suddenly absorbed in staring out the window—it's a sophisticated humour that we share.

He strokes the back of my head. 'I wonder who that could have been.'

A few minutes later, Scott's leaning over the armrest, about five inches from my face, staring at me. 'What's the girl doing?'

'What do you think I'm doing? I'm sitting on a bus.'

He turns to the invisible television reporter across the aisle. 'That's the thing I like about her. Full of surprises.'

Our seats offer an elevated view of the city. Up near the station, Seattle isn't as clean and ordered as I'd assumed. Graffiti. People sleeping in doorways. I look out the window for the iconic Space Needle but the driver cuts straight to the I-5 highway.

The bus is about half full. People are quiet, staring out the window or listening to music. A couple of older women are perched near the front, talking to the driver about the family politics of grandchildren—how much advice should they offer? This makes me laugh. My mother has children and grandchildren

32

the same age—Serena's daughter, Meme, is within a year of Lucas, my little brother.

I press play on my walkman and Paul Simon's 'Graceland' comes pounding through my headphones. Outside the city, the interstate is packed to a standstill. Eight lanes: the cars so wide, steroid-supersized, they barely fit within them. It takes an hour before we're on clear road, the traffic river flowing along the freeway, heading south. I'm staring out the window when Scott nudges me across the plastic armrest.

'What?' I unplug my headset. Someone in front of us is eating corn chips; the air smells of artificial cheese and salt.

'Portland. What do you know about it?' We're visiting the Oregon city because I have a friend there and it's often compared to Seattle—a fact most Portlanders I've met don't appreciate. There seems to be a one-sided rivalry between the two cities, not unlike that between Australia and New Zealand; the smaller place gets irritated with the overshadowing attention-hound.

'Not much.'

'Ever been there?'

I don't even hesitate, and give a single syllable reply: 'Nope.'

After three hours, we're in Portland. Despite the bright day outside and the bank of windows near the ceiling, the long, rectangular station is fluorescent dim. The heavy brick walls have diluted all strength from the light. Déjà vu: the brown floor tiles; the turnstile into the waiting area; the thick black plastic chairs with outdated television screens anchored to the armrests. I already know this. Beyond the benches and the partition—the restroom. Even though I haven't set foot inside, the bank of sinks is clear in my mind's eye. I've stood in front of them before. I remember the toilet door slamming closed behind me.

'Scott, this place is familiar.'

His head pulls forward from his backpack—a turtle unaware of its shell. He does his best to shrug under the weight.

'I'm serious. The door's moved, it was down there . . .' I point to our left, 'but I've been here.' I inhale deeply. The hall smells like the inside of a suitcase.

Scott lifts his baseball cap and pushes his hair back. 'You said you've never been to Portland.' Things are that straightforward for Scott. If you say you've never been to Portland, then you've never been to Portland. But in my family, there are secret passageways and hidden doors: it's obvious I've been to Portland.

We're five metres from the station entrance. Scott shifts towards it like I won't notice. 'You ready?'

'Scott.'

'It's nothing to worry about. Greyhound stations look alike.' The woman behind the counter laughs; the full-bodied sound doesn't match my uneasy impression of the room.

'No. It's something else. I've been here.'

'Fine, you've been here.'

Scott treads towards the automatic sliding exit doors but I'm not leaving yet. Another bus has unloaded—the passengers jostle past. A woman paces by like a stewardess with a wheeled suitcase streaming behind her. I edge back to let her pass and a kid whacks my arm with his skateboard.

Scott unlatches his pack's front waist clasp. 'Do you want to sit down then?'

I don't really. I don't want to be in this room any longer than I have to but this antipathy only makes me less able to leave.

'We're in the way here, Shady.'

Vague details come back to me. Not actual memories, but shadows of memories like hands imitating birds in front of a bare bulb. The last time I saw my biological father, Michael King Cosgrove, I was five years old and he was living in Portland. My older sister Serena and I would have taken the bus to see him. Why wouldn't I remember this? I suppose it's been over twenty years. People forget things. We stopped visiting when I was in kindergarten—his drinking had started up again and my mother didn't think it was safe.

Scott takes my arm and guides me to the wall. I study the other passengers as though more surprises might be waiting. A petite woman with red skin and heavy glasses bounces past. An army kid with a shaved head stares at me for staring at him.

'You'd think you'd remember being here,' Scott mumbles.

I can't remember anything else but the room is familiar and creepy at the same time, like a stranger who knows my name.

Outside the bus station, Portland is layered with railroad tracks and bridges as though the city was built around its train system. And again it feels like this place is in conspiracy with my past—I only have a handful of memories of my father and the strongest takes place on a train, back when he was getting regular shifts as a driver.

I would have been four and a half years old, my little hand gripping my father's as we carefully stepped over railway ties. Cargo boxes waited on steel rails like men hoping for work.

Michael hoisted me up the steep stairs and followed, pulling me onto his lap. Together, we were tucked into the driver's seat of the engine car. My pale blue gingham dress spread over his knees. To our right the window was open, his elbow perched on its thin ledge. He called out to someone below, a workmate, and gave me a lever to hold.

'Pull that down slowly. Good.' His hands were near in case anything went wrong. The train shunted beneath us, and we were moving—I was guiding its speed. Looking back, I realise it wasn't a token gesture: he was actually letting a kid run the controls. Anything could have happened. My fist was clamped tight around the steel; it dropped slightly and our speed quickened.

Michael glanced down at the readings. 'Keep it steady now.'

After a few minutes he stretched back as much as the cramped space would allow and clasped his hands behind his head. 'Look at you. You're smart—smarter than your sister.'

My little shoulders sat even taller with that news. I had to be the smartest person in the world because my sister was planning on going to college. This pride was buoying—I was his favourite—and my chest felt like it was packed with helium balloons. But I had the same sense of guilt as when he'd tell me what losers my mother and sister were. Even at that age, I knew there was something mean-spirited and illicit about his tone of voice.

Crossing bells started clanging for us—we were the final car in the parade. Outside, red lights flashed and a long striped arm dropped in front of the oncoming car traffic, an enforced audience of four vehicles. The first was a taxi. Its driver looked up absent-mindedly before his head jerked back again; he was still squinting at us when we pulled out of his vision.

'Did you see that?' Mike said, his voice too loud. 'Did you see that? Amazing. That was a man who's been driving taxis his whole life. He'll only ever drive taxis. He was born to drive taxis. And he looks up and there, in front of his eyes, is a little girl, *a little girl*, driving a train. Already exceeding him. Already beyond his wildest dreams.'

He was slapping the wall and I was grinning like rail transportation had just been invented. I remember this glee as though it's an old family video and there's another person holding the camera, pointing the lens at us. That person steadying the frame is myself now, looking back, and the experience reeks of a personal voyeurism that makes me uncomfortable. Even though I'm laughing when the tape zooms in on my little hands punching against the metal like my father's, there's something uneasy about the gesture.

★

I keep looking for Portland to be familiar—intersections, parks, restaurants—but nothing has the eerie presence of the bus station. Instead, I focus on Elvis and add 'Little Sister' to my repertoire. At first, the song appeals to me because I'd listen to it as a kid, but now I'm fascinated because the lyrics are so outrageous. The singer is insulting a prior date because she's not interested in him, and trying to score with her younger sister. It's so sleazy it's impossible to believe anyone could sing it straight-faced.

In Pioneer Courthouse Square, an inner city park, I listen to it all the way through. When Elvis's voice trails off, the twining guitar takes over—the two laughing at an inside joke. Then I run through the bar chords and move to a short brick wall opposite the bus interchange to sift through my three practised songs. Scott waits behind me on the courtyard steps, watching young boy-men kick a hacky sack around in a circle.

Buses whoosh past. Their heavy groaning makes it hard to be heard so I move up half a block. My guitar case swings open and my cheat notes flutter to the sidewalk. Despite this inauspicious start, it isn't hard breaking in—Portlanders take little notice of me. My fingers shape into the 'Little Sister' chords and I strum through the introduction, thinking of Serena. I used to imitate her, thrusting my hips back and forth as we danced to this song.

Along the street, a middle-aged woman with a bouffant hairstyle plods by slowly as though feeling each step through her shoes. Her movements are uneven—like river stones, not concrete, are underfoot. She doesn't look at me and keeps moving gingerly down the street.

After her, an old man wearing shorts comes from the opposite direction with his hands in front of him, feeling the air currents for direction. He pauses by the case but doesn't look up. Is the song drawing weirdos or is it Portland?

A second woman, mid-twenties, paces the sidewalk past us. Like me, she has brown eyes and pale skin. Glossy white shopping bags hang from her hands. Her suit looks fresh even in the late afternoon hour. Despite my relief at seeing her, she ignores both me and the old man and I realise I'm in the weirdo category now. It happened so easily. I used to work in an office, wearing nylons and heels, but to anyone walking by I'm now a card-carrying member of the Oddball League. It never felt like this busking in Australia—there was a feeling that people assumed you were a uni student clowning around, or a musician tired of practising at home. What's strange is that I care. I'm never going to see that lady or her shopping bags again in my life but I still care.

The old guy patters off and I'm alone. The next passer-by is another office worker in his mid-fifties with curly brown hair. When I was a kid, I'd always keep a lookout for men with curly hair. I worried they might actually be my father, travelling incognito. Before I went to live in Florida, there had been talk of kidnapping. In some versions of our family history, that's why I went to Florida when I was eleven years old. Around that time my mother made me swear on a telephone book that I wouldn't get into his car alone (if I did, I risked all the names in that book). But as I'm busking, running through 'Little Sister' for the eighth time, I realise there were equal parts fear and hope as I was scanning for him.

In Portland we end up staying with Lockett, a friend from college. She's always been slender, but she seems even taller and thinner than I remember. Her hair is long, almost to her waist. She grew up in the South of the United States, but migrated to New York for school and now to the Pacific Northwest where she teaches yoga and works for a local bakery. Even her house is healthy—clean wooden floors, retro fridge, futon guest mattress.

On our first full day together, I take my guitar to the markets where Lockett sells wholemeal breads and jam pastries. Despite the vigorous sun overhead, booths are clustered under white tarps in case of rain. Portland supposedly nudges out Seattle as the rainiest city in the country and it's obvious the booth vendors don't know what to do with the sun. They keep looking at the sky and shaking their heads.

I stand in front of a large rock in the shade just to the left of one of the entrances: a bold position. My case opens quickly and the guitar is already tuned. I use one of Lockett's beanies for donations. Weighted with my spare change, it looks like I'm a serious busker. After 'Heartbreak Hotel' I move into 'Can't Help Falling in Love', which Elvis recorded for his movie *Blue Hawaii* in 1961. It's another new one so my hands move slowly, picking the strings. Pride overwhelms me after each bar chord, so I mutter 'focus' to stay on track. After my four Elvis songs, I double back but for the first time I have a captive audience—the people manning the booths. Two hours of 'Heartbreak Hotel' and 'Little Sister' isn't going to impress anyone.

Well into the second round, a man with friendly eyes and thick glasses approaches. I pretend I'm stopping to talk with him but I really need to find my notes: 'That's All Right', 'Suspicious Minds' and 'Viva Las Vegas' will have to be piloted today.

Mr Glasses watches me for a moment. 'The Elvis is great. You don't hear a lot of him anymore. You play a lot of gigs?'

Is this guy deaf? 'No, not really. I—' Something's missing. Why would I play gigs?

'He's great, don't get me wrong. But most people of your generation don't appreciate him. Why Elvis?'

The sign. The sign isn't in front of me. My case is closed because I'm using the hat; my detailed explanation must be in the case. And this man thinks I'm a musician. He thinks I'm just playing here at the markets because that's the kind of thing a musician would do. This cracks me up and I have to concentrate on keeping a straight face.

'You know—' I'm about to tell him of the journey until my mind jumps to the man from Seattle, storming away, telling me I need a job.

Mr Glasses seems tired. His mouth is creased with wrinkles but his eyes are awake, a soft, thoughtful blue.

'Do you live here in Portland?' He emphasises the word 'Portland' as though it's code.

I think a moment: where do I live? 'No, not Portland.'

He nods. 'You know, you can sleep out of town in the forest. No one will hassle you and if you're hungry, the Salvation Army gives a good Saturday meal at three o'clock. Make sure you line up though, it's a favourite.'

'Good to know.'

He continues: 'Sorry I don't have much cash now, but here—' He props a copy of the Portland homeless newspaper against Lockett's hat.

I feel shy in front of this man's generosity and I'm sad my sign isn't out. I want to explain my trip to him. I want to talk about the layers of this journey and the complicated nature of 'home'—it seems like he'd have an interesting take on that—but I have trouble finding a way to start and end up mumbling, 'Thanks.'

'That's all right. The Elvis sounds good. Long live the King.' He shakes a fist at me in camaraderie but the gesture is softened by his gentle voice.

'"That's All Right",' I repeat back to him. 'I'll play that next.' Opening my guitar case for my notebook, I scan the chords quickly and start singing, kicking in with the guitar.

It's fitting that our journey began with 'That's All Right' back on Vashon—my mother dancing, the Greyhound revelation—because that song launched Elvis's career in 1954. He'd been stopping by Sun Studios for almost a year, asking if recording engineer Sam Phillips had any need for a singer. With Scotty Moore on guitar and Bill Black on bass, the three jammed together. It wasn't until Elvis clowned around during a break that Sam heard what he was looking for and asked him to play Arthur 'Big Boy' Crudup's 'That's All Right' again. Within a couple of days, Sam gave the recording to his friend, radio DJ Dewey Phillips (no relation), who played it seven times in a row on WHBQ, eliciting forty-seven phone calls and fourteen telegrams. The Elvis mania had begun.

All of this I've gleaned from Peter Guralnick's two-volume biography of Elvis—*Last Train to Memphis* and *Careless Love*. Scott raised his eyebrows when I loaded the hefty paperbacks into the backpack.

'You might as well carry bricks,' he said.

I gripped the books, showing off the two spines that joined together to make a picture of Elvis's face.

'I'm not bringing any others and maybe I'll learn something for our journey—maybe it'll make some kind of sense.'

I was three years old when Elvis died in 1977 and have no memory of him alive; he hovers like an urban legend that has been told so many times it's bloated out of proportion. These books had the research and detail (over a thousand footnotes) to peg Elvis back to earth.

Scott just crossed his arms over his broad chest. 'You going to carry them?'

'Can do. Here, this stuff can go.' Riffling through the pack, I started tossing out underwear and toiletries in a dramatic display of just how important these volumes were to me.

'Fine, bring them. We're still going to take deodorant.'

In the first book, I was surprised by how unworldly Elvis was. According to Guralnick, Sam Phillips and Marion Keisker of Sun Studios felt Elvis 'represented the *innocence* that had made the country great'. Before he entered the army in 1958, Elvis shunned alcohol and drugs. His travelling friend Cliff had to smoke outside and he even tried to get girlfriend Dottie Harmony to quit smoking in December 1956. I didn't imagine Elvis so pure, so straight, and liked him more for this—an awkward boy, stopping at Sun Studios again and again, controlling his frustration in the hope that he'd finally get into that studio. Just hang in there, Elvis, I found myself thinking, just record 'That's All Right'.

And once it hit the airwaves, everything went berserk. I try to imagine a radio station today so excited by a song, so excited by the discovery of a new voice, that a DJ plays the track on repeat. Certainly there's airwave saturation today, especially in the pop arena, but it's driven by record companies and promoters. Imagine playing a song over and over because you've never heard anything like it.

After a couple of days, Scott and I are back, waiting at the Portland Greyhound station. Next stop: Arcata, California, to visit my mother's oldest brother, Brooks, and his wife, Carolyn. Inside, the rectangular building still smells distantly familiar. The plastic seats and steel racks with rumpled brochures could easily be from the seventies. Grey lockers line the wall but they seem too new— maybe they've been added. How much does a bus station change in twenty years, I wonder.

'It's too weird, Scott. I know this room.' We wait in line for our tickets. Two people stand in front of us.

'What were you doing here?'

'I don't know.' Someone leaves the counter and the line pushes forward. Scott shoves the backpack with his foot and I nudge the guitar case.

'Who were you with?'

'I don't know, Serena probably. It's just the room. The place. There are some things I remember but I don't know if they all match up to the same story.'

My memories of my father are hazy at best. Much clearer are my memories without him—as a child, before the kidnapping threats, I used to spend hours waiting at the bottom of our driveway, organising the rocks by the mailboxes and drawing in the air with my stick-wand, in case he drove by. Of course I lived on an island—no one would happen to drive onto a ferry and then onto Vashon—but it seemed imperative that I be ready.

When I was nine, I focused on the piano, banging away through my arpeggios with a heightened sense of urgency, hoping that someday I'd be broadcast on the radio and he'd scroll by the station as the DJ introduced my latest classical track.

But here, in the bus station, I realise I'm comfortable with the story of Michael Cosgrove as an absent father: what makes me edgy is that I remember so little of him as a present father. My chest tightens and I continue, talking to myself like I'm trying to draw a dream into consciousness. 'Serena and I were visiting Mike. He lived outside of Portland. In a blue townhouse. I remember a balcony that overlooked the woods. An open-plan living room with stairs along the far wall.'

An announcement sounds over the loudspeaker: the Vancouver bus is now loading. It's not ours, but somebody behind us swears and calls out to the cashier to hurry it up.

'And?' Scott asks.

'I don't know.'

Scott lifts his eyebrows and prods the pack forward while I scan the bus station again. My voice is thin: 'I do know this building.'

'Fine.' Scott doesn't tell me to be quiet in public anymore but I hear it in his tone. My eyes can't blink I'm staring at him so hard. In a yelling whisper, I say: 'Just because you come from a family where everyone loves each other and you can't spend enough public holidays together.'

'Come on, it's okay. I believe you—you have a strong connection to this bus station. It's okay.'

The woman at the counter yells, 'Next.' I wait a long moment and then carry the guitar case to the open space. Scott follows with our backpack.

Scott Bazley is the fourth of five kids; it's obvious they're related— it's like they enjoy their own company so much they've decided to resemble each other. They all gather at the family beach house down at Jervis Bay for Christmas and Easter holidays. The kids, especially Scott's younger brother Craig, care for the property and all of them arrive each holiday to revel in making fun of each other. It's a wry sort of intimacy that I've only ever seen in large families.

One Christmas, Scott's sister, Gail, was chopping vegetables on the scuffed white bench. Gail has Scott's round nose and cheeks. Her hair was bleached honey blonde as though she was trying to escape the family's code of no-frills capability, but she was a nurse in a high-security jail—serial killers listened to her when she told them to stop whingeing and take their meds. Pausing, she set the knife down and took a swig from her stubby. 'Remember when Scott wanted to fly? He jumped off the top of the barn with a sheet for a cape.'

Scott was standing behind her at the sink and shook his head as the kettle whistled. According to photos, he was much leaner as a kid, a cross-country runner. I could imagine his desperate hands flapping alongside him, his thin body hovering in the air for an impossible cartoon moment before dropping.

Their brothers Kim and Craig were reading sections of the newspaper over by the fibre-optic tree that blinked slowly through the summer heat. Kim's face was thinner than Scott's but his frame was equally sturdy, his muscular arms emphasised by his loose tank top. He looked up. 'What about the time Scott, Shane and Craig sawed off the gate at Penrose? It took Dad a whole day to hang it the first time.' Penrose was a little town in the Southern Highlands where they all grew up on a farm. They had chooks, lambs and pigs. One of Scott's earliest memories is of being pecked by a turkey.

Scott crossed the kitchen and Gail shifted to the side so he could reach down to the wood-panelled cupboard for a mug.

Gail glanced at me and then piled the vegetables into a steamer. 'Have you heard about the trays?' she asked, pushing the strap of her singlet back along her shoulder.

I'd heard about the trays. Despite my nodding head, Gail smacked her lips and boomed: 'Scott went to Egypt and bought all these trays.'

She looked back over her shoulder at Scott, who was pouring himself a cup of tea. Her Australian accent was loud, rowdy. 'I'll have one too, Scott, thanks for offering . . . We were getting trays each Christmas for years. You've never seen so many trays. I bet there'll be more waiting for us under the tree. Scott, you'd better not be giving Shady a tray for Christmas this year.'

If Gail was trying to warn me, it was unnecessary: I was already well aware that Scott was a cheapskate. He was generous with his time but had an aversion to spending money, even on himself. This actually fitted well with me—it wasn't by chance the two of us met in a house with a weekly rent of $35 per room.

I'm not part of a family that makes fun of each other, maybe because so many years separate me and my siblings—I'm ten years younger than Serena and sixteen older than Grace. Lucas, my little brother, is eighteen years younger than me. But perhaps it's more specific than age. Scott's parents immigrated to Australia in 1960 after his father and uncle argued over the family farm in England. When Scott was eighteen, his father died of leukaemia without ever returning to Devon. Though Scott and his siblings journeyed back and reconciled with their relations, there's sadness in the family that his father couldn't do it himself. It's like the Bazleys are driven to enjoy every moment together as a form of protection against a similar fate.

As we were walking to the Greyhound station in Portland, Scott asked me if I wanted to track down Michael Cosgrove. The question surprised me and I realised he's been shaped by absence of a different kind. Scott misses his father, who would get up at 6 am on Saturday mornings to drive him and his brothers to hockey games in Kangaroo Valley. He misses hearing his father's Devon accent shouting, 'Go on!' when he made a break on the field.

'We're here. It wouldn't be hard,' Scott said.

I shook my head. 'I know you think I'm hanging onto grudges. It's not like that but I don't want to see him.'

GUITAR MAN

The bus arrives in Arcata, California, at nine in the morning after a twelve-hour ride. We walk the wide, slow streets to visit my aunt and uncle. The houses are tall, leaning towards the road like they're eavesdropping on the parked cars. Their porches were crafted by optimists expecting warmer weather.

Pushing through a white picket gate, we climb the concrete steps to the front verandah and knock on the door. It swings open and my uncle Brooks—co-owner of Wildwood Music, the man who shipped me the Martin six years earlier—welcomes us immediately. I can't remember the last time I saw him: ten years, maybe? He's still tall, but his shoulders roll slightly forward. Grey-white strands have claimed his dark hair. His tortoiseshell glasses are an updated model of the ones he's always worn and they sit like a familiar landmark on his face.

'Come in, come in.' His voice is animated and calm at the same time, reminding me of my mother, and for a brief moment I feel like I know him better than I do.

We follow Brooks inside and drop the pack and my guitar at the bottom of an old wooden stairwell. Stepping around the chunky black instrument cases on the floor, my uncle takes us through the living room where layers of built-in shelves are stacked with thousands of CDs—jazz, blues, country, bluegrass.

'The kitchen's out here—help yourself to anything . . .'

Above the stove, the wall is covered with my mother's ceramics: Brooks and Carolyn have tiles and plates from the 1970s when her images were hand-drawn with underglaze pencil. The lines are uneven compared to the newer ones silk-screened with wax resist. I pause on each one and it's like they're staring back at me, Irene is watching me. A few tiles are cracked and have been glued back together—a thin fracture interrupts the image of a kettle on a stovetop. The caption reads: 'It's time to take dreams off the back burner.' For the first time, I think of Brooks not as my uncle but as my mother's older brother, a proud older brother.

He sighs. 'Carolyn's out shopping, but should be back soon. And Dan, as you know, lives in Florida.' Dan is my cousin, Brooks's son; I haven't seen him in years. He lives near Molly and Andy, the same aunt and uncle I stayed with in sixth grade. According to the family photos stuck to the fridge he's grown into his father's lanky frame. His eyes are dark, like mine, with a hint of shyness in his expression. In one picture, I notice Brooks and Dan standing side by side, maybe in the backyard. Red flowers billow from a green bush behind them. Brooks has his arm around Dan in a proud gesture like it's a graduation, but his sweater has a hole in the arm and Dan's wearing shorts.

'How is Dan?'

'He's well.'

I'm aware it's my turn to speak but Brooks doesn't seem concerned: good conversation needs strong pauses. I take a deep breath—we're back in the living room and it smells of polished wood, herbal tea and dog hair. It occurs to me that Brooks is the kind of uncle who connects with adults, not children, as though he's been waiting for my generation to grow up. And funnily enough, I appreciate him in a way that's new: the idea of family carries a stronger currency with me now. In some ways, we're meeting for the first time and I'm surprised by how much I want this man to like me.

He motions to the couch. 'Have a seat.'

Scott plonks down but Brooks and I remain standing in front of the cast-iron wood stove, abandoned for the summer months.

'Irene tells me it's Elvis,' he says, chuckling. Even if he's laughing at me, I like the way his voice falls in register. He nods towards my case. 'How's the Martin going? We'll have to run through a few numbers.'

That afternoon, instead of busking in Arcata, I play with Brooks. He unpacks his Dobro and we start in on 'Heartbreak Hotel'. With the instrument on his lap, he slides through the notes behind me. No longer am I playing on the sidewalk, counting coins, singing as loud as possible to fill the empty street space—a deeper integrity has entered the room and I'm part of it. My fingers shift through the chorus an extra time to prolong the song.

He changes his finger slide. 'What other ones do you know?'

'"Hound Dog"?'

Of all the ones I've learned, this is the most fun. The downbeats are as certain as the lyrics. The clapping that keeps pace in the original has been embedded into the melody so it sounds like there's a rhythm section behind me. This song, more than the others, conjures Elvis. Before he was drafted, Elvis would close his shows with this number; it was his trademark.

I have to concentrate to keep myself steady. By the time we've run through it a few times, my voice and guitar can stay in time with my tapping foot. If Brooks is put off by my ineptitude, he doesn't show it but my other songs aren't as practised. When we finish I lean the Martin against the couch and fall back onto the pillows behind me. 'I've got the Elvis songbook here. There are some tricky chords.'

'Let's have a look.'

I scan the index for 'Blue Suede Shoes' and 'Jailhouse Rock'. Brooks pauses over the fingerings. 'They aren't hard, it's a matter of changing key.'

His fingers motion through the chords and it's obvious 'hard' is a matter of perspective.

'What about "Shady Grove"?' I ask. 'Do you know the chords for that?'

He hums to himself and his right hand follows a beat or so behind. 'It's E minor to D and back to E minor . . .'

I was named after 'Shady Grove', an Appalachian folk melody about a young girl whose husband has to travel away. Whenever Irene's had too much to drink, she says my dark eyes remind her of the woman in the song. According to family lore, I was supposed to change my name, dropping the C-O-S, and hit the road as a country and western star.

Brooks starts playing and I murmur the lyrics. 'Cheeks as red as a blooming rose. Eyes the prettiest brown . . .' The notes follow a skipping-rope rhythm. I wait, listening to a full verse before jumping in with the guitar.

Strumming along, I'm aware he's given me the chords to play myself into song. This should be a good thing—a musical catharsis, a moment of self-discovery for the protagonist. But there's something within me that's dark and not even particularly disguised. It has to do with Dan and the smiling image, the father–son sloped posture, pinned to the fridge with a magnet. I haven't seen my cousin in years but the photo has sparked something in my psyche that isn't loving or subtle: I'm envious in a kicking, crying kind of way that Brooks isn't my father.

The next morning, Scott and I walk four blocks to my uncle's store, Wildwood Music—Brooks has offered to replace my hard shell with a guitar backpack.

The door chimes and we're faced with the end of a counter. A thin young man with long hair is talking to a customer about guitar strings: both are wearing rock t-shirts—Pink Floyd is serving Led Zeppelin. Instruments hang off the wall and crowd the display cabinets. Long rows of sheet music are alphabetised, set in waist-high racks in the middle of the room. I can hear Brooks's low voice from the side office.

'Guitar packs?' I ask the t-shirts. Both point to the rear of the shop.

Leaning against a half-wall are basic soft shells with afterthought straps sewn on and middle-of-the-range ones with a bit more cushioning. Scott fingers a green one, reaching in to see how the padding has been sewn on. Behind these models, a deluxe pack is set to one side. Its tan fabric is thicker, more durable. With a waist strap, the guitar's weight is evenly distributed across the wearer's hips. It comes with a fancy side bag that clicks on and off—the Rolls Royce of guitar packs.

I'm gazing down at it when Brooks lopes up and nods. 'If you'll be walking, that's the only one that'll offer full support.'

He shrugs off my protests. Scott glances down at the price tag and his eyes bulge. On the money conscious scale, I'm not far from Scott: I'll opt for walking over catching a bus—it offers the bonus of free exercise. And it's never occurred to me to take a taxi, even in the rain. But I come from a family that adores presents. My mother once paid for Scott and me to stay in a hotel in Vancouver as we were flying back to Australia. It was the first time in Scott's adult life someone else paid for his accommodation (if you don't count the night he slept on his sister's motel-room floor, without a pillow, during the Rugby Union World Cup in Brisbane). Gifts are just something we do.

I spend the rest of the afternoon at Brooks's house zipping and unzipping all of the pack's secret pockets before trying it on.

'What do you think, Scotty?' I turn around with a wind-blown lingerie model pout. The juxtaposition of my prancing and the stiff canvas backpack makes him laugh.

At dinner, the round table is nestled in a nook near the kitchen. The overhead light is dimmed—there's a feeling of ritual to the meal that's less chaotic than Vashon. I'm sitting between Brooks and Carolyn; Scott is across from me.

After pouring us each a glass of red wine, Brooks turns to me. 'So, Australia. We're thinking of visiting Australia.' His tone is familiar and disbelieving, and he emphasises the word 'thinking'. Many Americans seem stunned by the cross-Pacific flight—twelve hundred dollars (minimum) and sixteen hours on a plane. While these figures may be off-putting, it could be worse: when Scott's mother emigrated from England, it took four weeks by boat.

Carolyn uses the tongs to drop a pile of spaghetti on her plate. She's heard the apprehension in Brooks's voice. 'No really, we're thinking about it.' Carolyn is practical; I imagine she's the one who handles their finances. I watch her to see if they have a blessing routine like my family—we all hold hands and each person offers thanks for some aspect of their day—but she just picks up her fork.

Scott follows her lead, slicing the pasta with his knife. 'It's a big country,' he says. Many Americans don't realise Australia is the size of the continental United States with one-tenth the population. And, as early pioneers discovered to their peril, the middle is desert.

Carolyn's titanium earrings glint in the light, their purple-gold reminding me of my mother, though Carolyn's nature is more solid. She has always struck me as wary of melodrama and, by extension, careful of our family. 'So why Australia, Shady?'

Though it's true, my answer sounds crafted, like I was thinking of a dinner just like this when I made the decision. 'At university, I wanted to go on a study exchange. I was deciding between Australia and Ireland and both names went in a hat . . . I picked Australia.'

Brooks stops drinking but keeps the wine glass to his lips, speaking over the rim. 'You weren't tempted by Ireland?'

'If you put it up to chance, you can't back out. Wouldn't want the furies offside.'

He laughs. 'I guess not. But why stay? Other than Scotty, of course.'

His question is a complicated one. I returned to the United States after that first year to finish my degree in New York, but as soon as I had saved enough money I flew back to see an old boyfriend and travel. Then circumstances—work, scholarship—kept me there. But I have a deeper connection to Australia that I notice especially when I'm driving alone on the Hume Highway to Canberra. The fields are pale brown with occasional clusters of sturdy, muscular trees. The sky is out of proportion, standing on the horizon. There's a particular stone hut from early settler days on the left-hand side of the road after the Goulburn exits—its door and roof gone, the sandstone exposed—and somehow its vulnerability feels honest. The barren landscape is comforting and with the mileage passing in kilometres and my car in the left-hand lane, I just know it's where I should be.

When I first moved to Australia, there were other things I adored—the wildlife that could have been spawned from a children's book written by CS Lewis or Maurice Sendak. Spiders bigger than my hand waited in my apartment foyer. Kangaroos watched us whack golf balls into the underbrush at a nine-hole course in Jervis Bay, their tails offering leverage as they pogo-ed across the green. Wombats—which looked to me like dog-sized bears—were a road-kill danger, waddling alongside country byways, eating grass when early evening fell.

And, too, I was smug. I'd visit the States and brag about my new home: we were the real democracy with strong public health cover that ensured everyone had equal access to medical facilities. We had a government-assisted loans scheme in place to enable university education, even for the financially disadvantaged. And before that, university study was free, like the British model. We had higher award rates, which meant the working poor wasn't the issue it was in the US. It was a national event when millions of people marched across the Sydney Harbour Bridge to acknowledge and pay tribute to Aboriginal Australians—I couldn't remember a similar event ever taking place in the States to honour indigenous peoples. With its dusty landscape and bizarre animals and social awareness, I'd found the promised land: an island sitting by itself, below Asia, on the other side of the world.

But that smugness was short-lived; Australia's changed since I first arrived in 1994, implementing policy to bring it in line with the United States. The public health system isn't adequately funded. University fees have skyrocketed. The minimum wage has been lowered.

Brooks watches me, his lenses reflecting the light hanging overhead.

'Unless you decide to leave, you end up staying,' I finally murmur. It feels like any deeper answer would take too long and there are other things I want to discuss.

Brooks leans back, stretching. 'That's true. It's been a while now . . . in Arcata for us.' Even though it's summer, the temperature is mild in northern California. My uncle pulls the cuffs of his sweater up along his forearms.

'Where were Grandpa Brooks and Christine when you moved here?'

'They'd already shifted to the University of North Carolina, Chapel Hill.' My grandfather had been a classics professor at Stanford when my mom was in high school.

'His death must have been a shock.' A brain aneurism on July 26, 1977.

Brooks nods.

'What was he like?'

I don't remember my grandfather. Apparently I would cup my hands over my ears and refuse to look at him. When he tried to talk to me, I babbled to drown out the sound of his voice. This was my response to most men but my mother was embarrassed. She was supposed to be the smart one in her family, her father had plans for her to go to college, but she ended up dropping out of high school when she was pregnant with Serena. Needless to say, I didn't represent her well.

Carolyn stands up, stacking the dishes, and Brooks clears his throat. 'My dad? He was absentminded like most academics. Passionate about teaching. We'd always have students over for dinner, visiting. He loved talking about Virgil.'

It's like a kaleidoscope, this conversation with Brooks. I can see my mother's influences and watch them tilt into mine: education was a family priority. When I was little, Irene read to me every night before I went to bed—Sherlock Holmes and 'The Adventure of the Speckled Band', *Oliver Twist*, *The Hobbit*. She made sure to have a working car (even if the door was wonky) so she could drive Serena to the south end of the island at 6 am every weekday morning. My sister had a scholarship to a private school in Tacoma, a city about thirty miles south of Seattle, and would catch the ferry to the mainland. Fifteen years later, when I was accepted into college, my mother took extra tile commissions so I could study English literature in New York. It didn't matter what I was studying, it was just important that I study.

Scott gathers the remaining plates and follows Carolyn into the kitchen. He doesn't come from a family that dissects personalities and motivations after dinner and I get the sense they have that in common.

Brooks too pushes his chair back and stands up, leaving the room. For a moment, I'm alone at the table. The kitchen sink is running: it's an excessive, beautiful noise after the drought back in New South Wales where water is rationed. Carolyn and Scott's voices murmur over it; they're talking about Australian movies— *The Castle*; *Priscilla, Queen of the Desert*; *Muriel's Wedding*.

After draining my wine, I reach for the bottle. The room feels hazy, as though wet earth has been packed around my brain. I top up the glass anyway, wondering if my conversation with Brooks is finished, but he returns a moment later with a deep red, hardcover volume. He sits down with a heavy motion and passes it to me. Along the spine, the author's name is outlined in gold—Brooks Otis. *Virgil: A Study in Civilized Poetry*. The cover creaks open. Its typeface reminds me of a PhD thesis, not a book. I move slowly through the pages as though it's an early family photo album.

'What did he think when Irene was pregnant with Serena?'

Brooks watches the book in front of me, unsurprised, speaking carefully like my mother might be listening in. 'It was a different time, you have to remember that. But they managed.'

Does he mean my parents (who didn't really manage) or Brooks Sr and Grandma Tine? My mother fell pregnant with my older sister when she was in high school and ten years later she had me. Serena and I are the only two siblings in our immediate family with the same biological parents.

Brooks rests his forearms on the table and the wooden circumference seems smaller. My fingers turn the thick pages slowly. When I speak, it's like I've been triggered by another picture in the album. 'And Michael Cosgrove, you knew him?'

'I was off at college most of the time. He was friends with Cheney. That's how Irene and Mike met.' Cheney, my mom's older brother, died in a car accident when he was twenty-one years old. Brooks continues: 'But when I came home, we jammed together.'

Irene, Mike and Cheney went to Palo Alto High. It was a high school with salubrious alumni: Joan Baez was two years in front of my mother. Members of the Grateful Dead, too.

'What did you think of Mike?'

'I didn't know him that well,' my uncle says. Of course he didn't—no one in my family admits to knowing Michael Cosgrove that well. But I've learned to wait through the long pauses and Brooks finally adds: 'He was a good guitar player.'

Every summer when I came home from college, I would wait until dinner to trap more stories about Michael Cosgrove. I was interested in the stories of my father, but I was also interested in the ways we remembered him, our family mythologies. Because he wasn't part of my life, it was easy to fall into a routine of absence, forgetting about him for months when I was at school, before coming home and bringing him up again at the table. It was only after the food was cleared and the dishwasher humming, the younger members of our clan in bed, that I asked about him. With Elvis as the family soundtrack behind me, my practised voice was casual. What was he like? What did he drink? What instruments could he play?

My older sister had taken enough women's studies classes in grad school that she was well versed in theorising the personal. She could talk of our biological father as though positioning him for a class discussion, but one night she was quiet, picking at the remains of her cobbler.

My mother was sitting beside her, staring at the wine bottle as if staring could be done slowly. At the end of the table, Jim leaned back to finish another beer and it felt like I had a secret ally. He, too, knew the strange stories but hadn't met my father. We waited for someone to start.

Irene eventually spoke, touching her temple as though steadying herself. 'He was charismatic, charming, and he could really play guitar. Blues. Country. There was natural talent there, the guy was a born musician. I think that was the saddest part about him—the potential that never got anywhere.' She smiled grimly, her thin lips disappearing for a moment.

'Alcohol?' I asked, even though I already knew this.

'Sweet cheap wine. He had a real sweet tooth.'

My sister kept quiet. With meditation-straight posture, she pushed her long fingers against the edge of the table, stretching her hands.

Jim watched her. 'How much?'

But my mother answered: 'A few bottles each night. And liqueurs. I remember all the glass. What was I supposed to do with all of that glass?' Irene's spine curved forward and Jim patted her hand like a séance was taking place.

'What did Grandma Bea think?' I asked.

Grandma Bea was a single mother to Michael and his older brother, George; she worked as the personal secretary to a bank director. When the boys were growing up, things weren't easy. Michael and George used to stay with Bea's mother, who wasn't of sound mind—she used to throw her skirt over her head and give George lead bullet casings as pacifiers, which provided yet another theory on why our family was so odd.

Irene glanced up, her voice clear and sober: 'Michael Cosgrove wasn't the only alcoholic. His father, his grandfather, his great-grandfather . . . Bea had a lot on her plate raising those two boys on her own. She did everything she could but Michael didn't buck his fate. At some point, you take responsibility for your actions.'

I had to pinch myself to keep from laughing. Irene wasn't renowned for taking responsibility herself. The family joke was that she became pregnant with Serena through immaculate conception, and I think part of her really believes Serena just happened to her, the way some people just happen to get glandular fever. She treated all of the kids this way—like we appeared on her doorstep and she sighed, setting another place at the table and marking another notch on her cross. It wasn't by chance she was building a Virgin Mary over the fireplace.

Serena read my expression and gave me a look closer to a parental nudge. She always had to save Irene, even though Irene was angriest with her for being born with such inconsiderate timing. The candles had melted over their holders onto the table. I broke off one of the bubbled seams and held it towards the flame. 'What happened when we left?'

I always asked this and yet it's not what really interested me. I wanted to know how glorious Michael Cosgrove was. I wanted to imagine all his talents, all the bands he could have played in and all the cities he could have conquered. Maybe he could have struck out on his own with only instruments as co-stars, laughing with the audience between songs. But even then I was aware that this desire was born out of a disturbing romanticism.

Serena was still watching her hands but her voice was sudden, buoyant. 'We packed the car and were going to stay with Barney and his girlfriend. Remember them?' Her head shifted slightly and the light caught on her glasses, reflecting the plaid table-cloth.

My mother nodded but the story was digressing from other versions I'd heard.

'I thought we stayed at Stell's,' I said. Stell was a friend of my mother's who lived on a boat.

'Whatever happened to Stell?' Serena asked.

'I think she died.'

I worried we were losing the main thread of the conversation until Serena looked up, making eye contact with me. 'We waited for the first ferry off the island.'

Irene and Serena, their voices overlapping: 'Every time a car came onto the dock, I thought it was him.' 'And then we got on the ferry and it just pulled away.'

My mother and sister were in sharp focus, though the background had blurred away—the walls, the kitchen. It was like we were onstage and the set had been carried off.

Irene trailed on, 'We didn't have the money for the toll bridge. We'd spent all our money on gas. I told the woman in the booth it was an emergency.'

'She let you through?' My words felt intrusive.

But Serena nodded and Irene continued, looking at me. 'You were really good. You were in the back in your baby seat.' Six months old.

Behind us, an Elvis ballad stopped with a bleary pause. I didn't want them to notice the finished CD. It had to seem timeless, our conversation around the dinner table. As soon as anyone looked at their watch or noticed the quiet, they would disband for bed.

'I'm one of the reasons you had to leave, right?'

Irene glanced towards the front door and it was like we were all leaving again. 'Mike was too erratic. It wasn't safe to have a baby in the house.'

In some versions of our family narrative, I'm a liberating force that inspired their departure. But the complicated theme in our family is that my mother's mistakes have been the making of our lives. It was a mistake for Irene to get pregnant with Serena and it was certainly a mistake marrying Michael Cosgrove and staying with him for ten years to make my life possible.

My wine glass was empty so I took a huge mouthful of water. It tasted clean.

I stood up and crept towards the stereo. 'And what did Mike do?'

'When?'

'When he realised we were gone.'

My mother's voice was off-hand. 'Oh. I must have told him that he'd have to move out. Eventually he did and we came back.'

I was wondering how long it took for him to leave. Was it a matter of days? Weeks? Did he leave the house in a mess, knowing it wasn't his anymore?

I was about to ask but Irene was shaking her head. 'That was a funky house.' At the north end of the island, the three-bedroom place was slipping off its foundations. The floor had never been finished so my mother had painted the plywood forest green. Mould laced up the walls and the only winter heating came from a wood-fire stove. Serena later told me she remembered rats climbing up the toilet. Eventually, when the tile business expanded and Irene had five employees, we pulled a trailer up the driveway and lived between the two buildings.

Irene filled our glasses. Jim was still watching her as she cleared her throat. 'The only legacy was the phone calls.'

Michael Cosgrove called us, off and on, for about five or six years after he moved out. Creepy late-night rants that turned into threats—generally a sign that Serena and I wouldn't be seeing him for a while. Years later, when Scott and I are visiting Vashon for Christmas, Irene won't remember the phone calls. We'll fight about this and my anger will be disproportionate and pitiless because they are one of the few things I remember. A red rotary dial phone plugged into the far wall of the house.

'There weren't any phone calls,' she'll insist. 'We just bought an answering machine.'

But I know this isn't true. I remember the ringing.

After Irene denied the calls, I talked to Garry, my first stepfather. Irene and Garry met in the late 1970s at The Grotto, a seafood dive next to the north-end ferry dock. This was before Irene became a tile-maker; she was working nights as a waitress. Garry would sit at the same corner table, with his beanie pulled low, and order the clam chowder. He had shy hazel eyes that didn't match his square steel glasses or stained work sleeves, but it wasn't until Irene left a note on his car—inviting him to Christmas dinner—and he arrived at our house without his cap that she realised he was almost bald.

Garry moved in with us when I was four years old—mid-1978. He was a welder until he quit commuting to Seattle and worked with Irene on the tiles. They eventually married, only to divorce during her Dire Straits infatuation (a period of about two years) and then remarry. While they were separated, I visited Garry in Seattle and we'd go to my favourite ice-cream parlour where I'd order cinnamon ice-cream. Grace, my younger sister, was born when Irene and Garry got back together and Lucas was adopted a few years later. In the end, it wasn't Garry's decision to separate, but Irene's. She'd met Jim. That saga—with the mix tapes and the dahlia-eating—began in late 1994.

Garry only met Michael Cosgrove a couple of times but he spent over fifteen years living with us after Michael had left, watching us recuperate. He's the man who drove me into Seattle for piano lessons once a week and to Girl Scouts on Saturday mornings. When Irene and I had such contrasting accounts about the phone calls, I asked Garry what he remembered. We were sitting with Scott at the Mexican restaurant on Vashon—it was the kind of place with huge platters of food, and plastic benches that stick to your legs.

'Irene says she bought an answering machine. Did they even have answering machines in the late seventies?' I asked.

Scott touched my knee under the table like he was trying to steady me. He knew the stories about Michael Cosgrove. My family didn't talk about my biological father as much as they used to but he'd heard enough.

Pushing his glasses along the bridge of his nose, Garry stared at me. A fringe of white hair circled his head. He'd grown thinner and greyer living alone. That afternoon, he'd come straight from work where he was welding again. His jeans were creased with black grease, stretched at the knees, but he'd changed into a clean shirt on the ferry—a plaid flannel I remembered from when we used to live together; it must have been at least ten years old.

He spoke quietly but it was a matter of habit, not out of deference to my mother. 'There's no way she had an answering machine. We were too poor. She'd just pull the cord out of the wall.'

The waiter splashed water into each of our glasses and then glided away.

Garry looked from me to Scott and then back to me again. We were poor. I'd forgotten that. Food stamps. Counting Irene's tips. Serena babysitting me, promising candy bars if I behaved. We shopped for clothing at second-hand stores in White Center, Seattle. Even my talk-along storybooks were homemade. Serena and Irene would record my stories on a little cassette recorder with different voices for each character, and Serena would gong a kitchen spoon against a pot when it was time to turn the page.

The waiter set a steaming plate in front of me and I picked up my fork. 'I wonder why she doesn't remember the phone calls.'

A few days after talking with Garry, I was sitting with my mother in Ruby, parked on a double-decker ferry. Irene and I were running errands in Seattle and she was wearing a black-and-white polka-dot dress and green-yellow cashmere sweater. Her head was recently shaved and the plan, this time, was to dye her hair purple.

My spiral-bound sketch diary was on my lap with half-hearted doodles lining the pages. I was asking about my father again.

'It wasn't a pleasant time.' Irene reached for a rag rug in the back seat—an ongoing craft project. She ripped the material in a long, curt gesture and started feeding it through a heavy needle, knotting it in place. Her eyes were focused on the patterned red cloth, its tension almost elastic as she yanked it through the matching fabric. 'What do you need at Costco?'

My questions weren't even original: the story of the long-lost father was too banal. In a family that had always spoken about everything with relentless intensity, her sudden reluctance seemed ridiculous.

'I'm going upstairs.' I slammed the door behind me and took the steps two at a time to the passenger deck.

That night, I spoke to Serena on the phone. 'Why isn't she proud of how far she's come, how successful she is? The woman who is our mother isn't the same woman who stayed with Mike. That incomprehensible distance, she should be proud of it.'

The distance *was* incomprehensible, I realised, as though both my parents were lost to me. The versions of Michael Cosgrove from the dining table didn't match my memories and the mother I knew would never have stayed: our family ground was unsteady.

'You have to remember, Shady . . .' My sister's voice was soft and patronising but I was old enough to listen through that. 'Mike used to tell Irene she was so stupid she couldn't even hang a picture straight.'

In Arcata, I'm trying to imagine that scene—my mother standing on a chair, tilting a glass-framed Matisse print, my father yelling at her—when Uncle Brooks hands me a photograph. A group of five men, barely out of high school, stare at the camera. Their postures are like rock stars but their expressions are young, honest. Jerry Garcia stands in the middle, a centrepiece, ready for his future successes. Brooks leans in on the left-hand side, the

most handsome of the group. And second from the right, standing
slightly behind the others, awkward: my father. He's holding a
guitar. I never imagined him so unsure.

Because the bus will be leaving before dawn, Brooks and Carolyn
say goodbye the night before. Scott still doesn't know whether
to hug those in my family or shake their hands. He moves in
slowly, prepared for either, but Carolyn just sidesteps his arm and
embraces him.

Brooks scratches his head and the gesture reminds me of
photographs of his father. 'You going through Arizona? I have
some friends in Prescott. Let me get their number for you.'

It's just another slip of paper in my journal but I feel more
secure when we set out the next morning, prowling back to the
bus station through Arcata's hollow streets—Brooks must trust
us to represent him.

Crossing an empty intersection, I pause and face Scott. 'I like
them, Brooks and Carolyn.'

He looks at me like I've told him it's nice to watch football
on Friday nights—some things are given—but my mother is
bubbling up inside me and I want to express everything in ripples
of words. 'My family has grown from stopping here, Scott; it's
larger than I realised. It's like another home here.'

'You want to live in Arcata?' He's making fun of me.

My voice is overly thoughtful, ironic: 'Yeah. I'm thinking of
moving here. With Brooks and Carolyn. They won't mind us
living in the guest room and we could drive up to Vashon whenever
we want. Dan should be fine on the couch.'

'That's the best place for him.'

'We'll tell them they can cook more pasta for us.'

'And play live music whenever we want it,' Scott says.

'And more guitar packs. One's not enough.'

'I want one too. Your family can't discriminate just 'cause I don't play.'

We're still laughing when we march into the parking lot, destination San Francisco, but I realise I could live in northern California. I could live near family.

In Australia, with holiday and birthday celebrations limited to phone calls, I would imagine the Vashon kitchen—the mismatching silverware, the blue-and-white china plates, the blown-glass cups. Each item pictured one by one in a slide-show sequence to stave off homesickness.

After Serena moved back to the island, she told me I was blessed to live on the other side of the world because whenever I came home, it was an event to be celebrated and Irene made sure we all had time together. It's harder to find that time in the everyday, Serena said. But that's exactly what I crave: being able to take my family for granted. I want to eat dinner without revelling in my mother's bright tablecloths or counting the number of meals before the next departure gate.

LONG LONELY HIGHWAY

San Francisco has a steel grey centre surrounded by water, dusty hills and pastel architecture. The terraced houses offer a mirage of grandeur but most of them are broken into separate flats. The mail slots are the only way to surmise how many families live in each building.

Scott and I stay in the Castro district with Amy, my best friend from college. She looks out of place meeting us at the Greyhound station. Her face is clean, without make-up, but she carries herself with the polished confidence I associate with upper-end department stores. Her yoga pants fall like crisp slacks—too loose on her frame.

'Training,' she says, hugging me. She's just qualified for the Boston Marathon.

It's only been a couple of years since we last saw each other. Her narrow blue eyes and heavy freckles are just as I remember them but her orange-gold hair has grown past her shoulders. It makes her look older and younger at the same time—the style is girlish but it lengthens her face. It's funny to imagine this Volvo driver as the same woman who'd almost joined the circus as a trapeze artist instead of going to college. When she laughs, though, it's an outrageous hiccup of sound and I remember her dorm room, painted 'Summer Sapphire' with sporadic white clouds so she could sleep in the sky.

When I meet her friends, Sarah and Daniel, it's with a certain voyeurism. If I'd moved to San Francisco after college, instead of Australia, maybe I'd be part of this circle of friends. I'd considered it—at least an ocean wouldn't separate me from my family, and there's security in knowing that you're connected by land, that you can drive home. For two years, when I first returned to Australia, I worried disaster might strike and I wouldn't have the money to fly back to Vashon.

Large bay windows invite the afternoon light into Amy's living room, lifting the texture of the deep maroon walls. Scott and I are sitting on a cushy L-shaped couch opposite a fireplace that's no longer used; the empty grille seems incongruous in the small room.

Downstairs, the doorbell rings and excited voices echo up the stairwell, and soon Amy's introducing us proudly and offering wine. Daniel wears dark square glasses. His almost-black hair is short, spiked up on top, and his shirt is collared, crisp: the fashion code of a graphic designer. I'm not surprised to find that Sarah is training as a hairdresser—dark wisps fringe her eyes; it's a glamorous cut. Her small lips are painted with pink-red lip-gloss. Daniel and Sarah have a whippet named Poppy. Whippets are oddly stylish dogs, gaunt like greyhounds, but smaller, breakable.

'Poppy's a little accident-prone,' Amy told me before they arrived.

When Poppy trots in and sniffs at the coffee table, it's clear Amy wasn't exaggerating: her tail is incarcerated in a pink cast.

Sarah strokes the dog's head. 'She was running across a field and tripped. Over nothing, really.'

I can't look at Scott. His commentary is already playing in my head: 'What next? The dog was running. The dog tripped. The dog broke its tail. Have you *ever* heard of a dog breaking its tail? You'd want to think long and hard before paying that vet bill.'

I try to imagine Scott living in San Francisco: owning a whippet, working as a graphic designer. The thought inspires nervous giggles and Amy glances at me before turning to Daniel. 'Shady and Scotty are going to Memphis. She's been playing Elvis covers in every town she stops at.'

'Yep.' I smile broadly, my head moving in agreement and no other words come. Sure, I can make fun of their dog but at least they're not busking to Graceland. Elvis is a ridiculed and contentious figure known for drugs, materialism, shooting televisions and careening in golf carts. Why on earth would I need to be received at Graceland? Here in this fancy living room, I feel like a freak.

Amy continues: 'They're going to get there for the twenty-fifth anniversary of his death.'

Again, I nod. No one notices—we're all staring at the ornate detailing on the fireplace.

'Come on, Shady. Play us a song.'

The last thing I want to do is retrieve my guitar but Scott's bobbing his head like he thinks it'll be a real showstopper: my boyfriend is either raving mad or deaf with love for me.

With the Martin on my lap, I scoot to the edge of the sofa. Amy fills my wine glass and I take a deep mouthful. Then, 'Heartbreak Hotel'. The chord changes come automatically. My chest is more relaxed, my voice loud. Drawing out the notes, I double-back on the chorus for a second time at the end. Everyone in the room claps enthusiastically, even Scott, who's heard it forty times. He grins: you're getting better, Grove.

In the last three minutes, the ice has broken—not in the room, but within myself, like a rubber galosh stomping down on a frozen puddle. I'm less insecure.

'Have you had any scary moments?' Sarah asks as I set the instrument down.

'What do you mean?'

'You know, on the street.'

'Nothing too bad. My sign weirded someone out.'

'Your sign?'

I reach down to the case and fish it out, handing it to Sarah. She squints at the white typeface and passes it around the circle. I shift to the floor, sitting with my back against the couch.

'There's a lot of text,' Daniel says when it reaches him. He's holding it so only the back is visible from my angle but he's right. Through my red wine buzz, I can picture the passage. The words are centred in the middle of the page in that white, fourteen-point font, not big enough to be read easily by passers-by.

I adjust the clip in my hair and lean back against the thick pillows. 'I take myself too seriously. Times New Roman is an earnest font. The sign's describing an Elvis pilgrimage, for God's sake. Of all the places you can't take yourself seriously. What was I thinking?' All of us are laughing.

Sarah glances over Daniel's shoulder. 'Do people stop to read it?'

'A few have. But most—no.'

Scott shakes his head. 'They stop, but I'd say they only get through the first few lines.'

Amy leans forward. 'It needs to be dramatic. Maybe with a photo of Elvis.'

'Yeah, old Elvis,' Sarah chimes in. 'Definitely old Elvis.'

Both women look at Daniel and he smiles. 'Let me work on it.'

The next day he draws up a few samples and emails them to me: simple lines, clean photographs, clear words: Going to Graceland. Please Help. Elvis Anniversary. August 16th, 2002.

Scott and I spend five days in San Francisco. Scott entertains himself with excursions to Alcatraz and the wharfs. I'm busy helping Amy pick out flowers and attend dress fittings—she's getting married in a couple of months. When the Elvis pilgrimage is finished, Scott and I will fly back to San Francisco where I'll be a bridesmaid at her wedding. Meanwhile, there's a large piece of butcher paper taped across a wall of her living room. It's a multi-tiered to-do list that resembles an intricate family tree; each morning we cross off items and add more to be done. The time with Amy should feel like I'm having a holiday from Elvis but it actually feels as though I've entered someone else's quest—like we're both undertaking rites of passage and for a few brief days they've overlapped.

The night before we're due to head out, Scott and I are sitting on the bed in Amy's guest room. I feel liberated and frightened by the fact that we could go anywhere the next morning.

'Where next? LA?' I ask.

The movies were a large part of Elvis as a capitalist machine: the movies promoted the soundtracks which promoted the movies which promoted the soundtracks ... Many Elvis hits, such as 'King Creole', 'Return to Sender' and 'Viva Las Vegas', had cinematic inspirations.

Scott's large shoulders lift slightly. 'Aren't we trying to get to Memphis? Isn't this about Graceland?'

'Yeah, but the movies. Hollywood. That's part of Elvis.'

'Name one you enjoyed.'

Serena's favourite Elvis movie was *Viva Las Vegas* and whenever it appeared on television, we'd make caramel popcorn and snuggle under blankets to watch it. When Elvis appeared on screen, she'd squeal and pinch me but even I have to admit the allure was spending time with my big sister rather than watching the cinematic work. Elvis never took acting lessons and in some films this is more apparent than others. His increased dependency on amphetamines during later shoots didn't help. To me, Hollywood symbolises the point where Elvis sold out. By 1960 he was disgruntled with his dialogue but Colonel Tom Parker, his manager, continued to negotiate contracts focused only on commercial returns, not artistic value. Elvis wanted both but never stood up to Tom Parker on this count. Or if he did, it never showed.

My pause says enough.

'So east then?' Scott asks.

On the sixteen-hour trip from San Francisco to Salt Lake City, the Greyhound soon loses any grubby allure it might have had. After suburbia, the landscape turns thirsty: even the trees have wilted. When dark begins to fall, my knees already ache. A sweater wadded up against the glass serves as a pillow but my neck reverberates with the steady motion of the bus.

Scott's already asleep, snoring softly. I shift around so my head is in his lap, my legs twisted against the window. The lights have been turned off and a quiet intimacy descends upon the bus like twenty strangers sharing a tent. Occasionally someone will brush along the aisle to the toilet but the road is so straight no one loses their balance.

The air-conditioning runs at a steady murmur so I pull my rain jacket close, tucking it between me and the seat to trap my body heat. Scott's lap is warm against my cheek. Then, four or five hours later, the cabin lights jerk on and the microphone shrieks with feedback. The driver's voice booms: 'We'll be arriving in Reno in about ten minutes. Please gather your things.'

Scott shifts beneath me. 'It's okay. It's not us.'

The driver cuts in again: 'Even if you're continuing on to Salt Lake City, you'll have to get off the bus for an hour. Make sure you take all of your belongings with you—the bus will be cleaned.'

Cleaned? At three in the morning?

When the engine cuts out in the parking lot, the driver's voice sounds again: 'You can collect coupons for the poker machines when you disembark.'

Gambling in the middle of the night? What's wrong with this place?

The other passengers are already stepping off. Scott rubs his eyes like it's no use fighting the inevitable; his hibernation's been interrupted.

'What if we refuse?' I ask blearily.

'Come on.' He's standing, easing my guitar down.

Inside, the station is hollow and coated with sallow, flickering light. The toilets are on the far side of the room. Just to the left, a woman swears at the lockers, kicking them, and I feel a strange sense of déjà vu that takes me back to the Seattle bus station with its broken lockers. It's been less than two weeks since Scott and I were waiting in line, buying our bus passes. Travelling can warp time, I think. It feels like we've been on the road for months.

Treading carefully around the angry woman, I enter the bathroom. My face looks dry, my skin yellow from the overhead grille light. Two of the toilet stalls are out of order, the others in various states of mess. I crouch over the cleanest bowl and then wash my hands but the soap dispensers are empty. Outside, I crumple into the seat beside Scott, locking the guitar case to my body.

'The romance of bus travel is wearing thin.' My legs, fully extended over the concrete floor tiles, are the only part of me that's content.

When the driver calls out, 'Salt Lake City—ready to board,' my semiconscious haze is interrupted.

The bus door is open, its tall black steps welcoming. Scott and I shunt down the aisle, back to our seats. I'm asleep before the bus leaves Reno.

Salt Lake City is named after the great salt plains that surround it. The land is cracked and white with craters, the temperature hot like California but drier, stern. It's been light for hours and we're still on the bus, stopping occasionally at lonesome casino dens. I take no chances of being left behind and use the toilet at the back of the bus.

When we pull into the station, I stand immediately. My journal, Elvis biographies and walkman have been packed into the guitar pack's click-on bag for the past hour and a half in case we happened to arrive early.

'No need to hurry. We're all going to get off the bus,' Scott says. He likes to wait for the entire bus—including those behind us—to unload. I don't get it. After the stretch we've just put in I'd leave without him but he has the aisle seat, trapping me in.

Outside, we scan the guidebook and trudge from the bus station along South Temple Street. The buildings are severe and looming. Their concrete façades imply a false longevity, as though the city is timeless and has always existed. Buildings and parks are labelled with embossed plaques. Even the public administration blocks resemble concrete steeples. It's the architectural equivalent of George Orwell's *1984* crossed with the Old Testament.

Despite the fact that he's wearing a baseball cap, Scott shields his eyes from the sun. 'Where're you going to busk?'

'Maybe up there?' But at the intersection, a sign is posted to a stone wall, 'No Begging', and I wonder if honouring Elvis is a form of begging.

The street is empty, shops closed, sidewalk abandoned. The only posters are those soliciting information about a missing girl. Her vacant-eyed photo stares out at us from the electricity poles. Scott eyes her warily. 'This is like a tomb.'

Salt Lake City's gardens are immaculate, the green shrubs in tidy rows. It doesn't feel that we're in a bad part of town, just an abandoned one. Outside the schools, the crosswalk flags are still in place, though no children are visible. This could be a science fiction Armageddon where everyone has died except us.

A red Toyota drives by—relief.

'I don't know if I can play Elvis here. It's a little weird.'

We pace along the perfectly moulded sidewalks and I can feel the sun burning the top of my head. 'I know what it is.' My voice snaps through the quiet air.

'What?'

'It's Sunday—everyone's at church.'

Scott nods sheepishly. 'Church. Guess that makes sense.'

I glance at the guidebook. 'If I'm not going to busk, we might just head to the hostel.'

'Don't you want to give it a go?'

I wish myself more nerve, imagining my voice loud and reckless: none of the ballads, only the boisterous ones. 'Hound Dog'. 'That's All Right'. But at the next stoplight, there's another sign that prohibits begging.

Scott scans behind us. 'Have you noticed—no benches?' It's true. The only place to sit is on the kerb.

My reluctance to play the guitar in Salt Lake City is not simply a fear of busking. It is specifically linked to my musical repertoire: Elvis. Certainly Elvis was a man of faith—his Grammys testify to the power of his gospel ballads. But in Utah, I'm also aware of Elvis as a symbol of sex and decadence with his twitching legs and gold lamé jacket. For the first time, I understand how rebellious he might have seemed in his early career. Elvis acted as a marker of his generation, especially in the late fifties. For those born in later years, after the pinnacle of his arc, it's difficult to fathom his influence.

My only comparable experience is from my first year of high school. I would listen to the Violent Femmes with the volume turned low so my mother wouldn't hear the anti-feminist lyrics in the song 'Gimme the Car'. Then, with my late eighties haircut— shaved on one side, long on the other—and my pointed, silver- buckled witch shoes, I'd sneak out of the house at midnight and meet boyfriends at the bottom of my driveway. But for generations after me, the Violent Femmes aren't rebellious and alternative: their music echoes in shopping malls. Every era has icons that separate it from those before.

Elvis may now be an established force in the rock-and-roll musical canon—old-fashioned even—but at the time, he was loathed by older generations. He was particularly reviled in newspaper reports because of the uncontrollable lust he inspired in his fans. This man incited riots—women tore at his clothes, ripped apart his vehicles and stormed buildings if he was rumoured to be inside. The saying 'Elvis has left the building' was originally broadcast via loudspeaker to his fans when they refused to leave his concert venues. In Salt Lake City, I realise this power still exists in his music.

Scott and I pause beneath a thin tree carefully guarded by concrete pylons. As I contemplate the meagre shade, a couple crosses the street in front of us. In the city emptiness, I'd usually be relieved to see other humans but their skin has an eerie whiteness. They both have the same hair colour—the palest brown I've ever seen—and their small steps seem haunted. I can't play Elvis here. Scott beckons towards my backpack but the guitar stays in its case.

Salt Lake City has two hostels. Scott and I play Rock, Scissors, Paper to see who has to call for reservations. We ball our hands together and shake them in perfect time so no one can cheat. On the count of three, I have a fisted rock and Scott an open paper hand: he wins. I dig into my pockets and slot coins into the phone.

A serene, female voice tells me the first one is full.

At the second, a man answers halfway through the first ring. I ask if he has a room available.

'For one or two?' He speaks quickly, like we're playing a phone equivalent of charades and the timer's running.

'Two.'

'Married?'

'I suppose.'

He pauses on that but only for a moment. 'What's your nationality?'

'American.'

Then, certain: 'Nup. Nothing for you.' The phone goes dead.

Scott watches me place the receiver down slowly. 'What happened?'

'I'm pretty sure he had a room but didn't want to give it to me . . . Maybe if you call?'

Scott eyes me as though I'm trying to subvert the power of Rock, Scissors, Paper.

I lean against the plastic window. 'Nothing else is within budget. What can we do?'

Reaching into his pocket for more coins, Scott dials the number: 'Hello? I'm looking for a room . . . Yeah, New South Wales, actually. South of Sydney . . . Yeah, I've been in the States before. Friendly people . . .' Scott motions for me to hand him a pen and scrounges in his pocket for something to write on. 'No, we're on the Greyhound . . .' He starts scribbling on the white scrap of paper. As Scott keeps talking, I stare absentmindedly at the photograph of the young blonde girl posted inside the telephone booth. It's like she's the personification of something deeper that this place is missing.

'So we follow that through and then go right? Small street, yep. Yep. Two of us. Yeah, she did call earlier . . . No worries. Thanks for that. See you soon.'

When he hangs the receiver back on the hook, Scott has a wide smile.

'You got a room?' It doesn't make sense.

He surveys the road and glances down at his notes. 'It's a bit of a trek.' His voice is even but he's smirking like his football team just won and he had twenty dollars riding on the outcome.

Scott starts walking and I stay planted by the phone booth. Partly it's his expression but more off-putting is the situation— either the hostel doesn't like Americans or it doesn't like women. Neither option seems particularly welcoming.

Scott calls back about ten paces away as a crow swoops by. My gaze is fixed on the bird, its claws clamped to an electrical line.

'Shady, where else are we going to go?'

I just want to lie down—I'm shattered from the bus trip and my stomach is growling. These two sensations—exhaustion and hunger—are so strong I'm overwhelmed with homesickness. For Australia or Vashon, it doesn't matter, but this city makes me uncomfortable. As an immigrant in Australia, I've always been defined as 'American' but I'm beginning to realise my homeland is much smaller—the Pacific Northwest.

I wonder if the bird is an omen in this strange place—maybe something will die, maybe my relationship to America is changing —but then it flaps away and I just feel overly superstitious.

Scott retraces his path and takes my uncooperative hand. 'Come on.'

When we finally arrive, Scott pushes through the door, eager for air-conditioning, but inside a series of fans are perched throughout the room, forcing air around in hot gusts. A man with a wiry frame and jeering teeth waits at the counter, his hands clasped in front of him.

He studies Scott, ignoring me. 'You must be the Australian,' he says and I recognise his voice.

Scott sets down the backpack, leaning it against the counter. 'Sure am.'

'You born there?' His tone is curious, not hostile, like he can't quite figure out what he's seeing.

Scott grins, nodding. He isn't pale like his mother and people often have trouble picking his ancestry—I've heard guesses from Native American to Aboriginal Australian, Islander to Spanish. Maybe it's his long ponytail or his round nose and lips. After a few beers, he tells people his forefathers were pirates who got shipwrecked off England.

Scott moves to the counter for the paperwork. The form is already lying out, waiting. He looks to me for a pen and the man tosses one to him.

Standing next to Scott, I'm unsure where to look. Beyond the counter, two backpackers are perched in front of a television like overheated birds. The volume is absurdly low.

The receptionist leans across the counter. 'I know you're not married.' He has the kind of face that would look better with a beard—his mouth is too small, his lean jaw hungry.

Scott glances down at his passport and keeps jotting the numbers in sequence.

Then, in a tone that's either threatening or conspiring, the man whispers: 'Don't worry. I won't tell anyone.'

'What?' My voice is sharp and Scott leans his leg against mine beneath the counter, but by now I'm hoping this freako kicks us out.

Our host's tongue darts out of his mouth, circling his top lip. 'In these parts, they don't look well on that.' He's smiling but his tone isn't quite joking. When he hands Scott the key, he winks.

'We don't know what we're travelling into,' I say, tripping on a frayed piece of synthetic carpet as Scott leads me upstairs.

After one night, we leave Salt Lake for Cedar City—a place with neither cedars nor city at the freeway turn-off—and eventually pioneer on to Las Vegas. Scott's upset about this. He likes the Utah capital because it hosted the 2002 Winter Olympics and he wants to see the facilities. I tell him I'll stay another night but only if he's willing to front up the cash for better accommodation: we end up moving on.

For the final Greyhound leg into Sin City, the air-conditioning is cold and immediate. Most of the seats are taken. Scott moves down the aisle ahead of me and sits next to a blond man whose frame is as wide as his own. Two rows further back, there's an empty spot. Next to it a young man, maybe eighteen, has a leg cocked up against the seat in front of him. His hair's slicked back and his glasses are too dark for the dimmed bus, the frames heavy on his pallid face—just enough attitude for a quiet ride to Vegas. He tweaks his head towards his shoulder in a crooked nod and I sit down, careful not to brush his elbow, which has taken ownership of the central armrest.

Before I'm settled, the bus has jerked towards the on-ramp to the highway. Through the window, the earth and sky are both brown-grey, mimicking one another. The monotony is almost intoxicating but I've got plans to finish the first volume of the Elvis biography.

'Where you going?' my new travel companion asks.

For a moment I think he's talking to someone else, maybe the couple in front of us—it's only when he turns his head and his dark lenses stare at me that I reply, 'What?'

'Las Vegas?' He's chewing gum like he has something to prove.

'Oh. Yeah.'

'Ever been in love?' His jaw stops and he lifts his sunglasses, peering intently at me.

The question seems so sudden I wonder if I've misheard. 'Sorry?'

'I'm in love.'

'Oh.' Maybe he's mistaken me for someone he knows. If I wasn't so eager to learn what happens next to Elvis—he's just broken into Hollywood—I could be more attentive. I'm on the rush of Elvis's breakthrough, the optimism that anything is possible. The kid sitting next to me seems the antithesis of this and he reeks of suburban hostility. If anything, he makes me nervous.

He's still staring at me. 'I've come from Colorado. Going back home to California.'

I reach down for the book, balancing it on my knees, and make a show of tucking my bag under the seat in front of me like I'm settling in for a long, quiet ride. 'Colorado's beautiful.'

He speaks with the drawl of a 1940s movie star gangster: 'I wouldn't know. Was there for fourteen hours. Fourteen hours.

I love that girl,' he sighs. 'Her dad thinks I'm bad news, won't let her see me. She's underage: sixteen.'

The book is beaming up from my lap but he turns fully towards me, waiting.

'Sounds like bad luck.'

'You said it.' He leans back and raps the window with the back of his fist. 'I just want to see her.'

I'm scanning the bus but there aren't any empty seats. 'You'll find a way. If it's meant to be—'

'By the way, I'm Jeremy.' He speaks so fast when he cuts me off that I wonder if Jeremy is on speed.

'Hi, Jeremy. Shady.'

He pauses, as though considering whether to shake hands. Instead, his whole body shifts towards me again, the window framing his silhouette. 'I've never been so in love. When my high school diploma comes through, I'm moving to Colorado, I tell you.'

I nod.

'You know. It's not fair. It's fucking not fair.' His face has gained a little colour; his eyes are an attractive brown and I think maybe he's okay, he's just a kid who's smitten, until he leans forward and swings his right fist hard against the window. The sound is anticlimactic, though his hand must hurt. The woman across the aisle is staring at us.

'Come on, Jeremy. Get it together,' I whisper.

Romeo's incarnation stares blackly at the window. 'Sorry. I just hate her dad. He's such an asshole. You know, I haven't slept in thirty-six hours. Can't sleep on the bus.'

That might explain it, I think, looking past him to the window. We aren't close to Vegas and the horizon is vacant—it must be three hours to the next petrol station.

He keeps smoothing his hair and checking his reflection in the window. 'Do you think I should call him, make a death threat?'

'What?' It's more exclamation than question. My mouth gawks open and I can't close it; this kid's all Montague.

He clears his throat. 'You know, so he takes me seriously. Knows I love her.'

Ahead, Scott is chatting away to his blond seatmate who, it will turn out, once lived in Wollongong and played rugby union for the Tech. I've got no chance of swapping places so I gently reach for the paperback on my lap as though easing it into the conversation. I'm not up to Vegas yet but I'm going to check the index and see what I can find out.

Jeremy is still breathing heavily beside me. 'Death is serious, you know.'

'I don't think threats would help the situation much.' The book eases open.

He lowers his arm from the sill and this seems to have a calming effect. He relaxes back into his seat. 'You're probably right.'

VIVA LAS VEGAS

If you want to hang off the eyeball of America, climb into the belly of the beast they call popular culture, Las Vegas is it: you are here.

This city may be known for Elvis and the white jumpsuit era but his first run in the Neon City began in late April 1956. I tell Scott as much while he scans the map.

'First time here, the older crowd didn't like him. It was 1969 when he broke all the attendance records. The International Hotel was so impressed they ripped up his contract and raised his performance fee. Imagine that.'

Scott doesn't care about my new Elvis trivia; he just gestures to the road. We're at least three kilometres from the Strip and Nevada is hot: the sun is beating down bullets and the mercury has heatstroke. Anyone with sense, a guitar case and a large backpack would catch a bus but Scott and I are wearing our trusty cheap skates and have plans to glide our way to the Strip on foot. It may be mid-afternoon in one of the hottest places on the planet but the bus will cost a full $1.50 each.

'We both walk, that's a three-dollar savings,' Scott says, flicking me the guidebook. If the situation weren't so absurd, you'd have to say we were made for each other. Who else would agree to heat exhaustion to save a few bucks?

82

Just ten paces from the bus station, any glide has disappeared from our step. The footpath radiates such vicious heat it feels like we're walking in the puddle of a mirage, and wet circles have already formed under Scott's arms.

On the corner, we're across from a cheap motel with a drive-through wedding chapel. The sign advertises Elvis impersonators as marriage celebrants.

'I think we're definitely headed in the right direction.' Scott points at the neon figure of the King.

I squint into the sunlight. 'You want to get married in Vegas?' I'm not wedding anxious like some of my friends who are waiting for proposals. Maybe it's my family history but I'm not convinced marriage is the most stable of unions.

Scott laughs. 'I wouldn't want to compromise you—marriage being such a patriarchal institution and all.' This is a joke stemming back to the Wollongong grouphouse where Scott and I met. Many of the residents were active in student politics—vegan lesbians, wannabe rock-stars, international exchange students, marijuana enthusiasts. Whenever there was a debate about the chore-wheel, patriarchy somehow got the blame.

'I meant the right direction for Elvis,' Scott adds.

I shrug. Scott and I joke that we're too cheap for a wedding so we just go to our friends' and pretend they're ours—like we picked them up second-hand from an op-shop wedding specialist. So far we've been 'married' in Kangaroo Valley, Melbourne and Wollongong. Amy's wedding will add San Francisco to the list but Scott's told me not to mention this to her. 'She's put a lot of time into it and might think we're trying to steal her thunder.'

Alongside us, a taxi slows down. Scott ignores it, pulling ahead of me. One-two, one-two: his wide steps follow a steady rhythm as unrelenting as the heat. Even the tops of my arms are sweating. Ahead, a bus pulls into the shelter. Scott tilts his head. 'What do you think?'

I sigh. 'If we catch it, we should have caught it five hundred metres ago.' There is a perverse logic to this: value for money. It makes sense to ride the bus as far as possible on the one fare. If we board it now, we've 'wasted' the walking we've already done so we may as well keep going.

The bus leaves, exhaling a hot cloud of exhaust. This heat is so absurd, so novel, I can't be irritated by it. 'I don't think I've ever been this hot in my life.' My tone is almost giddy.

Scott sighs in agreement, an uncharacteristic sound from him.

A large tower stands to the right. It reminds me of the Seattle Space Needle with its long, concrete stalk and restaurant hub at the top. I peer up at it, gazing against the midday light. 'It's a casino—the Stratosphere, I think.'

'Which one are we looking for?'

'Circus Circus. According to this, they're right next to each other.' But it's obvious I don't understand the scale of the map. The casinos in Vegas are among the largest hotels in the world. MGM Grand Casino, for instance, offers over fifteen square kilometres of gaming and accommodation. It's at least another twenty minutes before we open the door to the jet blast of air-conditioning that is Circus Circus.

Later that night, in our hotel room, I open the backpack, sifting through the camping supplies and dirty socks for 'the dress'. Purchased back in Australia, designed by Bang, it's the most expensive garment I've ever owned—a pale beige shift beneath an English rose–patterned lace overlay. Even though it's too elegant for Vegas, it's the only cocktail number travelling with us and I'm wearing it for Elvis: tonight I'm busking for the man.

'You ready?' Scott asks after we've both showered. My lips shimmer back at me in the bathroom mirror; I rub them together, somehow smearing gloss on my chin. I've been travelling too long. With grimy fingernails and damp underwear just washed in the basin, my femininity feels like a clownish approximation.

In the hotel corridor, Scott sets my guitar down and presses the button for the elevator. Inside, I focus on our faint, steel reflections and when the doors finally open, the foyer I am expecting has been replaced with a large gaming area. Animated groups are crowded around tables. A man close by throws the dice, his whole body part of the gesture, and a loud moan sounds in response. One of many roulette wheels spins behind him, uneven piles of chips waiting on the table for the motion to slow. A woman calls out to the marble as though it might listen. Beyond her, rows and rows of poker machines sit with images flickering across their screens. The room has the hustle of an auction and the sheer size of a stadium; it echoes the absurdity of my mission— I'm probably the only tourist in Vegas right now with no interest in gambling.

'Where are we?' Scott shifts the guitar carefully around the patrons as we cross the room. We navigate small staircases to make our way through the building but just when I think we're at an exit, we turn the corner to be faced with a carnival alley offering pinball machines and games. A crowd has formed in front of a racing competition and a large man at the end is winning—he's shooting a water pistol into a clown's mouth to seesaw his corresponding horse along the board above.

'Maybe down this way?' Scott turns to the right.

I'm tense, as though Elvis is expecting us and we're late. The walls have no windows or clocks—the gaming rooms are temporally and geographically suspended. For a moment, it seems we might not be able to leave. We're in a video game—the 'exit' is a luminous trophy only attainable if we manoeuvre through all the levels. We graduate out of the gaming corridor into an open room with a big-tent circus. The huge red and white awning is suspended from the ceiling, forcing me to re-evaluate the sheer vastness of the casino. This must be the namesake of the hotel. Trapeze artists swing from the ceiling, wearing lacy bathing suits. A ringmaster with a top hat is calling events from the sideline. He's too young and thin for the role—probably a college student on summer vacation. Even though it's getting late, kids gape eagerly from the audience—some with parents, many alone. When the jugglers and acrobats run onstage, Scott and I continue our search for the exit.

'You might have to busk in here,' he says when we round into a mirrored wall.

'We'll be the only fans that didn't make it to Graceland—sorry, Elvis, we got trapped in a Vegas casino.'

'You wouldn't want to write home with that beauty, would you? Especially when we were going so well.'

After backtracking through the gaming alley and down another set of stairs, we consult a glassed-in map beside a staircase.

'Do you need any assistance?' The concierge looks suspiciously like the ringmaster—maybe a recurring villain in this Circus Circus video game.

'Exit?'

He points behind us to an automatic doorway that didn't exist three seconds before. I nod meekly and hurry towards it—it could be a portal to the next level, only open for a limited time. Scott shuffles behind, unaware of my sudden urgency.

Every two hundred feet along the Strip, someone tries to hand me a leaflet advertising 'XXX' and 'GIRLS'. The city horizon is awake with synthetic lights. The spearing colours, flashing words and moving pictures are so vivid I can't imagine the dusted earth landscape along the I-15 highway. On the Strip, cars are paused at the stoplights like ponies, groomed and shiny. They shift into low gear with the green signal, though they don't move much faster than the people on foot.

We haven't gone far but we're close to the New Frontier Hotel where Elvis made his Las Vegas debut. Scott nods, handing me the guitar case. I'm sitting in front of a sign advertising 27-ounce margaritas for 99 cents and wondering if they do takeaway.

Obviously my first song has to be 'Viva Las Vegas'. I sing it twice. My tapping foot follows the rhythm of the lights across the street as they blink on and off. The pedestrians pass in sync like we're all connected through the steady pulse of the energy grid, and coins plunk together in front of me. Here, especially, Elvis is the symbol of the phoenix: the great return. By singing of him, it's like we're all returning—everyone who passes me on the street is part of a new cycle. They throw money at me like the performance is a charm and this song will watch over them inside the next casino.

I'm rounding back into the first verse once again when a security guard approaches. He's a stocky man about my age wearing a dark blue uniform. His face is pinched, a human bull terrier.

'Ma'am, I'm going to have to ask you to leave.' He speaks like a caricature of an American: the twang we hear on TV shows in Australia. I can't help smiling at this and that only seems to piss him off.

He speaks louder. 'We don't have begging here in Las Vegas.'

'I'm not begging, this is a pilgrimage.' A beggar wouldn't be wearing a designer gown to play Elvis songs. To emphasise this, I straighten my posture to make the dress fall straight.

He doesn't seem to notice and his voice is matter of fact, as though we're reciting dialogue. 'It's illegal.'

'Surely it's not illegal to pay tribute to the King of rock-and-roll in the city of his great return?' My words have an imitative formality to them and he glances at me, unsure if I'm making fun of him or not. Either way, it doesn't seem he's an Elvis fan.

'Ma'am, I'm going to ask you once again. Would you please leave the Strip?' There's not a lot of asking in his voice but I take advantage of our play at decorum.

'What about them?' I motion to the leaflet trawlers who are half a block ahead of me; a scrap of paper bearing a lurid sex kitten has fallen into my case.

He peers into the distance like he doesn't know what I'm talking about, until I reach down for the advertisement.

'The casinos own the sidewalks. I'm sure those gentlemen have casino approval and are participating in a legitimate trade,' he says.

I'm thinking this guy has missed his calling—he should be in politics, a press secretary—until his words sink in and I'm left gaping. 'The casinos own the sidewalks?' I turn to look at Scott as though he's a stranger, a neutral witness to this transpiring injustice.

'Yes. They sure do.'

'Well, that should be fine. I'm here in recognition of the casino that first brought Elvis to the people.' My voice is shiny, as though I really believe it's possible he'll be convinced.

He shakes his head. 'I repeat: we don't have begging on our streets.'

I'm aware there are just a few seconds left to state my case but the only thing I can think is that we're talking ourselves in circles. Samuel Beckett must be playing a joke on me. 'Begging?' I ask.

'The guitar case?' He shifts forward like he's going to step on it.

'Oh, I can put that away.' I zip it up and lean the tan soft shell against the concrete pylon beside me. 'I'm not here to make money. Good thing, eh?' Though it was a big haul for only ten minutes of playing, I nod back at him and align my fingers for 'Viva Las Vegas'.

He steps forward and the movement has an implied violence to it—his outstretched hand is only inches from the guitar neck. 'I don't believe you, ma'am.'

'What?'

'As soon as I leave, you'll put that back out.' Now it seems I'm not just a beggar, but a liar too.

I've thought a lot about what's motivating me since I set off on this trip and my voice comes back at him hard and low. The monologue's a bit pretentious, but it has convincing momentum. 'No. I'm on a quest, paying my respects to the King—he had 837 sold-out concerts in this town. By playing Elvis here I'm making a political statement, yeah I'm honouring the King, hell I'm honouring America, but I'm also using popular culture to deconstruct notions of the stage. By playing on the street, I'm questioning the whole issue of access. Access? Like who has money to pay to see "the performance" with minimum wage sitting at eight bucks an hour? Surely that's something you get being a security guard. Elvis is a total capitalist, so I'm questioning that aspect of him by playing him publicly. I'm adoring and questioning him at the same time, which is what we should be doing as Americans. It's the great irony, don't you think?'

The canine security guard takes a small step backwards, nodding his head slightly—the movement draws attention to his short neck and tight collar. Despite his thin mouth, something has shifted between us. We're actually seeing each other, I think. A bus pulls past, changing gears, and the street smells of car exhaust, alcohol and desert. Maybe he understands. Maybe my weird tirade wasn't as angry and uptight as it felt and he can see I'm not a beggar. I'm about to smile, to relinquish a tiny piece of myself. But he cocks his head into his neck, pinching his walkie-talkie: '5–12 here, I'm going to need back-up.'

Within seconds, twelve security officers appear and Scott watches as they escort me from the Strip.

Scott and I discover Las Vegas is the home of cheap alcohol (twenty dollars of judicious gambling can get you over sixty dollars of free drinks), cut-price entertainment (the casinos are free kitsch museums) and the unending breakfast buffet.

After exploring the city (sans guitar) until dawn, Scott and I comb our buffet dining options and decide on one that's beige and brown: walls, tables, even the bowls. The clientele is overweight and the benches and chairs are larger than average to cater for expansive girths.

Even though it's early morning, I tower my plate with desserts. Chocolate mousse, lemon meringue pie, chocolate chip cookies, fudge cake, doughnuts, carrot cake. Of course an all-you-can-eat brings out an unhealthy greedy streak in the economically aware. Scott has gone for the carnivore breakfast option—sausage (patties and links), bacon, steak, with eggs and hash browns.

Sitting down, I take a deep breath. My spoon cuts through the whipped cream into the mousse, breaking the gelatinous surface. The chocolate takes a moment to dissolve in my mouth; the stainless steel is rubbery with traces of it. After two bites of that, the lemon meringue has a similar texture but the citrus stings the back of my throat. The carrot cake is piled high with cream cheese frosting and I carve into it with my finger. The icing sugar mix melts to the roof of my mouth; despite the texture, I can't stop eating and soon circle back to the display for seconds. Chocolate chip cookies and an ice-cream sundae. My stomach has expanded, pressing against my belt, but the elaborate, frosted items are still calling out. Chocolate mud cake. Brownies. Another chocolate mousse.

When I return, my old plate has been cleared and a new set of cutlery awaits, replaced in my absence, as though I'm sitting down for the first time. Perhaps I've eaten too many desserts to differentiate between them or perhaps the fluorescent lights have stunned anything that vaguely resembles taste into compliance— every dish tastes the same. Even so, I can't stop.

The room is now packed, every table full. From our spot, it's impossible to see where the line to enter ends because it loops back into the main arcade of the hotel. One of the cashiers opens a side gate. A family—two boys, maybe eight and twelve years old, and their parents—file through. Their necks and bellies are swollen, their steps weighted as though carefully balancing the full mass of their bodies. They're too large to fit through the turnstile and I'm reminded of later Elvis, bloated and paunchy.

My fork stops in mid-air. The younger boy smiles and punches his brother, the gesture so quick and familiar I'm reminded of wrestling with my little brother. Sighing, the father tries to step between them but the space is too confined—he trips and sprawls on the side counter, his large girth wobbling as he struggles to regain his footing. When he stands up, he's more flustered than hurt, patting his glasses back into place, but this family's obesity feels personal—I'm part of a country that's consuming itself to death.

In the United States, it's not just physical but material—my need for an expensive designer frock a case in point. And Elvis, I think, pioneered both fronts: his weight was notorious and he loved to spend money. Leaning back against the bucket bench, I imagine Elvis lining up for the buffet. Of course he's polite, offering the serving tongs to the old lady creaking up behind him. His plate is piled with special-order fried peanut butter sandwiches. When he's done eating those, attendants wheel in a motorcycle and he rips off a shining silver hubcap and starts gnawing on that. The seat, the engine—he eats it all. Then they bring in his silk jackets, which he rips into with a big glass of milk, before finally crunching into his diamond 'TCB' brooches for dessert. That was Elvis's motto: taking care of business. I imagine him eating his way through all his possessions.

He died alone on the toilet, physically exhausted from consuming. Never mind that he was alone—he's our King.

That afternoon, Scott and I have our change ready. We're riding the public bus to the outskirts of the city on an unofficial poor-man's Vegas tour. We've even planned to change routes—our transfers will hold and we can negotiate the whole trip with one ticket. I plonk down right behind the driver, a greying man with an honest face.

Scott sits away from me, in the first row of seats. He knows I get friendly with bus drivers and it embarrasses him but I don't mind the distance. In fact, the two metres between us feel luxurious.

The indicator flashes and the bus pulls onto the street. I scoot forward, about to ask the driver how he likes working for the city, when his voice cuts over the sound of the engine. 'What brings you to Vegas—gambling?'

'Nah, I worked hard to earn what money I have. It breaks my heart to be separated from it and a twenty-dollar limit doesn't see you far in this town.'

He nods. 'Why you here, then?'

'Headed to Graceland.'

His gaze is fixed on the road and I can't help staring with him like there's some secret to the broken yellow line.

'Graceland, really?'

'I play Elvis covers on the street in each town. Except for Vegas, of course—security.'

The driver pushes his cap back. 'I suppose you can see if Americans are a generous people. That's a question. Are we a generous people? I think not.' His eyes gauge the intersection ahead and he turns the thin wheel hand over hand. 'We don't know our neighbours, we don't even know our fellow workers. The guy driving this bus, sitting in this very seat when I clock off? Needed a strike before we became friends and we'd been working the same run for ten years. If you don't know people, you can't be generous.'

Sometimes, even when you know people, generosity doesn't come easy. Elvis was famous for giving lavish, spontaneous gifts to friends and acquaintances—cars, horses, motorcycles—but his own band members went on strike in September 1957 because he wasn't paying them enough. The guitarist and bass player hadn't been given a raise in two years and were actually going into debt because they were paying their own expenses. Elvis, Scotty and Bill—there were personal politics between them, no doubt affected by the Colonel. But the driver is talking about a different kind of generosity. How do you judge the generosity of a nation?

We hit a pothole and someone pulls the cord. The bus eases over to a shelter, the doors flapping open.

'It reminds me of a joke I've heard in Australia,' I tell the driver. 'What's the best-kept secret of the United States?' I pause a moment for dramatic effect. 'The Americans.'

A woman with grocery bags moves past us and he tells her to have a nice day. Then to me, 'I don't get it.'

'When people travel here, they're surprised at how generous and polite and intelligent we are. From the world press and the television sitcoms, we look like idiots.'

He laughs slowly and the sound echoes the engine beneath us as we pull back into traffic. I think of Poncho Man giving me the artwork in Seattle or Mr Blue-Eyes who told me about the free feeds from the Salvation Army. I'd say we're generous but it's subject to flux, a matter of circumstance.

When I was a kid, Irene told me little kindnesses were important. We'd try the doors of parked cars if their lights were left on and most often I'd climb in and push the knob down by the driver's wheel, saving the battery. As an adult when I come across a car with its lights on, I still try the doors out of habit, but more often than not these days, I trip an alarm.

AMERICA THE BEAUTIFUL

After three nights, I leave Las Vegas like a kid who's finally ready to abandon a slumber party: exhausted and homesick. Our next stop is Prescott, Arizona. Back in the Neon City, I'd phoned Brooks's friends—Dorothy and Jeff, one-time residents of Arcata—and they invited us to stay with them.

Even though the Greyhound is late, Jeff's waiting in front of the Prescott bus station. 'Shady? Scott?' he asks, and I step into his open arms with a solid hug. With large shoulders and a thick frame, our host resembles a good-natured bear. 'Dorothy's home, just got back from work.'

Dorothy is a ranger. For the past few weeks, because of forest fires, she's been stationed at park entrances to keep visitors from entering danger zones. In the downtime, waiting by the barricaded road for more tourists (tell me, who would want to camp near a raging forest fire?), she's been practising magic tricks. So the first time we meet her, a wiry woman with round glasses and curly, shoulder-length red hair, she squeezes her arms around us and then produces a piece of rope.

'See this.' She dangles it before me. 'Try pulling it.'

I hold one end and yank it.

'Now I'm going to cut it.' Her scissors saw through the rope until there are three separate pieces.

Scott tests each one—there are certainly three distinct lengths. 'Watch this.' She wraps them around each other and—*voilà*—they've rejoined into one. Scott takes the cord in his hand and tugs at each end.

'I'm getting better, see?' she says to Jeff.

He nods. 'I've seen that one a few times. You guys eat burritos?'

Scott looks up from the cord and smiles. His eyebrows need to be trimmed—he looks like a happy jack-o'-lantern.

Half an hour later, we're seated at the wooden table in a nook off the kitchen. This homemade food could offer no greater contrast to the Las Vegas buffet. The beans have been stewed in spices and the flour tortillas are packed with meat and vegetables. The tastes demand attention, the salsa pungent with ripe tomatoes.

Dorothy sets her burrito down. 'How's Brooks doing?'

'Good. Still at Wildwood, though he's thinking of pulling back a bit.' I motion to Scott for the jug of water. The pitcher is heavy, ceramic, and he passes it to me with two hands.

Dorothy's still watching me. 'You know Brooks and I used to tour together.'

'Yeah. He got the Dobro out while we were there. You guys meet in Arcata?'

'Bay Area.'

The water flows quickly and my glass almost overfills. 'Did you know Michael Cosgrove?'

Scott looks up from his plate—my question is too eager.

Dorothy reaches for the salad. 'That was your dad, wasn't it? I didn't know him but he was a good musician from what I heard.'

'He once tried to teach me the fiddle.' My words sound hesitant, unnecessary, and Jeff's voice booms across the table, 'Dorothy plays the fiddle.'

After dinner, they unpack their instruments in the living room. We're sitting on a leather couch that looks heavy enough to keep Dorothy and Jeff from ever moving house. The coffee table has a similar sense of permanence about it, with thick wooden legs. Jeff's case is resting open on top of it. His hand moves along his guitar neck, easing through chords I've never learned as we hit 'Heartbreak Hotel', 'That's All Right' and 'Hound Dog'.

Jeff's harmonies offer depth, filling out the music; each number sounds suddenly complete. Like Dorothy's magic trick, I keep waiting for the gimmick to be revealed but it never is. It reminds me of playing with Brooks: these musicians are giving me deeper access to Elvis.

Even Scott chimes in, tapping on the coffee table. 'You could go on the road,' he says between songs.

We launch from one song to the next and the music sparks something in my brain. As I change chords, a memory slides to the surface of my consciousness. Late 1970s. I must have been in Portland with my father and older sister, one of the last times Serena and I visited Mike. We were standing in the living room of the blue townhouse. The kitchen to our left, a balcony behind us. All the blinds were pulled closed and only one glaring spotlight was on—we were pretending to be onstage. Mike strummed the guitar, Serena thumped through the bass and I played the electric violin. We were improvising a blues song, following Serena's thoughtful beat; she already had a whole riff mastered. My fingers gripped the neck of the violin and I moved the bow back and forth along one string, playing the note with exaggerated force.

When Mike lifted his head, Serena and I took our cue, playing the last chord triumphantly. Our father grinned, setting down his guitar. 'We should go on the road.'

Serena was watching me and I knew better than to disagree when she said: 'Not unless we call Irene.' That was the deal. No long trips in the car, no airplane rides.

Scott nudges my leg and the leather couch and coffee table

zoom back into focus. The latch on Jeff's guitar case glistens. 'You want to run through it again?' he asks.

Dorothy and Jeff are watching me. My fingers are still locked into place. 'Uh, sure.'

Later that night, stretched out on the guest room double bed, I talk Scott through the memory. 'It's funny, all that music and yet Serena and I had to concentrate on keeping him happy. There was this sense he could lose it at any moment. My sister's words seemed so brave, almost foolhardy . . .'

'Why?' Scott's voice is distant, his eyelids dropping.

At this point, I'm still thinking this trip is only about understanding my homeland. I don't realise Portland was only the first stop in a parade of five, maybe six, memories and that these will affect the way I view this trip. It's not that they're taking me in a different direction—but they're taking me deeper, adding layers and complexity to the journey. This quest began as a way to understand where I've come from. But now I realise that the question of where I come from is bigger than my nationality. Understanding America and the country where I was born is certainly part of it, but there's more—understanding the family I was born into. I'm about to reply when a small snore punctuates the air. My finger needles his rib cage but Scott's well asleep. He's been known to drift off in as little as eight seconds—I used to time him when we started going out. A loud snort wheezes from his throat and he shifts onto his side, his arm wrapping around me.

'Scott.' My foot darts through the sheets, connecting with his shin.

'Mmm.' His voice is bleary. 'St George really should have won that '99 final.'

I try to roll over but Scott's face is tucked into my neck, his body solid against my back. My mouth stretches into a resigned yawn. 'Your Australian sensitivity is just knocking me out.'

★

If the first sign from Elvis came around the Vashon dining room table, then Scott receives the second one from the King a few days later when Jeff and Dorothy lend us their car to visit the Grand Canyon. A borrowed map rests open on my lap, large creases imposing an artificial grid on the state of Arizona. Outside, it's the kind of hot that makes the news: record temperatures, children dying of heat exhaustion in locked cars. Along the two-lane road, second-rate tourist shops roost beside their hand-painted signs. Ahead of us, a large black Mercedes starts to slow down. Scott touches the brakes and then needs to step harder: the Mercedes has stopped.

Scott wipes the windshield with his hand. 'What's going on?'

The traffic moves in two-car increments like we're about to merge onto a freeway, but it's just the line to enter the Grand Canyon national park. Forty-five minutes later, we've finally passed through the ticket booths. With restaurants and hotel accommodation, the complex is closer to an amusement arena than a national park.

I slam the guidebook closed. 'I guess we won't be hiking to the bottom. Camping spots on the floor of the canyon are booked out a year in advance.' I don't mind the idea of descending—it's the mile-long vertical climb back out that puts me off.

'Maybe someone's cancelled.' Scott wants to hike the Grand Canyon because it's famous. If it were the exact same phenomenon without the notoriety, or long lines, he wouldn't be so eager. It's the same argument we've had before about celebrity—Scott loves autographs and having his picture taken with famous people whereas I find it all a bit tacky.

He cranks the wheel, following a sign for parking. I reach down for the sunscreen, smoothing another sweaty layer onto my window-side arm. 'Why does this canyon matter any more or less than any other?'

'Because it's *grand*. A natural wonder of the world. Americans do hype things up, don't get me wrong, but this one's worth it.' I've never been to Arizona but Scott visited the Canyon with mates from high school years ago and this makes him an expert.

In the lot, every spot is filled. We pull onto another road that leads to more parking. A sign for campsite reservations points to a nearby hut.

'I suppose Elvis was pretty hyped,' I say.

'Yeah, and he came up with the goods.'

'So we need to hike down the Grand Canyon because it's like Elvis?'

I don't know of any stories that link Elvis to the Grand Canyon but Scott nods like the logic is obvious. 'Sometimes I have to put things in terms you can understand.' He reaches over with his left hand and pinches my leg. 'You can be a little slow.' Scott left school at age fifteen and often tells me he has to simplify his arguments because he doesn't want to intimidate me. Another of his favourite jokes is that he has to keep things basic because 'you'll have a PhD soon and I don't want you to feel pressured by my intellect'.

We wait as a truck backs out of a parking spot. After locking the car, Scott hikes away from the lookouts, straight towards the reservation hut. 'The view's not going anywhere and we don't want to miss out on a campsite at the bottom.'

'Certainly not.' My eyes roll in a large arc for anyone watching this reality TV experience.

Inside, a young woman with long, polished fingernails at odds with her park uniform taps our request into the computer. 'Nah. Nothing available.'

I'm already edging towards the door. 'Oh well.'

Scott strolls to the postcard rack and plucks cards out, passing the small pile to me.

'What do you think of these?' The Canyon at dawn. A view up the rock face from the Colorado River. A mule-train plodding along the uneven path. My shoulders lift without conviction.

Scott steps back to the counter and the attendant scans the barcodes, sliding the cards into a paper bag. As Scott takes the package, he leans forward like he's trying to get a glimpse of the computer screen. 'Could you check availability on the Canyon floor again?'

She glances behind us but there's no one else in line. She sighs and looks back at the screen. 'Bright Angel Campground?'

'Yes, please.'

'Tomorrow night?'

Scott bobs his head. 'We're already booked in for tonight, up the top.'

'You do realise there aren't even forty camping spots on the ground and we have over a million visitors each year. And tomorrow is the fourth of July.'

'Yes.' Then he adds, 'Ma'am.' His formality surprises me. He winks then, his head swaggering with '68 Comeback flair as though trying to channel the power of the King—how did I end up with this absurd and beautiful man?

Again, her fingers press on the keyboard and she stares at the screen for a long moment before looking up at Scott. 'What do you know? In the last thirty seconds, a spot's opened up.'

'It's a sign,' Scott says.

Thank you, Elvis.

At 6.30 am on Independence Day, we're already standing on the edge. Morning views of the Canyon lack the snapping cameras and pushing tourists and the gaping absence seems deeper, more resilient, than the afternoon before. As we hike, anything close— nearby trees and patches of earth—turns deep red in the burgeoning sunlight but far away, the jagged points and rock depressions seem washed out and grey. An increasing heat adds to this sense of duality and by eight o'clock we're guzzling water in grateful shadowed nooks.

We were warned that a ranger waits about a quarter of the way down to assess potential hikers and turn back the under- prepared. As we've been winding our way along the path, I've plotted our arguments: water rations, food supplies, first-aid knowledge. My mistake is to tell Scott. He's keeping a steady pace ahead of me and doesn't turn around. When I'm finished he just says, 'You know what Amy told me in San Francisco?'

'Amy from college?' I'm so gullible I wonder if she had a secret outdoor life I hadn't picked up on—maybe she's given Scott a clue that will help us bypass the keeper of the Canyon.

'Yep. She said you guys took three classes together.'

'What?' There were more than that, I'm sure there were more than that, and start counting them in my head.

Scott waits a moment, only responding when we're about ten paces from the ranger. 'Introduction to List-Making, Intermediate List-Making and Advanced List-Making. Apparently you topped the class.'

He's timed it well—the ranger's standing with a clipboard, eyeing our packs—so I can't slug him. Scott stops and pushes his hands into his pockets, looking up at the sky like he's pondering the chances of rain. With his big pack, it's not a graceful gesture.

'We've a spot at Bright Angel,' Scott says proudly.

'And water?' The ranger glances down at our shoes.

'Two gallons.'

We pause for another drink, proving ourselves.

'Okay then.'

I wait for more. Surely there's got to be some deeper proof that we need to offer but Scott grabs my hand like we're passing a familiar bouncer at his favourite pub and the ranger is already gazing at the next hiking group. We passed them on the way down—the two teenagers are wearing strappy sandals. On average, one person a year dies from falling into the Canyon and I wonder if their wedding-party shoes will turn those girls into virgin offerings.

By three-thirty we're scaling into the belly and with each step the temperature rises. It turns out the bottom is ten degrees hotter than the top; the warm air can't escape and the heat feels solid. We swim in the Colorado River to cool down but within thirty seconds of climbing out, we're dry again.

Scott and I traipse along the floor, following trails between the campsites and cabins. Even with the heavy growth, it feels low-lying, like I could climb a tree and see across this ceiling-less room to the other wall.

We won't be seeing any fireworks this Fourth of July. Instead, the park rangers stationed at the bottom will march along the main path in costume—it's an annual event that has me thinking about Elvis and patriotism. In 1956, he was linked to US independence when Memphis City named the Fourth of July 'Elvis Presley Day'. He honoured soldiers at Pearl Harbor and took up the draft without protest; even the famous white eagle jumpsuit was an emblem of his dedication to country. It all has me wondering what constitutes patriotism. I may question the United States more than Elvis did but I don't think that makes me less patriotic. There is devotion in the way I assess my homeland—I want the best possible America and wouldn't give it as much thought if I didn't care so much.

'I love this place, Scott.'

'It's *grand*.' He thinks he's funny, talking about the Canyon. I don't correct him and the trail opens to a clearing where a screened café serves overpriced Coronas. Scott and I buy one and pass it between us, taking each watery sip slowly. Scanning the families and older couples around us, I'm reminded of stumbling alone into a hostel where everyone else is chatting in the TV room and I don't have the courage to introduce myself. Then a drum sounds and we bustle out, lining up along the path. Rangers and volunteers march by in groups of two and three, banging homemade drums. A girl is being pulled in a red wagon. Behind her, a boy with curly hair plays a beat-up trumpet. Their costumes are made from whatever they were willing to carry down the steep trail—face paint, fairy wings, long johns pulled over someone's head, sheets as capes, fishnet stockings with hiking boots.

Scott points to a woman wearing bright stockings and a rainbow wig. 'Is that Irene? Surely the pink hair was enough?'

My voice mimics Scott's dry tone. 'What's she doing here?'

'You just can't go anywhere without your family turning up, can you?'

The rainbow ranger must have overheard us despite the noise of her soda can maracas because she turns, her heavily lined eyes glaring at us. She whispers to a fairy elf in army fatigues and they both snigger.

Obviously there's been some miscommunication—maybe the rainbow ranger thought we were making fun of her—but I don't really feel like applauding this odd menagerie. Most of the rangers are my age, maybe a little younger. They laugh and flirt along the 500-metre trail, performing for themselves in a way that seems distinctly American. When I played in Amy's living room, I gradually felt more comfortable. Here, it's the opposite—the longer I stand the stranger I feel, like everyone understands this place except me. Campers line the edges clapping and cheering but there aren't quite enough of us. I should feel enthusiastic— this parade is a celebration of country and nature, two things I adore—but my position on the sidelines feels emblematic and I wonder if the traveller can ever return home.

The next day after climbing out, I busk to the Canyon. Facing the ledge along one of the side trails, I strum through my Elvis numbers, pointedly ignoring the few holidaying pedestrians that pass. The massive crevasse isn't visible from my position but I can feel it: a meekness has entered my songs. Maybe it's because Elvis saw us to the bottom of the Grand Canyon with the open campsite or maybe it's because the Canyon is an American icon and I'm surprised by it: the wonder of its nothingness, the *absence* that makes it so spectacular. But I'm thinking again about Elvis and wondering why he's such a powerful figure in American culture.

I have trouble thinking and singing at the same time so my right hand practises fingerpicking and my voice just hums along. Because it's still hot, there's not a lot of foot traffic.

Part of Elvis's currency rests in the fact that he represented the American dream in extreme proportions—the idea that success is achieved by working hard, no matter where you come from. He was born into poverty in 1935. His father Vernon had trouble holding down a steady job in Tupelo so the Presleys moved around before settling in the Memphis Lauderdale Courts, a public housing estate. Elvis worked nights during his senior year of high school for the furniture assembler MARL Metal to help supplement his family's income. The day he graduated, he went to the Tennessee Employment Security Office and got a job as a machinist for thirty-three dollars a week—most of which he handed over to his parents.

I respect Elvis for this but it wasn't just humility that made his story compelling; Elvis was also shadowed by loss. His twin, Jesse Garon, died at birth—an absence that permeated his entire life. And his mother died when he joined the army, something from which he never fully recovered. Then, there's the loss of Elvis himself—so much potential lost to drugs and alcohol. This, I think, is the sadness that his biographer Peter Guralnick was referring to when he said there was no sadder story. This decline, this loss of potential, makes me think suddenly of my father.

Despite the calluses on my fingertips, my hands are sore and swollen from the midday warmth. Three condors circle overhead, their bodies motionless as they ride lifting air currents. Their wings are fully expanded and they are too large, otherworldly harbingers that make me uneasy. Suddenly I don't want to be alone in front of this huge earthly abyss. I want to join Scott in the bar where he's having a beer and probably making fun of the bartender for all the helmets and padding in gridiron, American football. I don't want to think about Elvis and all the *lack* standing before me, endless as a horizon. Maybe some things just happen and Elvis just happened to be in the right place at the right time. Maybe there's nothing more to it.

LITTLE SISTER

After journeying back to Prescott and saying our goodbyes to Jeff and Dorothy, Scott and I board the Greyhound. Our next stop: Santa Fe.

After eighteen hours, we finally disembark, our legs eager for the five-kilometre trek to the hostel where the reception area has low ceilings and little light, like the room itself is recovering from a hangover. The competing decorations remind me of the grouphouse lounge room where Scott and I met—Indonesian tie-dyed saris, creased photo collages and ageing rock posters. A motorcycle helmet claims the closest computer terminal. It reminds me of the urban myth about a guy who found a Harley Davidson in an abandoned barn and tracked the serial number to Elvis. Somehow in my mind this translates to the idea that the motorcycle helmet is Elvis's and he's here in Santa Fe, staying at the hostel, and I start giggling.

Two women wait at the desk to the right of the doorway. The first has olive skin and heavy brown hair that weighs down her features. Her sidekick is blonde, pale, with red-rimmed eyes. Their complexions couldn't contrast more, but both have the same downturned mouth—thin lips, brows set in a casual frown—and the resemblance is almost familial.

Scott waits a moment like we could be in the wrong place and then approaches the counter. 'Do you have any doubles?'

The blonde steps back to sort through a pile of papers and as she moves, a quiet ring sounds. It's coming from her skirt—a small metallic bell is fastened to the drawstring. The long, tiered Indian fabric is a little too delicate for her large frame.

The brunette watches Scott. 'Reservation?'

'No.'

'You'll have to pay up-front.'

He nods and she pushes a registration slip and ballpoint pen across the counter. I'm no help in these negotiations—I'm too busy checking out the door in case Elvis comes in; I'm wondering how he's aged.

When Scott's finished, she shakes her bare wrist over the form—the movement sudden and quick like a territorial ritual. 'Well?' she says.

We're staring at her.

'Payment?'

I wonder if she's going to hex us but she just looks at the blonde who's paused, one hand keeping her place in the pile of paperwork. Scott reaches into his money belt for a traveller's cheque.

'I'll need to verify that.' The brunette takes the purple-scribed note and paces from the room.

I turn to Scott. 'Have we offended them?'

'I think it's me.' Scott's right—both women watch him with a peculiar animosity, as though he represents something archetypal and untrustworthy. I wonder if it's Elvis—maybe he's been staying here and holding court over loud drunken parties and they're tired of men.

Scott nudges me. 'Could be she's a Parramatta supporter—still carrying a grudge about the 1977 grand final.'

'What are you talking about?' I emphasise 'talking' and my voice sounds foreign to me: the American accent has become stronger.

'St George towelled up Parramatta. If she's an Eels supporter, it makes sense. They let that one slip out of their hands. I'd be in a bad mood, too.'

The blonde raises her head, tilting it like she's trying to translate, but he's speaking Australian rugby league. The thought of these two women barracking for the Parramatta Eels, wearing yellow and blue jumpers, is absurd and I start laughing again. First, we're so far from Australia: they wouldn't know what rugby league is. Second, you don't see a lot of hippie skirts and Wiccan rituals at the games. In fact, women at rugby league stand-offs think nothing of shouting at the players and insulting the referee. I once heard an old lady with a handkerchief tucked over her hair yell that she hoped the 'ref's legs broke off' so she could 'stuff them up his arse'.

The motorcycle helmet is still sitting there and with Scott hammering on about the rugby league it's like I've entered a Jim Jarmusch film. My mirth is no longer hushed or nervous and air rushes from my chest in loud guffaws. Part of what's so funny, I realise, is the contrast—Scott's referencing rugby league and I'm dreaming of Elvis. By the time the Parramatta brunette reappears in the doorway, my stomach aches.

Our host flicks a dark strand of hair over her shoulder and storms back to the register; even her posture is grim. This makes me double over. I have to turn away, circling the room and concentrating on my breath, to regain composure. The guest book is open. I riffle through the wide pages: a woman from Wollongong was here six months earlier and had an amazing time. Better not trust people from the 'Gong, I think, but then again maybe the Parramatta Eels weren't on duty and Elvis hadn't checked in.

The next morning I'm convinced the Parramatta Eels have tried to hex Scott but their spell missed and landed on me. Another person might blame bedbugs for the itching rash all over my face and arms but it's uncanny that Scott, who was sleeping beside me, isn't affected.

As we walk the five kilometres to central Santa Fe, it takes willpower to keep from scratching away my top layer of skin. I'm wearing the guitar pack and it rubs gently against my back where more hives are forming. Even so, I want nothing more than to lean against a fence post like a cow.

In the city square, short buildings squat along the narrow, cobbled roads. My inner busker sizes up the brightly painted doorways and rendered adobe exteriors but there's a practised tourism to the hanging cords of chillies that doesn't invite newcomers.

'Gallery?' Scott asks.

I nod, ready to stall my musical foray into Santa Fe.

We tramp into one with hardwood floors and stainless steel fittings that reflect each other. Angled bulbs spotlight works by emerging artists and the owner—a woman with a bobbed, blonde hairdo and clacking high heels—watches me carefully as we enter. I try not to dig my fingernails into my itching neck.

'Can I help you?' She steps out from behind the counter. Her perfume is light, expensive: the boutique variety where the sculpted bottle is as much the product as the accompanying scent.

'Uh, no. Just looking,' I stammer.

I'm dirty in front of this art: my shirt is sticking to my back, we've run out of deodorant, my face is pulsing and all I want is to submerge my head in a basin of calamine lotion. My instinct is to leave immediately but there's an etiquette of interest that needs to be played out so Scott and I walk the gallery's perimeter.

Beside the long, bright canvases, the titles and prices are detailed on laminated placards. Sixteen hundred dollars. Twenty-two hundred dollars. The same people who can afford to stay in the city centre have money to buy this artwork. My gaze is longing—not for the art itself, but for the comfort it represents. When I turn back to the counter, the owner is staring at me as though I'm going to hoist down a picture and pocket it.

'Can we leave?' I whisper to Scott.

After an overdue lunch of corn tamales, my blood sugar levels and social courage are renewed and we stroll along the shopfronts. The clothing stores seem contradictory—mud exteriors pitted against polished floor-tile interiors. With mannequins artfully posed, the clothing could be an exhibit—every shop a gallery of things I can't afford.

Suddenly I want to be in a place where beauty is not for sale. 'Maybe we could visit a museum, Scott. Georgia O'Keefe's permanent collection is in town.' I've taken to pressing my fingers into my skin to relieve the throbbing.

'But you have to busk.' What he means is: 'I'm here to support you and you're on a mission.' Though I'm too tired and itchy to translate.

'I don't have to do anything.' When I look up, the only thing in focus is my boyfriend's big, goofy face. Sweat is beading along his hairline and his complexion is clear. The bedbugs veered squarely for me.

My reflection bounces back from a shop window—because the guitar pack is shaped to the instrument, my head has a long, thin arm probing behind it. I look like an alien from a B-grade movie and my swollen forehead doesn't help. I realise, vehemently, that I hate Santa Fe with its Parramatta supporters and sleek-rich tourists, and busking is not an option. I can't bear for anyone to look at me like a beggar right now, as though performing will involve losing some intangible and core piece of myself.

I start pacing towards the Georgia O'Keefe museum, tears scratching my eyes.

Scott trails after me. 'We're on the same side . . . We're on the same side . . .' This is our mantra, an effort to assert ourselves as a united front, but I can't turn around. Focusing on the roofline of an adobe building in front of me, I concentrate on each word to keep my voice calm. I know it's not his fault that I'm cracking up but even so, my self-control is wearing thin. 'Please. I need some time alone. Meet you back at the hostel, okay?'

Mentioning the hostel reminds me of the bedbugs and the ratty box spring mattress; we're going to have to negotiate for another room. I want my bed in Australia—the low-lying pale timber, the Japanese angles along the headboard, the worn flannel sheets and medium-firm mattress. I want it with a homesickness that surprises me: it's Australia that I want, not Vashon.

The next morning Scott and I are waiting at the Santa Fe bus station when the bus arcs into the parking lot. When the door sighs open, the driver is the only one to disembark. He's a short man with a dedicated paunch who doesn't look up as he scurries down the stairs. 'I'm sorry, every seat's filled.'

When he comes out of the station, I'm standing between him and the bus door. My arms are folded over my chest and my face is pulsing. 'We've been waiting for over an hour.'

Greyhound offers two trips to Taos a day and the next one leaves in the late afternoon. I have a sudden vision of being trapped here—Sartre's *No Exit* set in the box hut bus station of Santa Fe, New Mexico, linoleum squares covering the stage.

The driver shrugs, his Greyhound polo shirt barely moving.

I concentrate on speaking slowly, still edgy from the day before. 'We don't mind standing.'

He glances down and jots something on his clipboard before looking up. I'm ready when he does, my face beaming through the calamine war paint. 'Please. We've got to get out of Santa Fe.'

His moustache twitches. 'It's a two-hour journey.'

I shift my weight back on my heels like a relaxed and rational human being and he nods his head. 'All right then, but it's a long trip. I warned you.'

We stand in the aisle about halfway back, brushing against the other passengers, smiling apologies, our packs nestled at our feet. My anxiety turns to excitement as the motor powers up and everyone on board seems to share it—eavesdropping is unavoidable.

An old man wearing a suit jacket far too warm for the increasing heat tugs my shirt. 'I've never been on the bus when passengers couldn't sit down.'

'I hope you didn't pay full fare,' the round woman beside him adds, her neck creased with sunburn.

The bus turns and I grip the back of a nearby seat to keep from falling onto another passenger. Half an hour passes and someone on the other side of the aisle presses my shoulder. It's a blond man with a sweet face and a green backpack. 'If you'd like to sit, I'll stand for a while.' His English accent is clean and familiar, like the British television voices in Australia.

I glance back at Scott, whose jaw has dropped in mock incredulity, and manoeuvre around the Pommie into his seat. The woman beside me, by the window, is sleeping. Across her, the hills are dry, like someone has peeled back the top layer of landscape to expose the gravel rocks beneath. We're climbing in low gear along ridges balanced between valleys; my ears pop with the altitude.

Across the aisle, the man with the heavy jacket clears his throat, his eyes peering up at the English traveller. 'And where are you from?'

'Manchester.'

'What brings you here?'

In the surrounding rows, we all listen as John introduces himself and tells of his two-month trip across the United States: he started in New York and will fly out of Los Angeles. The highlight of his adventure so far was staying up two days straight in New Orleans.

After ten minutes, the woman sitting two seats in front of me stands up and turns to Scott. 'Would you like to sit down?'

In regular shifts, other passengers offer their seats too, so the aisle position is rotated. It's a game—whoever stands is the subject and those sitting around ask how they've come to be on this bus to Taos.

When I stand for the second time, the older man has finally taken off his jacket. He's enjoying this communal bus and isn't going to let the momentum fade. 'With that backpack, you look like you're travelling too.'

'Yeah, but I grew up here.' Technically, this isn't true. I'm nowhere near Vashon. For a hot, strange moment I have no idea how to explain myself. 'I grew up in Seattle and we've been living in Australia. This trip is about resolving my home.'

Everyone along the aisles is staring at me, waiting, so I continue, 'And we're journeying to Graceland for the twenty-fifth anniversary of Elvis's death. I'm searching for . . .'

I don't finish. It sounds incongruous—home and Elvis—but, I realise, he *is* central to resolving my relationship with America. And that's why Scott wanted to travel with me, that's why he took a leave of absence and kept saying he'd carry my bags—on some level my boyfriend is making sure I understand where I've come from so I can commit to our life in Australia. This thought makes me wonder where, in fact, I have come from and an image of Vashon springs to mind—Irene at the dinner table, cutting into pizza with sewing scissors, Elvis on the turntable. And then I think of Michael Cosgrove and Serena, microphones set up in the lounge room, and I know it's not just presence that dictates where you've come from but absence too.

No one asks any questions as the straining motor guns into gear beneath us. 'I don't know. Elvis. America. Family. They kind of seem connected,' I add as a lame afterthought.

The old man on the aisle nods and I wonder why I couldn't just tell an amusing and banal anecdote about getting drunk in a foreign city. Why do I take everything so seriously?

Eventually it's my turn to sit and I plonk down next to Lee. Because of a steel plate lodged in his neck, Lee can't lift his head: it's permanently locked at a forty-five-degree angle. With a sinewy body and black, frizzy hair, he wears dark glasses that make his thin face seem even thinner. He too is on a Greyhound bus pass.

'It's the cheapest, safest accommodation I've been able to find. Sixty nights, after all.' He laughs like he's gotten one over on Greyhound but it's a nervous sound. This is a guy who knows what it's like getting harassed and beaten up, I think.

'So where you going after Taos?' I ask, leaning forward so we can make eye contact. Both of our heads rest on the seats in front of us.

'Depends how it goes. Sometimes I zigzag across the country if I need to sleep. Not easy with this.' He points to his neck and chuckles. His laugh is light, almost impersonal, as though he's amused with a television show.

'Happen recently?'

'Oh no. An accident. God, what . . . fifteen years ago now?' As he talks, he seems to embody something kind and endangered, and this gives his words an aura of wisdom. 'They kept operating, never got any better. Would have been hard, but I've found . . . have you heard of this?'

Lee reaches under the seat in front of him and pulls up his backpack. He opens the top and starts unloading the contents onto his lap. Finally, wedged in towards the bottom, he finds what he's looking for and hands me a book about Servas International. I haven't heard of it—an organisation that connects host families and travellers with the hope that shared experiences will promote peace.

Notes are written beside the text; Lee has spidery handwriting that's crawled all along the margins. He takes the book and thumbs through it like he's looking for something but then pauses without finding it. 'It's funny how much talking can give you another sense of the world.'

I'm thinking this bus trip has done just that for me, and it seems to have had that effect on the other passengers too. When we finally arrive at the station, everyone says goodbye to each other, many shaking hands as they disembark.

Lee starts walking towards town, his thin body leaning forward, and then he pauses and turns around to me. If there was a movie camera behind him, it would pan out and the bus would be outlined against the clear sky. 'Good luck in Graceland. You'll find it, whatever you're looking for.'

Scott and I visit Taos Pueblo, a traditional Native American community. It's the biggest operational pueblo in the country and dates back 1000 years. The adobe houses, squares propped on top of one another, can comfortably accommodate 10,000 residents, roughly the winter population of Vashon Island.

Many of the buildings are accessible only by ladders—a strategy to help the community evade attack. Doors were built into ceilings as though the residents were inviting the constellations to dinner.

'But the threat now is from the televisions and promises of work,' the guide says, shuffling us along the path between the outdoor exhibits. 'The cities are drawing our younger inhabitants away. Attrition. We're down to one hundred and fifty full-time residents.'

Scott pulls me aside: 'This is an ancient civilisation. It's survived thousands of years—weather, colonists, wars.' He shakes his head. 'But it might not survive a big screen and a remote control.'

I don't busk in Taos. I know Elvis wasn't responsible for the advent of television but he's a symbol of its cultural power and it just doesn't feel right. I leave my guitar in its case.

★

The next day we move on to Albuquerque, New Mexico. We have about half a day in the state capital before our connecting bus leaves for the town of Truth or Consequences.

Scott stores the red backpack in a locker and we begin the hour's walk to Old Town. In the historical centre, some of the buildings have been painted bright turquoise in an effort to outbid the cloudless sky. Murals of the Virgin Mary gaze out from alleyway nooks, quiet courtyards and store fronts, reminiscent of my mother's ceramic altar over our fireplace. I feel close to Irene and Serena strolling through this icon-clad city. The dusty roads and vivid buildings are an antidote to the haunted Portland bus station.

With the sense that my mother and sister are watching over me, I perch on a concrete wall in the middle of a park and open the guitar pack. The grassland is square, a large space that seems even bigger because of the empty surrounding streets.

'I should be okay if you want to look around,' I tell Scott, but he stretches out on a shaded patch of grass for a nap, his baseball cap perched over his face. In front of me, elderly men dressed in white play chess at picnic tables in the shade. Their feminine counterparts sit on nearby benches with knitting and embroidery. I begin 'Heartbreak Hotel' about fifteen metres away and shift towards them with the moving shade. After each song, they clap with a dry sense of duty as though I'm a charity act in a nursing home and they approve of my intentions even if they don't care much for the execution.

Then an older gentleman steps forward, gently placing a dollar in my case. 'Would you play "Suspicious Minds"?'

After I swing through the chorus a second time and he moves back to his board game, a security guard steps into the square, aimed at me. Despite the excessive heat, my pulse quickens. A hurried scan tells me the officer is alone but he may have comrades in hiding, Las Vegas style. Scott's been teasing me since the Strip, saying I was trying to resist arrest, that he didn't know I was an outlaw and that he thinks the real reason I came to Australia was because I was up to do time in the States. He's trying to make light of it all but I'm still nervous playing. I keep waiting for someone to tell me I have to leave. The sense of entitlement that

I had—that the street was fair game—is gone. The guard is within ten metres, his stride uneven.

I take a deep breath and, willing myself to be brave, finish the song with a loud, strong note. One of the men playing chess looks up and smiles, nodding his head. He's the only one to applaud, apparently unaware of the impending drama.

'No begging's allowed here.' The officer is a short man with a round gut. He doesn't have a walkie-talkie.

My lips move into a strong smile. 'I'm not begging, I'm playing music.'

'Then you won't mind putting that guitar case away?'

'No.' The zipper catches as I close it, and I shove the tan pack behind me.

'Thanks for that. I know it's a pain.' Then, as though to explain his cordiality, he says: 'I play too.'

Since Seattle, I've given up any thought of making money on this trip and since Vegas, I've wondered whether to play with an open case. I do receive donations (usually enough to buy a cold beer after an hour of playing) but I like the idea of free music. The case is an option for passers-by, not an expectation, even if it implies begging.

'I'm not worried about the money; I'm just on a mission to honour Elvis.'

The officer shrugs like it's good to honour things. 'You know, the anniversary of his death is coming up.'

'Yeah. I'm headed there. August sixteenth.'

My sign is still on display but he's watching my face, squinting: 'You wouldn't know "Little Sister", would you? I just got married. I had this girlfriend in high school. For years. And then, out of the blue, she left me. Went to college. I was crushed. Anyhow, things happened and I started seeing her younger sister. And we just got married. Last month. It's a joke between us, that song.' He pauses frequently, smiling each time, but when he starts speaking again his features slip back into earnest alignment.

'No worries.' I strum the guitar especially hard and launch in. The song reminds me of Serena. I'm eight or nine years old, swing dancing with her in the foyer of a college dorm. We're surrounded by her friends and roommates and I've never felt so grown up. When the beat really kicks in, she breaks away, waving her arms in the air and wiggling her bum. She can't help herself and soon she's climbing on a table. Her hair is cut short but has a purple tail that catches the light. Now, in Albuquerque, I know my sister's alive and well—she's living on Vashon Island—but still, I have the eerie sense Serena is actually a ghost and she's with me now, watching over me.

After the song rounds back into the chorus, the security guard waves and continues on. I realise, as I keep playing, that he's an antidote to the one in Las Vegas and some kind of karmic equalising has taken place. As he was walking towards me, I was ready for things to pan out in the worst possible way. It's funny— he'd have no idea, he'd just be making his rounds through Old Town—but his simple act of telling a story has reminded me that America can be friendly and generous.

LADY MADONNA

Our next destination is Truth or Consequences, New Mexico. The town was named after the radio show of the same name in 1950 when television and radio producer Ralph Edwards started a campaign to honour the show on its tenth anniversary. After a series of special elections, the citizens of Hot Springs voted to change their town's name to Truth or Consequences.

The town borders the Rio Grande and, as its original name suggests, boasts natural hot springs. Our hostel is comprised of a series of trailers and teepees centred around a main house that has endured many additions over the years. It's tucked next to the river and the kitchen is packed with free food left by travellers: tea, cookies, pasta, lentils. At any given time, three or four guests will be lounging at the table, drinking and talking. About thirty paces from the front door, the hot baths are set down along the water—they're open for resident use in the mornings and late afternoons. Sitting in one of the three square stone tubs, visitors can see the Rio Grande moving with gentle, majestic urgency. After soaking, Scott and I walk a hundred metres upstream and jump in, floating back to the hostel.

It's the kind of place where people—British backpackers especially—stop for the night and forget to leave. Many subsidise their rent with daily chores and I imagine them brainstorming more duties to avoid leaving. When a South Londoner shows us to our room, he points to the hundred-odd cement Virgin Mary statues clustered beneath a tree—each about two feet tall. 'If you're looking for work, they need to be painted.' Who dreamt up this one—Virgin painting in a place called Truth or Consequences?

The streets are paved but have the dusty vacancy of dirt roads. They radiate too much heat so I sit beneath a water-starved tree and busk to the vacant-eyed statues, playing my Elvis numbers. If only Irene could see me now. In honour of her fireplace Madonna I sing 'Silent Night', an Elvis favourite.

The concrete figures have me thinking—the Virgin Mary is a religious icon, Elvis a cultural one. In both senses, the icon is representative: it's a vessel filled with the longing of the observer. The woman praying in church isn't praying to a painting: she's praying to what the Virgin represents. And likewise, most people who celebrate Elvis are celebrating what he represents to them. I'm not sure what it means exactly, but absence seems central to this flexibility—in order for people to decide what the icon means, there must be space for that projection. And maybe that's why I could romanticise Michael Cosgrove in such dangerous ways during the dinners with my family.

I start the slow lullaby again and it's a relief playing away from the street. My captive audience doesn't contribute much to my beer fund but, on the other hand, I don't have to field any complaints.

The next day, I'm back in position, playing 'Don't Be Cruel' to the Virgin statuettes when a lanky guy in his late twenties joins me under the tree. I recognise him—he drove up in a clapped-out station wagon the night before, asking about vacancies. His brown hair falls in his eyes and his face is thin and brooding.

'Josh,' he says. We've never been introduced but he asserts his name as though I've forgotten it.

'Shady. What are you doing in T or C?' I ask.

'Road trip—I want to know if I'm making the right choices with my life.' He doesn't look up as he says this and I wonder if he's fled a wedding. I can see him shrugging off the layers of his nuptial attire—tuxedo jacket, cummerbund, bow tie—as he speeds west along the freeway.

My fingers slide through the one impressive blues riff I know. 'You play?'

'Got a guitar in my car? Might go get it?' Whatever he's wondering about has affected his speech—even his statements sound like questions.

I'm not surprised when Josh tells me he usually plays the drums. His dark eyes and heavy eyebrows would suit a front-man position but his nature seems too quiet, compliant. Before the hot pools reopen for the afternoon shift, he's heard all of the Elvis covers I can play and most of the three-chord songs I've written over the past year. He strums along with me, watching my left hand intently for chord changes.

'I like the one about Noah's Ark,' he says when I finally pause between numbers. It's a dramatic one I composed about believing in yourself when the world thinks you're crazy. I play it again. And again. The religious sentiment seems fitting with our audience of Virgin Marys.

'There's a nice rhythm to the lyrics.' He's watching my face with the same concentrated focus that he watched my fingers.

I glance down at my Martin and shift it out of the direct sunlight. 'I don't mind the chorus—I think that's catchy. It's the verses, they sound a little too wailing-woman-angry-at-the-world.'

He bites the underside of his lip and follows the progression on his guitar. 'Let me think . . . What about trying D there?'

He plays the riff, his hands stretching for the chords. I follow suit. The changes are jerky but even so, it sounds smoother, less homemade.

'And what about a different strum?' He increases the pace of the song.

Repeating our changes, I cement the rhythms into my hands, concentrating on how my voice follows on the up-beats.

Josh doesn't edge away like my guitar teacher in Australia and I actively discourage myself from imagining us on a shared road trip. My friendships tend to be intense and searing, usually with women. When I happen to connect with men, I have to make a conscious effort to draw mental boundaries. My role models aren't great for this: my mother's passions have been the mythological making of our family. Part of me wants to climb into every beat-up station wagon just to see where it's headed. But with a steady partner, I've had to learn other ways of having male friends.

Even so, Scott doesn't appreciate Josh. Later that evening, when I play him the improved version of the song, he shrugs. 'I liked it before.'

'Are you deaf?'

Despite his jealousy, it's obvious Scott appreciates a little time without Elvis. He paddles down the Rio Grande and talks to the British backpackers about the rugby—Australia trounced them. And Josh seems safely out of reach because he's running from a fiancée. I have her well imagined now: blonde and needy, without a passion for music.

Josh and I are still playing guitars the following afternoon. We've shifted position from the day before but we're still within sight of the holy mother congregation when Sam joins us. I met Sam in the kitchen that morning—he has flyaway red hair that's already receding: he'll be bald by his twenty-fifth birthday.

'Mind if I sit down?'

Josh moves back to offer space but I'm wary of playing for anyone new and I realise I've already become used to having Josh to myself. In my mind's eye, I see a flash of freeway. Josh is driving, the seat fully back to accommodate his long legs. My hand adjusts the radio dial, moving the needle along the stations. The fantasy reminds me of my mother and a slow blush creeps over my face.

When I look up, both men are staring at me. 'Um, I should probably move on.' My head tilts towards the hostel but Sam is squinting at me.

'Please, don't go.' His voice is shy and panicked—he thinks it's his fault I'm leaving. No, Sam, I'm just a jerk who needs to get back to her boyfriend.

Josh peers at me, nothing complicit or romantic in his expression. 'Shady'll play a song. Won't you?'

Sam is nodding.

There's no choice—I'll just have to get over myself. Sighing, I lift the guitar into position, thinking through my repertoire for a song I haven't played. 'Sad one, okay?'

The music and lyrics came to me about a year before, in Australia, when the mother of one of my friends died. The song is about fleeing to Mexico where they have a day to honour their dead. It's about wanting some sense of cultural recognition for death that's deeper than colour catalogues with price lists for coffins. It's about missing your mother with crippling intensity. I draw a deep breath. 'I know there's angels south of the border . . .'

The pace is too quick during the first verse but then the song settles into a firm rhythm and the final verse rounds back to the chorus. 'If the dead can dance, let the music free. If the dead can dance, then dance with me . . .'

Sam is clapping. His hands join in a repeating echo that's swallowed up by the hot afternoon. 'That's amazing.'

I must look sceptical because he says, 'No really. You lose your mother?'

'Oh, no. My friend did—I wrote it for her.'

'Lucky.'

'She wasn't really, her mother died.' My voice is harder than intended. Sam just shrugs, his collarbone visible through his wash-worn t-shirt.

'I meant lucky to have a friend who cared so much. My mother died three months ago.'

The triangle between us is quiet for an embarrassed moment. 'You okay?' I ask.

He laughs. 'Not really. This trip is about piecing myself together.' His hand rests on his chest and he laughs again. The sound that comes from his mouth isn't much different from crying and I'm aware that some things actually matter, really matter, and you can't always pick them.

He turns to Josh as though he bears some level of ecclesiastic privilege. 'Why would God do this?'

Josh looks up suddenly, scanning our faces one at a time. 'I'm trying to figure that out.'

The Madonnas are all facing us. A couple have been painted in the last day, blue robes and brown hair, but most of them are still concrete grey.

That night, a bluegrass trio sets up beside the campfire. Josh and Sam are playing cards by a light that's plugged into the house with an extension cord. I'm lying on a blanket, staring up at the trees. Scott's next to me with an open beer.

The lead singer—a wispy girl with plain brown hair—counts off, her foot tapping into the moon-blanched grass. She's so skilled on the mandolin that she gets prettier and prettier with each song. When they take a break halfway through, I decide that I, too, want to play the mandolin. It's our last night in Truth or Consequences and the thin beer has made everything seem possible.

Scott stands up and moves to the fire, near the musicians. 'Hey, do you know "Shady Grove"?'

The singer rests her instrument in its case. 'Of course—it's an Appalachian staple.'

When the band reconvenes, they play through my namesake. I've never heard this version before: the theme is the same but the lyrics are different. Her mandolin plinks through, racing around the notes as she sings. Two other band members, both male, back her up with double bass and guitar. Every now and then, they chime in with well-placed harmonies. The stars are slightly woozy overhead. My foot taps along.

'Shady Grove—that's you.' Scott's hand finds my leg in the darkness; his warm palm rests on my shin.

The mandolin player counts in for another song and I stand, moving towards the cooler. After fishing through the ice for a couple of Heinekens, I nudge the lid back and straighten up. Josh is standing beside me.

I point down. 'Want one?'

'Nah. Thanks.'

Over at the card table, Josh's place has been taken: Sam's now engrossed in conversation with a woman wearing a cowgirl hat who has a strong Californian accent.

'Can I talk to you for a moment?' Josh asks. I have the sense that he's holding my arm but he's not. A few inches separate us.

'Yeah, sure.' I spritz open one of the aluminium cans.

'You know, you've made an impact on me?' His words lift again as though asking a question.

'Good, right?'

'Yeah. There's something . . .'

I lower the beer from my mouth. In the last three seconds, the campfire has become impossibly remote, as though the twenty paces to the cooler is actually much further. The music, too, seems to fade with this newfound distance.

Josh waits a moment, looking up to the clouded moon. His Adam's apple is pronounced, his throat shadowed. 'I just wanted to thank you.'

Scott's over on the blanket, waiting for his beer.

'Yeah?' I'm worried about where this conversation might be going. I've enjoyed playing the guitar with Josh. I liked the break from daily-grind travel but that doesn't mean my highway daydream was anything more than that.

'I was trying to figure out my life. That's why I started this trip. See, before . . .' Josh stops and tilts his head so he's staring at me. 'I was going to be a Jesuit priest. I was confused but you really helped clear it up for me.'

My hand lifts the can automatically to my mouth and I take a long, slow sip. 'What are you going to do?'

'I'm going to join.'

'Really?' My voice falls out of my gaping mouth: loud, jarring. There may be relief in my tone but my pride is rolling around on the ground in shock.

'It's about faith.'

I wonder if I've had too much to drink.

Josh clears his throat. 'I really like you, Shady.'

'Me, too. I mean: you. I like you. I like me, too, but . . .'

'That song about the Ark. About following your passions when no one understands. My parents . . . they won't be happy about this decision.'

I nod in agreement but wonder if that's lying—like I have any idea what he's going through.

He takes a deep breath. 'You got a pen? I'll give you my email address.'

We walk to the kitchen where the fluorescent light overpowers the quiet night. Josh riffles through the scrap paper on the table.

'Let me get my journal. Otherwise I'll lose it.' The door creaks open to my room, just off the kitchen. My guitar backpack and latched-on carry case lean against the wardrobe. All of my things are packed, contained, for our morning departure. There's a tidiness to the room that makes me pause: it's as if I've already left. I wonder what it is that I'm looking for, exactly, and dig into the outside bag for my journal. I'm coherent enough to know I won't forgive myself if I wake up and can't find his address. In the end, we'll email for a few weeks but distance and time will bring a shyness to our computer-screen letters that can't be covered with guitars.

'Good luck with it all,' I say as he writes his name and details carefully.

'Thanks. I hope you find the King.'

'You too.'

He hugs me goodbye, his whole body committing to the firm embrace. Even though she doesn't exist, I'm drunk enough to wonder about his fiancée. How has she taken this news of the priesthood?

'Take care.' He waves and then turns around abruptly, heading towards his trailer. I stare after him for a moment and then open my door, tucking the journal into my pack. In the half-light from the kitchen, I stare at the empty room and finish my beer before shuffling outside to give Scott his drink.

Because Elvis is such a ridiculed and contentious character in American culture, it's hard to consider his religious life with solemnity, but by all accounts he was deeply spiritual. He grew up singing hymns and saw music as a sacred experience: his three Grammys were awarded for gospel albums. I'm now into the second volume of his biography and talking with Josh makes me take more of an interest in Elvis's spiritual life. The King was a member of the Self-Realization Fellowship and at one point he even wanted to become a monk.

I never asked Josh but wondered what it was, exactly, that decided him on a path to God. For Elvis, it came from a deeper sense that something was responsible for his life and this was later confirmed when he had a religious experience outside Flagstaff, Arizona, with his spiritual mentor Larry Geller. Elvis was thirty years old. As the two were driving across the desert, a clearly defined image appeared in the clouds before them—Joseph Stalin.

According to biographer Peter Guralnick, Elvis called out, his voice breaking, 'Why Stalin? Why Stalin? Of all people, what's he doing up there?' Then he pulled the bus to a violent halt, climbed out, and began running across the sand as the face above turned into that of Jesus. 'Oh God. Oh, God,' Elvis kept saying. And in a moment of self-awareness or vanity that only endears him to me more, he said: 'Can you imagine what the fans would think if they saw me like this?'

I don't understand the spirituality of visions or priesthoods but I do understand the ideas of karma and humility. And I believe that sometimes the hardest thing in life is to make use of the gifts you've been given. Elvis may have believed in God but he was still derailed by fame and drugs, and this idea of derailment raises a whole set of questions that begin with 'What if . . . ?' But the danger with lost potential is that those questions don't lead anywhere useful and run the risk of consuming those who have been left behind.

SUSPICIOUS MINDS

Scott and I arrive in the Texan border town of El Paso. Across the bridge: Juarez, Mexico. Because Scott is an Australian, he needs to leave the United States to renew his visa and the rest of our trip depends on this bureaucratic negotiation.

The Greyhound station is six blocks from the river. We store the red backpack in the trusty grey lockers and cut south, following a stretch of open-air vendors to the river where the Rio Grande has dwindled to little more than a muddy trickle. Its banks are fully carved out but they're filled with rocks and garbage, not water.

Scott and I follow the trail of people streaming across the bridge, our pace dictated by the crowd. We're on a walkway alongside lanes of traffic; we pass a building that says US Immigration but it's on the other side of the road. I pause, scanning for an official booth or someone in uniform.

'Maybe you get stamped here,' I say, but the tunnel-bridge opens slightly and we're funnelled into open air. Within a matter of seconds we're walking alongside a potholed road in Mexico without any record that we've left the United States.

The air smells of fish, perfume and tortillas. Stereo speakers call out in English and Spanish: sales, bargains, cheap cheap cheap! Duty-free shops line the road with bright signs—yellow and orange, blue and white. The stores are so close together they're

practically inside one another. Scott picks up a bottle of Kahlúa
and has to pop next door to find out how much it costs. It must
be a good deal because he gestures at me but I don't care about
cheap booze right now. I'm worried about his visa.

After a nervous lunch in an upscale Mexican diner that's
decked out in shades of bright pink, we walk along the other side
of the bridge to the US immigration office, passing traffic stopped
in gridlock. Car windows are open, drivers fanning themselves.
Despite the temperature, people are calling to each other and
laughing from 1970s Fords and Chevrolets.

On the El Paso side, inside the US government building, the
foyer is cluttered: generations of families; prams with sleeping
babies; luggage on wheels. Every group has someone in command
of the passports—the immigration slips poke out like bookmarks.
Beside us, a matriarch speaks Spanish to her grandchildren.

Pointing to the line in front of us, I use my college Spanish:
'¿Por los Estados Unidos?'

She nods. All up, there are eight booths with corresponding
queues. Some move quicker than others. I step forward to see
what the officials look like. Ours is a large woman with short,
spiky hair.

When Scott and I move forward to her window, I make
sure to smile brightly as my hand presses our documents onto
the counter.

'Mm-hmm.' She pauses at the photo in Scott's passport. He'd
showered right before the picture was taken. With his wet hair
pulled back and bulging eyes, he looks like an escapee from the
jail where his sister Gail works.

I nod as though in reply. She frowns, which doesn't seem like
a good omen, and then her lower jaw relaxes; she's either chewing
gum or trying to dislodge something caught between her teeth.
'You been here already?' She's talking to Scott.

My head moves up and down vigorously. 'Yes. Scott is
Australian and I'm American—we've been travelling.'

She flattens his open passport with one hand and looks only at him. 'You been working?'

'No, ma'am.' His formality reminds me of Elvis and I realise he's taking this seriously: I love him for taking my country seriously.

She thinks on that, her bovine jaw moving up and down. 'Well. Just to your right over there is a series of offices. Before the offices, on the right, a room. You need to go there, take a number. They'll help you.'

As we scurry away, my immediate impulse is to talk: why are we going over here, what does this mean, why didn't we just go through? But Scott presses my arm and I take a deep breath.

A thin corridor stretches along the side of the hall and we open the first door. Inside, the walls are green, the blinds tweaked closed. In the administrative twilight, a tall bank of three granite windows waits in front of us. Two are occupied. A large red sign indicates 'forty-seven' and Scott takes a ticket.

'What number?' I ask.

'Fifty. That's good luck.'

On the plastic chairs by the door, two women, sitting separately, are crying. Attentive men pat their arms, murmuring in Spanish. One of the women clutches her partner. The other just stares ahead, tears dripping off her face.

'Cheery place,' Scott whispers, sitting down. He picks up a newspaper left on a seat.

I lower myself gingerly beside him and start counting backwards from one hundred. If our number is called before I reach zero, then we'll be fine—we'll pick up the backpack from the El Paso locker and continue to San Antonio.

100 . . . 99 . . . 98 . . .

'Look at this.' Scott pushes the tabloid at me. A mass grave of Mexican illegal immigrants was discovered in the Texas desert. Vigilante border patrols are suspected of the slayings but no one's been charged. 'You can't just round up people and kill them.'

'Apparently you can.'

81 . . . 80 . . . 79 . . .

'Number forty-eight.' The immigration agent at the centre booth has a New York accent and I wonder how he ended up in El Paso.

An older man at the end of our row stands up and walks to the counter with heavy, measured steps. His English is just as laboured as he explains why he overstayed his last visa.

55 . . . 54 . . . 53 . . .

'Number forty-nine,' a bored voice calls out. The line is moving. Good, we'll get in before zero. A few seats down, one of the couples stands up and sidles to the opening. The boyfriend starts speaking quickly in Spanish and the official picks up the phone and requests an interpreter.

35 . . . 34 . . . 33 . . .

The interpreter arrives. Within a few minutes, though, it's obvious she doesn't get along with the agent because they're fighting over which form the couple should fill in.

20 . . . 19 . . . 18 . . .

My lips mouth the words in some effort to slow them down. It's obvious the man with poor English made a mistake—he didn't mean to overstay his visa by a day and a half; it was an oversight. For God's sake, stamp his passport. I imagine the quick, decisive punch of the rubber in an effort to will it to happen. The entire quest to see Elvis is hanging in the balance at an office on a river. Stamp. His. Passport.

12 . . . 11 . . . 10 . . .

Fuck! We're going to be marched back to Juarez, Mexico. Despite the frigid air-conditioning, uneven patches of sweat have formed under my arms. Scott and I aren't new to official interviews—back in Australia I applied for residency as Scott's de facto partner. Our immigration agent was ultra-polite, nodding at my blow-by-blow account of our photographs. She was wearing sandals and it felt like she was counting the hours before she could hit the road for a weekend down the coast. This experience is different—it feels like no one is planning on going anywhere and if this takes months to sort out, then so be it. US immigration doesn't care that Elvis is waiting for us and I don't want to continue the quest without Scott. It's funny, I've spent years considering the cultural implications of loving someone from the other side of the world but I've underestimated the practical ones—like visas and entry points.

I imagine that I'm blowing up a paper bag. Long, slow deep breaths. There has to be a silver lining—maybe Elvis isn't dead: he's hiding out in Acapulco and this is going to afford me the chance to find him. Or maybe his spirit is lurking in the desert and I'll start hallucinating Elvis-style. I'll get the real quest this way. I can go back and get the red backpack and join Scott in Mexico. Surely there are worse things. I have my health. I have a loyal partner. My mother is still alive.

5 . . . 4 . . . 3 . . .

Then from nowhere, a woman steps up behind the last counter. She wears the same grey uniform but her face is round and friendly. 'Number fifty.'

I hurry to the counter in case she changes her mind. Scott presses the newspaper down and ambles behind, laying his passport on the counter. She thumbs through it.

'Why'd they send you here?'

Scott shrugs.

'You don't need to be here. Go back out where you were. But don't wait in line again. Go to the furthest right-hand window— there shouldn't be anyone waiting. Just give them this.' She reaches into her drawer for a form, stamps it, and pushes it towards us.

The heavy door swings closed behind us.

Our new counter is occupied by a man who looks like he would rather be playing the guitar than working for Immigration. His long hair is pulled back in a bright rainbow band and I'd be willing to bet he's a fan of the *Sun Sessions*. Grinning, he tells us everything is in order before looking at our forms.

'I like Australia,' he says.

The man gives the passport a loud, decisive stamp and Scott secures another three months in the States. He turns to me. 'More faith, Shady. Elvis is waiting for us.'

After a night in El Paso, Scott and I set off on the eleven-hour bus trip to San Antonio. The city is known for the Alamo, a battle that went down between Mexicans and Texans in 1836. It began as a siege—the Mexicans were fighting to reclaim the province of Texas and the Texans, though they rebuffed initial advances, eventually fell. Despite this, the battle proved a rallying point for the Texans and they eventually gained independence.

The lockers at the Greyhound station are out of order so Scott and I carry our packs through the city to visit the Alamo Mission. After the tour we head to the city hub around the river. The restaurants and bars along its banks are bright and plastic, making me wonder if the water itself is actually an elaborate prop. We could be inside a Vegas casino or a massive water theme park.

In front of a minor tributary, I strum through my songs. My pack is tucked behind me to avoid security guard alerts but this just seems to perplex those walking by. The case provided a purpose—money—which passers-by could understand. Without it, people just give me a wide berth. After two rounds of my Elvis song list, Scott returns from scoping out accommodation prices and the guitar goes back into hiding.

'You done?'

I nod wearily. 'Find anything?'

'Too expensive.'

I don't ask if this means another night on the Greyhound, the words refuse to form, but we start walking back towards the station. Inside, there aren't enough buses departing the city and the station is packed: all the chairs filled, the café overcrowded, families on the floor. When an announcement sounds over the loudspeaker detailing the next departure bay, everyone collectively stands up and rushes to join the queue. It doesn't make sense—surely they're not all heading to the same destination?—but they all migrate to the open door that leads to the buses. There's no way we're going to get out of here, I think. We may have survived Scott's visa trial but now we're stranded in San Antonio and the chaos tops any other station we've passed through.

A call for Austin sounds and a throng forms in front of the bus. Scott and I don't even get close to boarding.

Greyhound bus stations used to be elegant terminals, located in the centres of towns. They were prestigious buildings, on a par with railway stations. They had high, ballroom ceilings and carved cornices. Ticket counters were crafted from polished hardwood and baggage attendants handled your check-ins. When Elvis was drafted in 1958, he rode a chartered Greyhound from Fort Chaffee to Fort Hood with his army cohorts: his bus in the middle of the fan motorcade.

After four hours of missing buses to Austin, Scott and I start second-guessing them before details are posted. They're parked in the lot, doors open. We sit in the front seats, fanning ourselves until the driver climbs onboard.

'Where you headed, folks?'

'Austin.'

'This bus is going to Dallas.'

And again: 'This bus is going to Corpus Christi.'

And again: 'This bus is going to El Paso.'

Eventually: 'Well, you're in the right place. Let me look at your tickets. You want to store anything below? I don't know how you found me, this run hasn't been announced yet.'

Scott received a sign from Elvis at the Grand Canyon and he's convinced the King helped him through the visa checkpoint at El Paso. Our next Elvis revelation comes within an hour of arriving in Austin, Texas.

The heart of the city spans about thirty blocks—the CBD down near Congress Avenue Bridge, the university north of the State Capitol, the music row on East Sixth Street. We haven't stopped at a pronounced hub but the city bus has been travelling for well over forty minutes since we left the Austin Greyhound station. We have to be close.

I'm searching through the guidebook for a landmark and Scott moves forward to talk to the driver. 'We downtown?'

'It's all downtown.' The man behind the wheel looks like an automaton. When his shift finishes, I imagine he turns off and waits for the next route before powering up again.

Clambering off, we're surrounded by steel-grey, lanky-thin buildings. The late afternoon sun glistens against the glass overhead and the empty streets give the impression that concrete takes up more than its fair share of the city.

My fingers mark the page of the map. 'I think we want to head east and then north. If you see anything open for food . . .' It's an awkward time: too late for lunch, too early for dinner. Scott shakes his head and I have to remind myself it's not his fault we haven't eaten. We're-on-the-same-side, we're-on-the-same-side. It seems fairly certain that if we follow Guadalupe Street, we'll intersect with the university district where there has to be cheap food.

After twenty minutes, this supposition isn't enough. My stomach groans with hypoglycaemic panic and I stop in the middle of the sidewalk. 'Elvis, I'm asking for a miracle.'

Scott keeps pacing forward so I raise my voice. 'I'm asking for a miracle. I want a shop to be open and I'd like a fresh green salad. Maybe a veggie burger or some chunky soup. What do you want?'

Scott glances back, pausing. 'A steak.'

'Do you hear that?' My voice carries through the quiet office precinct around us and I adjust the guitar pack straps so they hit my shoulders at a slightly different angle. About two hundred metres ahead of us, on the left, the sidewalk breaks for trees and grass.

We're almost to the park when a silver-plated truck heading in the opposite direction dives across the empty lanes and pulls up on the kerb in front of us, brakes squealing against the superhero momentum. A man, late sixties with blond-grey hair, leans out of the passenger window: 'You guys hungry?'

'What?' I step up to the vehicle wary of any hidden cameras (funniest home videos meets reality TV travel). Scott actually gawps.

'You hungry?' the man asks again.

'Yeah, we're famished.'

The driver is younger, late twenties, beaming a broad smile of straight teeth. 'Well, we've been on the lunch run. We don't have much left but I'll see what we have.'

Scott is hitting my arm like I've planned this and I try to shove him away. We're like kids who have entered some fairytale land with crystal buildings and magic trucks.

Both men open their doors and hop down from the cab. I squint at the driver to see if I can make out an aura of white light but he seems human and looks nothing like Elvis. He's too tall, his shoulders awkward. At the rear of the van, he shunts up a roller door and the sudden gesture straightens his posture. 'You guys travelling?'

'Yeah, from Seattle. And Australia.' I nudge Scott, who's staring at the truck. Inside, shelves have been installed: this is a portable lunch canteen.

'We're out of sandwiches, but here you go—hot dogs, chocolate milk, hmm . . . a couple apples, an orange.'

It turns out the silver-van angels are part of a church organisation. After refusing any money, the driver tells us they've just been feeding homeless people in the park.

'You kind of looked like you qualify,' the older one says.

'And toothbrushes? You guys want toothbrushes?' the driver asks.

Scott and I can't pass up anything free, certainly not toothbrushes. 'Throw them at us.'

'Here. We won't Bible bash you. Keep this for reading.' He gives me a card: it asks that I let Jesus into my heart and I wonder if he's in cahoots with Elvis—the remarkable timing of it all is impressive. It isn't a sighting at Lourdes, but a free hotdog in Austin almost has me convinced.

Out near Austin's Barton Springs, Scott and I are walking to the 'Dillo—a trolley that's part of the city's public transportation system—when we pass a sign guarding an empty parking lot: the Shady Grove Café. An arrow points inwards, beyond a row of semi-industrial shops.

'Scott, look.'

He's eyeing his watch with a tired expression—we have ten minutes until the next 'Dillo departure. 'Hurry.'

I duck across a warehouse parking lot and arrive at the back entrance. It's like I'm cutting through a stranger's yard as I circle the large balcony with white palings. The hostess is outside, behind a podium by the gated entrance. Tables and chairs are fenced off behind her. She's peering down, counting lunchtime reservations and writing names onto a map of tables. I wait for her to look up.

'For lunch?' She's wearing a white Shady Grove Café t-shirt that fits her but the straight cut isn't flattering. The red writing lassoed across her chest is stiff, like her thick brown braid.

'No, actually. I'm travelling and we came out to the Springs today.'

Her make-up—even the blush—is severe. After staring at me for a long moment, she blinks twice, showing off a smear of blue eye shadow, and I take this as a sign to continue: 'And I happened to be walking by . . . and my name is Shady Cosgrove.'

Her expression doesn't change.

'Get it? Like Shady Grove. Like your café.' As a kid, I didn't understand my name was unusual. Tourist shops with licence plates and key rings always had 'Sandy' and 'Shannon' but (funnily enough) never 'Shady'. I'm waiting for some due, some reckoning, here at the Shady Grove Café.

The hostess is still peering at me and I wonder if I should spell out my name. Instead, I pull out my wallet and set my driver's licence in front of her—the final flourish.

Her gaze hasn't shifted but her hands move up, smoothing her hair. It's already pulled so tight she'll have a headache before the afternoon's finished.

I push the identification across the stand; the photo is decidedly unflattering. The morning of my Australian driver's test, Scott and I had been fighting and my face is tired from crying. My hair hangs limply in an unfortunate blonde-growing-out stage.

I can't blame the hostess when she looks at it dubiously. She lifts her head and squints. 'So you want a table?'

'Uh, no.' Something's amiss in this interaction. I don't need handstands and streamers but some acknowledgement of the kooky coincidence wouldn't go astray. Even if it never made the tourist top ten, it's a good name. According to family lore, Irene and Serena chose it—Michael wasn't involved—and this seems like the place to honour them for that.

'So what do you want?'

I don't know exactly so I sigh and stare back at her. We wait, gridlocked. Finally, 'Do you sell t-shirts?'

Apparently they do quite a trade in merchandising because she points to a display on the ground behind her. Five different styles, each pinned to a billboard. Despite the thick cotton, one of them is actually sexy and I point to it—a muted red, fitted, v-neck tee. The white emblem across the front shows a woman, reminiscent of 1920s cartoons, kicking her legs out. The words 'Shady Grove Café' appear in discreet cursive behind her head.

After debating sizes, I pay inside and scurry back to the 'Dillo stop where Scott's still waiting. Scanning the street, I duck into the shelter behind him and peel my black t-shirt over my head.

'What are you doing? The trolley's rounded the corner,' he says.

The new fabric smells clean and rubbery as I slide my arms into the sleeves.

The 'Dillo snorts to a halt in front of us just as the red shirt falls into place. From the glass door, a tidy reflection peers back at me. It fits perfectly.

Along Austin's East Sixth Street, bars line the streets like cafés. Buskers are celebrated and musicians play the sidewalks but there's a casual ambience about the place, as though we've all stepped out of our living rooms. It's dark out but I feel safe and Scott ducks into a bar with a movie-sized television screen to watch baseball while I set up thirty metres down. Within fifteen minutes, bills and coins are dropping into my case.

A throng of college students has funnelled into a pub across the street and I'm playing 'Viva Las Vegas' as a thin man with curly black hair stops in front of me. He's wearing angel-white jogging pants and a shimmery basketball tank top. When he steps forward, he teeters, standing slightly too close, staring slightly too long at the change in my guitar case.

'Three-twenty. Three-fifty. Four.' It takes a moment for me to realise he's counting my money: there's probably nine bucks. I look at his hands—one is firmly planted in his pocket, the other rests on his hip. He glances up without meeting my eyes and starts counting again from the beginning.

I've never been mugged before and I'm not keen for an initiation—I'm certainly not going to stand here while he debates whether there's enough cash to make it worthwhile. When he's up to seven dollars, I stop playing and stare him straight on. 'You must really enjoy Elvis.'

'What?' The whites of his eyes are yellow and the contrast with his dark, large pupils isn't a healthy one.

I focus on standing with strength in my posture; my voice is smooth and confiding. 'The King. You must like him. You've listened to most of my repertoire. I tell you, I've been playing my way across America and no one's done that yet.'

'Really?' The word is drawn out like he's talking to a dream, unsure if I exist.

I'm all too aware that he exists and wonder why I've chosen this corner, so far away from Scott. The street that seemed busy just moments ago now feels uncomfortably empty. My mind is hammering for anything to keep him talking. 'What's your name?'

'Joseph.'

'Hi Joseph. I'm Shady.' A voice in my head is wondering about statistics: is someone less likely to mug you if they know your name? Or maybe I can just keep him talking and he'll forget. He keeps bending his knees as though seeing if they still work. Every time he goes down, the white fabric of his sweat pants bunches over his shoes.

I watch his eyes as he straightens up. 'Do you have a favourite song?'

'Favourite song?' It's like we're talking across a freeway and he has to listen hard to hear my voice.

'By Elvis. Is there one you're waiting for?'

'Uh. "Suspicious Minds"?' His tone is hopeful, as though he's not quite certain whether it's a song by Mr Presley. He steps towards me and I can smell something artificial on his breath— green toffee or purple bubblegum. With his body odour, it's like dust and sugar.

'You know, I've been practising that one. After "Heartbreak Hotel" it's one of my favourites.' A couple walks by behind Joseph. The man looks at my sign and by the way he nudges his wife I can tell they're Elvis fans but they glance at my new friend and keep walking.

Joseph nods. 'Yeah?'

My fingers move into position and I concentrate on maintaining eye contact. 'I'll give it a go, but you've got to be patient with me. Sometimes I have trouble with the chord changes.'

I start strumming. G major. Change to C.

Joseph starts rocking back and forth as though something's finally kicked in. His hands stop jittering and there's a sweetness to his closed eyes. I don't mind him in this moment, swaying in front of me. He's not quite moving in time, though he's more engaged than most of the pedestrians who've passed.

When the song finishes, I wait for him to groove off down the street but his lids open and he's back staring at my guitar case. The counting starts again and he seems to be hovering even closer. 'A dollar fifty. Two dollars.'

No one is coming towards us from either direction so I try a different tack. I'm thinking of my conversation with the bus driver in Las Vegas and wondering how to be generous here in a way that doesn't put me in danger. 'You know, Joseph, I've got a few songs I've written myself. Maybe you'd like to hear one of those.'

He looks up at me as though he can't figure out how I know his name. 'Um, okay.'

His enthusiasm isn't bowling me over but I keep going. 'I wrote this for a friend when her mother died.'

Joseph's head snaps up and he's staring at me, his eyes too wide. 'I know that song. My brother's dead: shot. Best friend dead: dosing it. Mother, don't know, haven't seen her for a while. But I know that song you're singing.'

The introduction ripples by in 4/4 as my fingers pluck the eighth notes. The plaintive chord changes don't quite fit into the Austin musicscape but Joseph's humming along when I round back on the chorus for a second time. His voice is deeper than I would have expected and the combination is powerful. I close my eyes and sing as loud as the quiet melody will let me; his volume lifts too. When the guitar fades at the end, it's like we're both coming up for air.

Joseph steps around the case. 'Let me play you a song I wrote.'

I pause, gripping the neck of the guitar with my left hand, the body with my right. He waits, his gaze focused on my face. I can't think of any excuse. Later I will ('I don't let strangers play my guitar'; 'I need to meet someone') but at the time, a polite paralysis takes over my brain and I lift the strap over my head, handing him the Martin.

Joseph nestles the guitar close to his body and plays carefully, his fingers plucking and strumming the strings. He taps against the body of the guitar, adding a back rhythm. The contrast is funky, the lyrics sombre—we're trading death lullabies. It's a good song, a really good song, but it doesn't end and this makes me increasingly uncomfortable. The verses are long and he keeps doubling back to the chorus. The one time Scott isn't standing nearby, I think.

When Joseph finally finishes, he turns so the guitar is against his far side and I'm aware he could outpace me easily.

'You're too good,' I say. 'You're going to take all the earnings.'

My words seem to settle into his brain. After I've had about twenty slow seconds to map out each and every outcome of this interaction—I have to tell Scott I gave the guitar to a speed addict who ran away with it or said speed addict swipes my change or else he overdoses in front of me—and Joseph just grins, swinging around to face me. 'You think so?'

'You'd better give that back to me. I'll lose my business here and I've got to make some money for drinks.'

He hands the guitar to me easily, the frets glistening in the streetlight.

'Shady—good luck.' He's remembered my name and something about this makes us both human. I try to make eye contact with him, to thank him in some way, but he's jogging in place and staring straight ahead.

'Hey, take this.' I reach down and hand him the first fiver I've made on the whole trip.

He takes the money as if it's nothing to him and nods a smiling goodbye before bouncing down the block. When there's a respectable distance between us, I count to ten, pack up the sign and pour the leftover change into my pocket.

DEVIL IN DISGUISE

Scott and I have finally crossed the state of Texas and we're headed into Louisiana. From our bus perch, the Mississippi river is too wide: an ocean current caught between two narrow coastlines. We roll onto a heavy, grated bridge that's sturdy enough to hold trains and I'm thinking of Huck Finn—his rafting journey suddenly scaled to a new level. In my early readings of Mark Twain I imagined him winding along smaller tributaries, streams, but this river is so thick and certain it seems even the sun overhead has been convinced to follow the rush of water.

I was ten years old when I first read *Huckleberry Finn*, a library copy with a broken spine and creased pages. I remember sitting with the open book at one of Irene's workbenches—a card table covered with newspaper—while she dabbed thick pastel glaze along the edges of a tile. Upon reaching the end of a chapter, I'd lean back in the olive green office chair and twirl around, making sure not to bump the table. It was during one of these spinning breaks that the phone rang.

Irene leaned over for the receiver, holding it to her ear with her shoulder so she could keep glazing. 'Hello, Irene's Tiles . . . Oh, hi, Bea.' It was my father's mother, Grandma Bea. Irene glanced over and I looked down at the book, careful not to appear interested.

144

My mother's voice was soft. 'Really? With Rhonda? I'll tell the girls they have a brother.'

Over the next few years, my grandmother delivered regular updates on my half-brother: he was walking, starting school, playing soccer. I began listening in on these phone calls to deduce what Michael Cosgrove Jr's life was like. Apparently this new stint at parenthood had inspired my father to give up drinking, which seemed to imply a failure on my part—he certainly hadn't given up drinking for me. It's hard to compete with someone you don't know and who's ten years younger than you but I wasn't one to give up easily and soon became a show-off in the most unattractive ways. At Pegasus School, students were allowed to set their own curricula so I accelerated through two grades of arithmetic. I made sure to let my friends know, saying things like, 'Yes, but do you know what X to the nth power means?' At the same time I began reading Charles Dickens and Irving Stone so I could ponder aloud 'the state of Pip' and whether Michelangelo was 'man or myth'. I'd always been an avid reader but these books became sites of performance, the drama one of increasing pretension. Of course I never had the chance to compete with Michael Cosgrove Jr directly. I never even shared my newfound knowledge with our father—I'd given up waiting at the bottom of the driveway and he never phoned.

When Michael Cosgrove Jr turned eight years old, Grandma Bea called again. I was about to graduate from high school and had been shopping in Seattle for a dress to wear for the event. I'd just got home and padded downstairs to show Irene, who I assumed was applying china paint to a batch of tiles and talking on the phone. The red rotary phone had been replaced with a headset so she could work and talk at the same time. 'It's very strange. Eight years. Eight years—that's what I can't believe,' she was saying.

I wove through the wheeled glaze shelves and roller tables stacked with silk-screened tiles. Irene smiled at me but her eyebrows lifted like she wasn't certain of the gesture. Her hair was pulled back in a limp ponytail—this was before the crew-cut, hair-dye days.

'Serena?' I mouthed. She shook her head, waving her hand for me to wait. It was only then I realised the plastic tub of china paint was closed and the table empty. She wasn't working on a tile at all: she was downstairs for the privacy.

When she finally hung up, Irene took the headpiece off and pressed her forehead like she could rub out the two parallel lines between her eyes. 'Oh boy . . .'

It turned out that Michael Cosgrove Jr didn't exist. He'd never existed. My father invented him, giving my grandmother photographs and stories that belonged to his neighbour. Since they lived in different states, she didn't consider it too odd that she'd never met her grandson in person. Until suddenly, the updates became vague. There were no more photographs and Grandma kept pressing for information about her only grandson: 'Michael Cosgrove Jr', the kid from next door, had moved away.

On the Greyhound I'm wondering why you would make up a child for eight years. And too, who was the performance for? Grandma Bea? My mother? I don't think he planned it for me but I was one of those most affected. I'd spent years plotting ways to outsmart Michael Cosgrove Jr and even planned a special episode of *Jeopardy* where he and I would mark off against one another. Maybe it was a lark for my father, a practical joke that got out of hand. Maybe he was too aware of his failings and imagined a nuclear family to save face.

I'm still thinking about my counterfeit brother as the bus pulls into Baton Rouge. Jo Curtis, a friend from high school, is already waiting at the station. Her parents are more mainstream than mine but she too has a funny Vashon name. Jo Curtis is her given name—she was named after her aunt—and she's always explaining that it's two words but one name. Her surname is Lester. It's been five years since we last saw each other and she's now teaching acting and voice at Louisiana State University. Jo Curtis smiles, and I remember her publicity shot for our high school production of *The Crucible*. She played Elizabeth Proctor and I've always connected her with that role, perhaps because the two share an emotional resilience.

For a moment, it feels like I'm caught between different parts of my past but Jo Curtis was one of my best friends and confidantes when I found out about Michael Cosgrove Jr. It makes sense to be with her now as I'm re-evaluating my relationship with my father. She hugs me tightly and I'm brought back to the present, surprised to realise how much I've missed her. Her make-up is still striking—brown pencil emphasising her slim green eyes. Her hair is a richer blonde, well below her shoulders.

'You been home?' she asks. She means Vashon.

'Started there. June.'

'How's the island look?'

'More houses. More cars.' She raises an eyebrow and I can't help smiling. We talk about the Puget Sound in the same tone of voice we use to discuss shared ex-boyfriends. Next, we'll be carrying on about how much we miss the rain.

During our stay, I think about Michael Cosgrove and growing up on Vashon. On a drive out to the bayous, Jo Curtis lets Scott drive her ageing Volvo and I sit in the front seat. We hum along the cracked and hesitant two-lane road. The heat is wet—even the trees seem to be sweating. Trailers and houses litter the side of the road—screen doors propped open, barking dogs, vehicle carcasses splayed in the yards.

My mother started her artistic tile business when I was four years old. There wasn't enough room in our small house so a couple of years later she pulled a double-wide trailer into the yard. The long workbenches and kilns stayed in our living room but the kitchen and my mother's bedroom moved into the trailer. It was about ten paces from the front door, tucked up the driveway, shy.

When the business grew, we built a three-metre-square cabin for my sister, out behind the trailer. Serena wasn't afraid of the dark—she had a roll of toilet paper and a flashlight for night-time emergencies—and she'd relocate all the spiders that hung in the corners of her room so I could stay for sleepovers.

But my favourite parts of that north-end island residence were the fireplace and the bathtub. The cast-iron wood stove had a thick pipe that led to the chimney and a metal grille so we could watch the fire catch. Wearing pyjamas, I'd curl up behind it with Serena and the cats. My mother had grouted the nook with green and blue ceramic tiles pressed with images of palm trees—now I see the fantasy in this gesture, a reminder that warmer days were coming. I also loved the bathtub—a long white basin with a silver, swan-curve faucet. I remember sitting naked on the toilet, waiting for Serena to finish washing her hair so I could climb in and have a bath with her.

Long after we'd moved out of the north-end house, after Scott had joined the family, Irene said she'd hated that bathroom. We were eating dinner and she grabbed a small pile of salad and set it on her plate—a fist of leaves. Jim passed her the sesame seeds.

'No shower. I always thought, "What kind of people don't have a shower?"' she said.

I was drinking beer instead of wine and the unstained window frames were the only part of our house that seemed steady—crisp, measured rectangles. Beyond them, the darkness was convincing: the kind of night that held creatures from storybooks.

'I loved that bathtub.' I thought I'd spoken but it was actually Serena's voice that carried across the table. She tucked her blonde hair behind her ear and the gesture had a certain seriousness about it.

I nodded. 'It was warm and steamy. I don't think I could live in a place without a tub now.'

Serena rested her elbow on the table. 'Me either.'

Irene looked up from her salad. 'Isn't it funny. I couldn't wait for a shower.'

Jim turned to Scott, his voice crooning. 'Watch out, they're getting nostalgic. Remember the good old days when we were so poor we didn't have a shower? Haven't times changed?'

When it comes to being earnest, my mother beats even me. She laughed but the corners of her mouth were embarrassed. 'Well, they have.'

Jim eased back in his chair. 'And remember the wife-bashing husband? Wasn't he a great guy?'

Everyone at the table was giggling except Scott. Jim was right: this conversation was only going to lead to Michael Cosgrove. I stood, plucking an empty wine bottle off the table and crossing the kitchen. Carefully I leaned it on one of the recycling piles by the fridge and raided the laundry corner for another.

Scott reaches over and rests his arm against my car seat and suddenly I'm back in Louisiana where the sun is shoving more than enough heat through the windscreen.

I turn around to face Jo Curtis. 'Do you think Vashon will always be our point of reference?'

'Yeah.'

'Even if we move across the country?'

'Even if you've moved around the world, you mean?'

To get from Baton Rouge to New Orleans, the three of us drive on long, grey bridges suspended over swamps. They reach for miles, thin concrete lanes over the marshland, like we're balanced on the surface of a place that's breathing beneath us.

New Orleans is a top contender for having the highest murder rate of any US city. In the French Quarter, women flash their breasts in exchange for Mardi Gras beads and drinks are weighted like violent slushies—Hurricanes, Hand Grenades, even absinthe is available. This neighbourhood—the buildings, the streets themselves—seems drunk. Even on this weekday afternoon, the revellers are a little too loud, the fun a little too angry. We park

the car at a nice enough hotel that we booked over the internet
and wander outside.

The buildings are dressed up with colour. Green walls and
salmon-pink doors. Red walls and blue shutters. Sturdy wrought-
iron lace encloses the balconies—some are wraparound porches
with only enough room for one person and others are long thin
verandahs with access via many doors.

At the intersection of Bourbon Street and Orleans Avenue, a
woman teeters. Her shoes have spikes for heels and her black lace
skirt is short, drawing attention to the muscles protruding from
her skinny legs. A man in faded jeans and a tired rock band t-shirt
grabs her arm. There's no irony in his mullet haircut.

His voice is low. 'Jess, listen to me . . .'

'Oh fuck off. I'm tired of you.' Her body shifts forward with
the syllables and her legs follow as though to catch herself.

He leans back, waits a moment and then reaches for her arm
again. 'Jess, I'm sorry.'

This time, he holds her wrist forcefully and she crumples into
his chest, crying.

'It's going to be okay,' he says.

'It's not going to be okay.' Her voice is shrill, mocking. Sighing,
he disentangles himself from her sloppy embrace.

'What, you're gonna walk away? Figures.' Her tone is loud,
wanting for witnesses. She stumbles along the bricked gutter
towards a lamppost.

'You listening?' He sounds softer.

'Sure am.' But she's sassing him, stepping away again.

He grabs at her. 'Jess, listen to me . . .'

They drift from one corner of the intersection to the next.
Overhead, the clouds are moving faster than they are, against a
sun-faded sky. Scott tugs my arm, embarrassed that I'm staring,
but I'm captivated as though it's convincing street art.

★

In adolescence, I yelled and slammed doors. Over the course of my years in high school, my mother slapped me four or five times, with good reason. My stepfather Garry physically threatened me on a few occasions and my older sister, Serena, once threw rocks at him in my defence. I was a picky eater and stubborn about texture: I still won't eat mushrooms.

This degree of violence seemed minimal after Michael Cosgrove—no one had to go to hospital, furniture was never broken—but when I started seeing Scott, I realised my accepted volume levels weren't universal.

One Sunday afternoon, Scott and I were recovering in our flat post-argument. He spoke quietly, staring at the floor: 'I just don't understand why you get so *angry* at me. Why do you shout? It hurts my feelings when you say you hate me.' Scott's a solid man who's fought on a rugby field. He's been in brawls and punched grown men in the face. That morning, when I yelled at him over the orange laminate counter, his expression was small, his posture scared. On that sun-streaked autumn day the fact was inescapable: if I didn't do something about myself, I'd yell him away.

I began to see a therapist in Canberra where I was studying. I commuted every two weeks to meet with my postgrad supervisor and before returning to Wollongong, I would arrive at my counsellor's private practice. We sat in her study, surrounded by books—the titles spanning Jungian therapy to the tarot. She asked about my family.

'It's women,' I said. 'My mother is charismatic, passion personified. My sister—the strongest person I've ever met. They raised me, the two of them. I remember everyone else at school had boring mothers and fathers. I thought I was the luckiest—no one else had a mother and an older sister like mine.' Irene and Serena were like mythological birds—part eagle, part lion, part snake. It was important to describe every nuance so she could understand how breathtaking they were.

'What about your father?'

'Which one?'

'Start with the first. How did he handle anger?'

'I don't think he has much to do with it.' Of course he had everything to do with it but I was convinced my rage was about my last boyfriend—the law student.

'Well, let's start there anyway.' My therapist was the kind of woman who could have lived on Vashon. It wasn't difficult to imagine her running a cooperative day care centre or being friends with my mother. When her office moved to a renovated school bus in the backyard, it was established beyond a doubt: she was one of the few Australians I'd met who understood my hippie cultural heritage.

At the beginning of each session, she always offered a cup of tea and together we analysed my outbursts and dreams. She asked me about early role models and gave me homework—'Draw yourself in a way no one would recognise'—and I brought in artworks that took days to create. My self-portrait had been a blind crocodile, falling through space in the foetal position, and of course I thought there was nothing in it but she took one look and grinned like we were getting somewhere.

Eventually I faced into my anger with Michael Cosgrove—years of unanswered longing can make a girl spiteful, I realised—and at the time I thought, 'So what? So I'm angry, how is acknowledging that going to help anything?' But then my rages began to ease with the slow release of a steam valve and after eight months, I was sitting in my usual chair, staring at a tree in her backyard that needed pruning, and realised there was nothing to report: no outbursts, no tantrums. I didn't throw plates or rip up Scott's magazines when he wasn't paying attention to me.

'I'm not sure what to say. Everything's good.' Usually, I had a list of topics to discuss—questions from how to negotiate equal shares of the housework to ensuring I had time to write. The last few sessions had been closer to conversation than therapy.

'Any incidents?'

That afternoon, I was drinking milky tea out of a purple mug. The liquid was warm and pungent—Ceylon. My fingers gripped the handle for a moment and then set the cup onto the short table between us. 'Well, Scott was four hours late picking me up from a friend's house. He was playing golf.'

'What did you do?'

'Well, usually I'd yell and curse. "How can you waste my time? I have things to do." But this time, I just presented him with a bill—twenty dollars for each hour I'd been waiting. It was enough to buy a black sweater I'd been eyeing. He was happy because I didn't yell; I was happy with my new cardigan. But you know, I don't think he'll ever be late again—he doesn't like spending money.'

'You know what I think?' my counsellor asked.

'What?'

'I think you're done here.'

During an impromptu tour of New Orleans, Jo Curtis takes Scott and me to an above-ground graveyard. Any excavations are quickly filled with water so the dead here aren't buried, they're entombed. The cemetery downtown is like a white granite maze—sunbaked stone angels stare down from the eaves and thick crosses guard the departed. On top of one, a concrete girl kneels. Behind her, the sky billows with white-dry clouds that seem oblivious to the moist heat.

'Look at this . . .' Jo Curtis says. I follow her voice, wondering if our excursion is appropriate—she lost a close friend from work to suicide the year before—but she's humming to herself, looking at a small memorial. From the dates inscribed, the baby only lived a few months.

Down from us, a long series of graves has been bricked up—three rows stacked on top of one another, extending for thirty metres. It reminds me of storage, a morgue.

Scott is standing around the corner in front of a gravestone.

He waits until I'm next to him and then speaks without looking at me. 'Do you want to visit your father?'

'What?' I wonder briefly if Michael Cosgrove has died and no one remembered to tell me, maybe he's buried here. Then I wonder why Scott's bringing him up.

When my boyfriend turns, I have a sense that a deeper history than the one we share is staring at me but as soon as he speaks, this eerie feeling fades. 'He's come up a few times, that's all . . .'

A tour group streams around us. The guide is a fat man with a heavy southern accent—it's so strong it has to be affected for northerners. 'Come on, y'all,' he urges. Most of the tourists are 'lai-deez' wearing too much hairspray; their combined scent makes the muggy air even heavier.

'Why would I want to visit him?'

Someone jostles me but Scott's frame is large, anchored. 'People die.'

'We can always hope.'

At college, I wrote stories that celebrated Michael Cosgrove's imagined death. In one, Serena and I were in a department store, trying on high heels. Scouring the racks, debating styles—red pumps, black stilettos, tiger-print platforms—we were going to wear them to dance on his grave. Given this, you wouldn't think I'd have needed a therapist to discover my anger with Michael Cosgrove.

Scott's face is sweaty and tired. He steps forward to read the plaque in front of us and I realise he's probably thinking of his own father who died of leukaemia. Cemeteries, like wedding halls, are places of projection—the ritual of death an encounter that only becomes more familiar the longer you live.

The guide points to a plot down from us, and cameras snap. 'This gentleman was instrumental in the early town planning . . .'

I take Scott's arm. I know his father left for Australia on bad terms with his brother and when he died, so too did any hope of reconciliation for the two men. But it's ludicrous to consider the story of Michael Cosgrove in light of the Bazleys, a salt-solid people. At first, Scott's question seems like a dooming one—we will never understand each other, he can't fathom how bizarre and aggressive my father was—and then I realise it's not dooming at all: his incomprehension proves that violence is escapable. I've ended up with a man who can't fathom my dysfunctional background, let alone reproduce it. I should be rejoicing.

SUPPOSE

The next morning, the Montgomery-bound bus is packed. Scott sits up front and I'm lucky to get a seat near the bathroom. The demographic on the bus has changed again. From California through Texas, most of the passengers were Latinos. In the south, more than ninety per cent are African-Americans. I'm aware of this each time someone boards the bus. And then, in a fit of western liberal paranoia, I wonder if anyone notices that I'm noticing this. Unconcerned, the black kid next to me yawns. He wears his new clothes—a green alligator polo shirt and khakis— like they don't fit. I wonder where he's going, who's meeting him at the other end of his journey. He stares straight ahead, listening to a shiny discman.

The bus swings out of the station, the front wheel hitting a pothole—since Texas, the roads have dropped in quality. My hands thumb through the guidebook but it shakes and my stomach starts to churn.

Forty-five minutes later, the Greyhound pulls up at the kerb thirty metres from a service station, the motor humming beneath us. After a few minutes, the engine cuts out completely and passengers begin to rustle in their seats.

'What's going on?' I ask my companion, who shrugs.

He takes off his earphones as the driver's loudspeaker whines. 'Passengers. We're having engine trouble. I apologise for the inconvenience but we're going to have to wait for the Greyhound mechanic.'

An older man calls out: 'Just put us on another bus.' He's wearing a 1940s felt fedora hat. Looking around, he lifts his hands, a wide grin on his face. It's a relaxed expression, like he's used to smiling even in his sleep.

'Wouldn't that be the way? I'm almost home,' the kid next to me says with the exhaustion of a fellow traveller. He isn't as young as I thought but he has the easy grace of a high-school track star—someone who could break state records even if he'd been studying all night before.

The driver continues: 'There's a service station if you want to purchase any refreshments. But alcohol is not to be consumed on the bus.'

'Purchase any refreshments?' my seatmate says, still sitting. 'Who makes this shit up?'

Most of the passengers rise at the same time and push up the aisle. I grab my guitar off the rack and sit back down, the instrument on my lap. There's no hurry—the bus isn't going anywhere.

From the front of the bus, Scott motions that he's getting a drink and drops down the steps.

'You know—' The man in the fedora hat, two rows ahead, turns around. 'I'm going to New York.'

I can't help smiling back at him. 'Yeah?'

'Dream of mine. Whole life. Fifty-nine years old and I'm finally going to sing "Start Spreading the News" on Broadway. I love Frank Sinatra, just love him. I'll be on the street and I'll just start singing. No one can stop you singing. The name's Ray, by the way.'

I have the crazy sense that the bus has broken down so the two of us could find each other—an ageing black man on a Sinatra pilgrimage and a late-twenties white girl who's channelling the power of Elvis.

The guy next to me holds out his hand to Ray. 'Tyrone.'

After the three of us shake our introductions, Ray nods at the case. 'You play any Sinatra?'

'No, only Elvis. It's all Elvis. I'm on a trek to Graceland for the twenty-fifth anniversary of his death.'

'I like the King.'

I'm surprised he calls Elvis 'the King'. Some have argued Elvis was an impostor whose reign was only made possible by exploiting the music of African-Americans. After all, in the *Charlotte Observer*, Elvis himself said, 'The colored folks been singing it and playing it just like I'm doin' now, man, for more years than I know . . . and nobody paid it no mind 'til I goosed it up. I got it from them . . .'

Tyrone perks up. 'You think he's the King?'

'No one beats Sinatra but he was pretty big.'

I'm thinking Elvis was pretty big in part because he was white and he made black music more palatable to the white audiences of the late 1950s. He didn't invent the system that marginalised and oppressed African-Americans but he sure did benefit from it.

Tyrone doesn't seem convinced by the power of Elvis. 'I don't know. He seems like an old dead white guy now.'

Ray lets out a crackly guffaw. 'I guess he is.'

'Part of the controversy about Elvis and African-American music is the songs.' I've been reading the biography and have to control my voice so I don't sound like a textbook Elvis nerd. 'He didn't write them but took some of the credit for them. Otis Blackwell, the guy who wrote "Don't Be Cruel", was told he'd have to make a deal if Elvis was going to sing his songs. Elvis never even met him but he made a lot of money off that guy's music.'

They're both staring at me and I realise neither one cares about Elvis Presley and race politics—I've read that into the conversation; they were just talking about Elvis's place in the musical scheme of things. The awkward moment reminds me of riding the Greyhound through Beaumont, Texas, a few days before—a place with a history of racial tension. I was staring out the window as though expecting pointy white hats to be perched on the chimneys. My naivety seems painfully northern—like if we could all just hold hands around the bus we could sing ourselves to racial harmony.

I'm beating myself up over the stupid Elvis comments when a skinny white girl at the front calls out: 'I'm gonna dump the jerk. I don't need his shit.' She's perched on her knees, facing sideways. Her tank top is too small, the tag popping out between her shoulderblades, and when she reaches behind to yank her red ponytail tighter, the gesture seems crass. Besides Scott and me, she's the only other white person riding the bus. She's been talking to an elderly black woman across the aisle, who nods wearily. 'I have potential, you know. Potential.'

The girl shifts in her seat, smiling back at us, and her face crinkles; her eyes look young. She can't be any older than seventeen.

Tyrone turns to me. 'That your sister?'

My eyes widen. 'What, 'cause I have potential?'

He laughs. 'Not a lot of white people on the bus, that's all.'

I ease back in the seat and shrug. If I'm going to assume he cares about Elvis and the politics of race, he can assume we're related. 'No, there's not. But unfortunately: no. Never seen her before.' I shake my head and Tyrone and I both giggle. Ray's still leaning over the seat ahead of us, watching like a mildly disapproving parent.

The redhead's voice bounces through the bus. 'You know, I might join the army.'

'Pity that,' Ray says. 'Don't matter if you're black or white—you poor, the army starts looking okay. There weren't many rich kids lining up for Desert Storm.'

I think of how unhappy Elvis was to receive his draft notice, as though he knew the irrevocable change it would bring—it was during his army stint that his mother died and he discovered pills.

The girl is still talking; she can't decide—maybe she'll join the navy and perform underwater missions. 'Because I really like to swim,' she says.

Even Ray can't keep from smiling at that one and turns to Tyrone. 'So where you coming from?'

'Jail. Been free for two and a half hours now. Couldn't see a horizon. Didn't step on anything that wasn't concrete. Felt like I was always being watched, you know.'

'You probably were,' I say.

He laughs again and Ray rests his elbows on the headrest and stares down at Tyrone. 'How you going to keep out?' He speaks with the authority of a family member.

Tyrone reaches into his bag and pulls out a Bible.

'Good man. What were you in for?'

'Cocaine. Dealing.'

'You got clean friends?'

Tyrone looks at both of us before nodding. It's a quick, deep gesture. His chin drops low, almost to his chest.

'Good. Your family miss you?'

Again, Tyrone nods and I imagine older sisters that'll fuss and tease him when he steps off the bus. 'Tyrone, what on earth are you wearing?' the oldest will ask, lifting his shirt to check he's still there beneath the green knit fabric.

Ray's voice is deep and forceful. 'You'll be okay then. But you don't want to go back there.'

'No sir,' Tyrone's voice follows in litany.

Ray turns to me. 'You going to play us some Elvis or what?'

A few days later, Scott and I are in Birmingham, a city with shiny red-brick buildings. Modern structures—with sheets of glass and glinting steel—offset this historical architecture. Women wear high heels that clip across the pavement; their long strides seem uniquely southern.

At the entrance to the Civil Rights Institute, Scott and I wait for a gaggle of schoolchildren to push ahead. The teachers speak in museum-calm voices. Most of the girls hold hands, attentive to a buddy system, while the boys run around the foyer—a couple are pretending they're airplanes.

Inside, once the kids have moved along, the dark hallways are silent. After passing timelines of the Civil Rights Movement and a life-sized model of a segregated soda parlour, we pause in front of a replica of Martin Luther King Jr's jail cell. When we round a bend, an old Greyhound is modelled into the wall.

'A bus!' My enthusiasm is too loud, mismatched with the solemn corridor. Scott nods to hush me up and I realise it's only a remnant of the vehicle. The silver insignia has been charred with smoke. It's a model of the bus that was burned in the Freedom Rides, when Klan supporters attacked it.

Black and white members of the Congress of Racial Equality and the Student Nonviolent Coordinating Committee boarded a similar bus in Washington DC in May 1961, headed to New Orleans to test the desegregation court case *Boynton vs Virginia*. Travelling through Alabama, the Freedom Riders encountered mob violence in Anniston and Birmingham. When they arrived in Montgomery, their police escort disappeared and over 200 anti-integrationists set upon the bus. Eventually Attorney General Robert F Kennedy sent in US marshals to dispel the mob.

'That bus would have been on the same stretch of freeway as us,' Scott murmurs.

We're quiet for a moment. I think of all the rides we've taken across the United States: the swishing doors, the passengers ahead of me cranking their seats back, the overhead compartments.

'I never thought of the Greyhound as part of civil rights history.' My whisper hangs in the passageway. But of course it was, and indeed the bus itself had been a symbol of the Civil Rights Movement since December 1955 when Rosa Parks refused to move to the 'coloured' section of a Montgomery city bus, instigating her arrest. In response, the civil rights community began boycotting Montgomery's public transportation—the boycott officially ended a year later, after the US Supreme Court ruled that segregation was unconstitutional on November 13, 1956.

'You know, Rosa Parks may have won the battle, but buses are still segregated: white people just don't ride them,' I say to Scott.

He nods and I think of Elvis, whose music was gaining momentum at that time. The year of the Montgomery bus boycott saw him record hits like 'Heartbreak Hotel', 'Hound Dog' and 'Don't Be Cruel', as well as launch a movie career with *Love Me Tender*. Elvis did proudly thank BB King backstage for early lessons at a benefit in December 1956, and according to the black press *Memphis World*, reports also surfaced that year that he ignored 'segregation laws by attending the Fairgrounds Memphis amusement park on East Parkway, during what is designated as "colored night"'. But for someone with such influence, I wonder if this was enough. How much does context justify a man's (in)action?

And this isn't a question confined to individuals. The broader South is still negotiating its relationship to history. Just down the street from the museum, the Sixteenth Street Baptist Church looks unassuming, but on September 15, 1963, a Ku Klux Klan splinter group planted a bomb beneath its steps. The bomb exploded, killing four African-American girls between the ages of eleven and fourteen: Cynthia Wesley, Addie Mae Collins, Denise McNair and Carole Robertson. They'd been preparing for Sunday school. None of the prime suspects was charged at the time and eventually the FBI officially closed the case, citing lack of local cooperation. It was reopened in 1971 and Robert Chambliss was convicted six years later. In 2001, Thomas Blanton Jr was convicted and sentenced to life in prison but it wasn't until May 2002—just two months before Scott and I arrived in Birmingham—that the last living suspect, 71-year-old Bobby Cherry, was finally sentenced to life in prison.

Forty-five minutes north of Birmingham, we stay with my mother's cousin and her husband in a town so small it doesn't rate a mention in the guidebook.

My mother and her cousin Sylvia share the same birthday (date and year) and measure the same height (almost five feet tall), but the woman who picks us up from the bus station has regular manicures, and a tennis racquet sits in the back seat. I've never seen my mother on a tennis court and can only imagine her staring vehemently at the ball and whacking it too hard.

Sylvia asks about my siblings. 'Serena, Grace and Lucas, right? How are they?'

I'm feeling a little self-conscious. Scott and I haven't showered in five days, since Baton Rouge—the fleabag hotel we were staying at didn't have running water. The pipes would just moan and shudder if you turned the taps. This wouldn't have mattered so much except the summer heat has been so ferocious that Scott and I have a combined body odour that could knock out a small child. Sylvia ignores the stench and follows a code of hospitality: we may never have met but I'm family. We start talking as though we're already mid-conversation and within minutes I'm telling her the gossip about Serena's new boyfriend: 'Get this—they went out in high school and have come back together after twenty years.' They actually lost their virginity to each other, though I hold off on that detail—it doesn't quite go with the sealed windows and air-conditioned new-car smell.

When we pull up at the house, I've gotten the rundown on all the extended cousins in the state of Alabama. Sylvia shows us to the guest quarters—an upper wing of the house with its own bedroom, sitting area and bathroom. Fabric-softened white towels and washcloths are folded on the bed.

'You'll like the bathroom,' she says, and Scott looks at me as if to ask whether it's an American custom to pass judgment on your host's toilet. But as soon as we walk through the door, her meaning is apparent: the shower has been grouted with my mother's tiles. There must be at least thirty or forty of her images—sandcastles and palm trees, couples dancing, goldfish bowls on checkerboard tables. And beneath them, captions: 'Take time to play'; 'Save the last dance for me'; 'Tides change'. The colourful jolt of my mother almost starts me crying.

As soon as Scott and I are alone, I pull the smelly Shady Grove t-shirt over my head and start the water running. It storms out of the nozzle and I step in, scalding myself. A clean plastic suction mat keeps my feet from slipping and I reach for the full bottle of shampoo waiting in the shiny rack—for the first time in weeks, my hair's going to smell like a make-believe garden.

In Montgomery, I had a meltdown in a phone booth, crying in loud gusts because I couldn't find Sylvia's number. With my four quarters chunking into the machine, I asked Irene to check her address book, talking in a slight falsetto so she wouldn't hear the sobbing in my voice. Afterwards, when I was busking in front of the Hank Williams tribute statue, people scowled at me as though I'd gotten my icons mixed up: they didn't understand I was honouring Hank with Elvis (and I didn't have much else in my musical repertoire). And then, at the Greyhound station, I smashed my head against the doorway as we were running for the bus. Tears were seeping from my eyes when we boarded and all the women on the bus looked at Scott as though he were to blame. This probably wasn't helped by the fact that he kept repeating, 'We're on the same side, we're on the same side,' as we moved up the aisle.

Travelling had become the hard work of finding a place to sleep each night, playing my Elvis, and staying within budget. But here—wriggling naked in the water, stomping and singing—I feel safe: my mother surrounds me, hugging me through her bright tiles.

Scott and I spend five days with my relatives. We take a rowboat out on the lake where my grandmother used to go fishing. I learn the best recipe for macaroni and cheese the South has to offer and eat homemade ice-cream. I even go to church. Alabama may boggle me as a place (especially the sign alongside the road into town that says 'Evolution Is Science Fiction') but I'm forced to take the South seriously: people who I like live here. I realise too that I've taken a break from travelling. The traveller doesn't have to commit to the places where she stops. In Salt Lake City, for example, I felt uncomfortable so I boarded a bus and got out of there. Now, I'm wondering what my life would have been like if I'd grown up here in the South, if I'd been born into another branch of my family tree.

Sylvia and her husband Wesley take us out to dinner before we leave. When we're parked outside the restaurant, Sylvia bends down and pulls out a bottle of red and four plastic glasses from a chest at her feet. The wine must have been opened before leaving the house because the cork comes out easily. She pours us each a glass, passing them back one at a time. 'We can't drink inside the restaurant.'

'No licence?'

'You can't serve alcohol here: we're in a dry county. We miss out on the taxes, of course. And we have to buy our wine across the county line, but you get used to it.'

The plastic cup is at odds with the expensive wine. I imagine trying to explain this to my friends in Australia, where Scott can judge the population of a country town by the number of pubs on the main street. In a weird way, it kind of reminds me of Vashon. My mother is so passionate about Vipassana meditation that it's not unusual for her to stop drinking when she's gearing up for a retreat.

Sylvia tells me there are hundreds of dry counties in the United States, located mainly in the southern states. In Mississippi, almost half of the counties are dry and in Texas, almost a fifth of the 254 counties are completely dry and about half are 'moist' (laws vary from county to county: in some, only up to four per cent beer is legal, while in others the alcohol percentage can be higher). The terms—moist, dry—remind me of weather forecasts.

If the South is still wary of alcohol, I can only imagine what it would have been like in the fifties and sixties. Like my epiphany in Utah, I'm reminded of Elvis as rebellious. I picture the King swaggering into a cowboy bar, drawing back a long shot of whiskey and slamming the empty glass onto the counter.

That night, I start writing down everything that surprises me about the United States: top of the list are the fact that it's legal to ride your bicycle without a helmet and the noticeable lack of clotheslines, especially in hotter areas. The Aussies have turned the Hills hoist into a national icon and I'm used to seeing them at attention in suburban yards. The water consumption, too, astounds me after living with water restrictions. On Vashon, I was gobsmacked when my younger sister took an hour-long shower: she'd actually lain down in the streaming water and fallen asleep.

'What else is weird about this place?' I ask Scott.

'Condoms. In Australia, you can get them at petrol stations, supermarkets, public bathrooms, chemists. Here, you practically need a warrant to find them.' Scott has been keeping track of how the availability of sexual protection varies from state to state. He seems to think this restraint is novel and I can imagine him gleefully telling his friends in Australia about this puritanical streak in American culture.

'Not on Vashon.'

'Especially Vashon. Even you hippies are weird about sex.'

Despite Scott's claim, I'd always considered my family open about sexuality. Irene said if her example was anything to go by, it was obvious her daughters would need to be informed. When I started menstruating in eighth grade, she responded with cheers and applause. 'Shady, this is a rite of passage.'

'OH-my-God, can you please keep your voice down. And we are *not* having a party like Serena.'

A few years later, much to my chagrin, my mother and aunt set up a betting pool as to when I'd lose my virginity to my high school sweetheart. He and I were allowed to have weekend sleepovers in the same bed—still, it was months before anything transpired: sometimes my conservatism surprises even me.

Yet, in spite of her openness, I'd never regarded my mother as sexual. It was in Australia, when my mother's best friend from high school visited, that I was forced to reconsider this. Lucy had attended Palo Alto High with Irene—they were due to graduate the same year and she'd been my mother's closest confidante when Irene discovered she was pregnant with Serena.

But Lucy and I weren't discussing that as we walked along the North Beach cycleway—we were talking about Elvis. 'Some think his cultural power was through music . . .' My voice trailed off as I cleaned my sunglasses with the edge of my shirt. 'Others cite his image. I think it's something else: his story. Sure the image and the music are there too, but it's the story that's so powerful. Poor beginnings. Meteoric rise to fame.' I delivered my thesis in compact sentences that matched our steady pace.

A bicyclist streamed past, his helmet pivoting as Lucy started laughing in unafraid, loud whoops. 'Bah! It's none of that. It was sex! When we were swooning and screaming, adolescent girls going wild, it was all about the sex.' Her accent was exciting and brash and East Coast American. I wasn't sure I'd ever heard the word 'sex' resound with such stinging force before.

Even so, I'd spent a lot of time thinking about Elvis and why he inspired my trip. I was convinced it was about his story—he followed the great hero trajectory. 'But Elvis was so polite.'

'Not on stage.'

'But—'

'Sex.'

'Really?'

'Sex. Honey, we were all about sex.' Lucy's red hair bobbed unapologetically.

Even with the family conversations over the years—my mother and sister using bananas to demonstrate how to put on condoms—I'd never seen Irene as 'all about sex'. Maybe it was self-induced ignorance: there's a creepiness to thinking of your parents as sexual.

The following day, Lucy, Scott and I drove out to Wombeyan Caves, a natural reserve about two hours west of Wollongong. The single-lane dirt road followed the Great Dividing Range, twisting along mountain ridges. On tight corners, I slowed to forty kilometres per hour and pulled up when cars approached from the opposite direction. Anyone in the passenger seat had a view seventy metres down to the ragged, dry eucalypts. In the distance, the horizon was layered with trees blue from haze.

When we finally arrived at the reserve, Lucy and I sat beneath a small gum tree in fold-out chairs, watching airplanes cross the sky.

'So you knew Irene when she got pregnant.' My words hovered between assertion and question.

'Your mother was wild. She had this crazy, sexual energy.' She spoke in a sassing voice and I imagined Lucy and my mother in front of their lockers, piling in textbooks and scouting the hallway for boys.

'Did you know Michael at all?'

A cockatoo squawked overhead like a warning and Lucy smoothed her hair with a slick, purposeful motion. 'You have to remember, he was a few years older. But they had a fierce and intense connection. Did I understand it? Not really. She and I would skip classes and smoke cigarettes in my black Nash Rambler—the "Roach". It was all about risk.' She said the word 'risk' with the same energy as 'sex', and again I tried to connect the single syllables with my mother.

'Risk?'

Lucy leaned back fully into the green canvas and smacked her lips together—I could see her and my mother in the parked Roach, my mother cranking the rear-view mirror out of position to inspect her face.

'The whole era was about risk. As we drove here today, you kept to the speed limit, honking on blind corners. There was none of that. We'd all pile into a car, drunk, drugged, seatbelts loose, whatever, and we'd speed along these winding mountain roads.'

As Lucy spoke, another airplane eased across the sky. Staring up at the red and white tail, I remembered another story about Michael Cosgrove: in some test of faith, he used to drive wearing a blindfold. Irene would sit in the front seat and give him directions. 'Okay, you're in the middle of the road, that's good. You want to slow down now. Turn to the right, sharper . . .'

When he hit a parked car, he raged at my mother: 'Why didn't you *tell* me?'

Serena later told me she remembered the story differently. In her version, Michael was driving blindfolded with a friend when he hit the car. When police asked what he was doing, he said he'd 'bent down to pick up a dime' while driving.

Staring up at the cloudless blue with Lucy, I realised part of the reason why my mother was embarrassed to talk about Michael Cosgrove: crazy as he was, she chose to sit in the front seat with him. Whether she was actually in the Ford station wagon or not, she was in his car—metaphorically speaking—for ten years.

After nearly a week with Sylvia and Wesley (and a weight gain for me of three kilos), Scott and I reluctantly continue on, zigzagging back to Mississippi. When we arrive in Natchez, the bus barely stops at the depot. It lets us off and scoots out of the station as though trying to catch up with its schedule. After dropping our packs at a dive on the cheap motel strip, Scott and I explore the other side of town with its decaying mansions. In the centre, buildings have nooks and decorative cement work—white angel faces nestled into chipped red brickwork. A shop features posters of the King, his body leaning back, his mouth stretched open: somehow this indicates the new line of Elvis furniture now available. I'm surprised the King is an icon of homeware style—images of him strutting onstage hardly fit with coffee table catalogues.

On the Mississippi, white-grey water blends into the white-grey sky and a steel bridge like the one in Baton Rouge reaches skyward in peaks. In front of us, a gambling-den paddle steamer is tied to a small pier. Tourist buses unload middle-aged couples in the parking lot above: the women are dressed up with powdered faces and thick, sturdy heels; the men wear bumbags.

Scott has a grimy collar and sweat stains beneath his arms. I'm wearing running shoes. 'I'm not sure we fit the dress code,' I say.

'How about a pub?'

We walk upriver to a tavern nestled on the footpath and Scott swings the heavy door open. Beneath the thick wooden rafters, we're faced with the end of a bar where two people are sitting—a blonde woman and a guy with a baseball cap perched backwards on his head.

The woman grins. 'My name's Kate and this is my cousin Sam.'

Her eagerness makes me wonder if we made a mistake sitting near them. She has a pleasant round face and compact figure but the straps on her pink tank top are too long; the sagging fabric doesn't suit her frame.

'Shady and Scotty,' I say while Scott nods to the bartender for a beer.

'Where y'all from?' Kate's voice lilts, her accent comfortable in the empty room.

'Australia.'

'Australia?' Sam asks, his blue-green eyes twitching back and forth between us. His gaze is one of curious hostility, and I can't help wondering if he was a reptile in a previous life. Maybe he's noticed my American accent and it's confusing him.

'Yeah.' I nod to Scott as though he's an authentic South Pacific specimen.

'That's the place with really weird gun laws, isn't it?' Sam turns his baseball cap around like he needs to shield his eyes.

'I don't think so.'

The bartender plonks our drinks in front of us.

'Yeah, I'm sure it is. I was reading about it.'

I prod Scott like it's his patriotic duty to know the specifics of Australian gun legislation and he stares back at me like I've gotten it all wrong: the only guns he cares about are ones that win gold medals in Olympic shooting. 'Not that I know of,' Scott says.

Australia actually has progressive gun laws. Following the law reforms after the 1996 Port Arthur massacre in Tasmania and the buy-back scheme, Australia only had 333 firearm deaths in 2000. The US had almost 30,000. Even if you take the population difference into account, you're almost ten times more likely to die from a firearm injury in the States than in Australia.

Sam sets his beer on the counter and inches forward in his chair. He's the kind of guy who would rather keep quiet and roll his eyes moodily while his cousin chats us up, but he can't help himself. 'No, I'm sure it was Australia. You need to get permits for your guns and mostly they're reserved for farmers.'

'Oh. Yeah. That's true.'

He gapes at me as though I've just told him we like to feed our young to rabid kangaroos. 'That's pretty fucked up. Who's the government to tell me what I can buy?'

Scott takes a long sip. 'I guess that's one way of looking at it.'

Kate beams at me like we're doing great—Sam never talks this much and we all deserve a big pat on the back for bringing him out of his shell—but Scott and I won't be ordering another drink.

Sam purses his lips. 'Yeah, I was interested in going there until I heard that.'

As we're walking out, Elvis comes to mind. He loved his gold-plated Beretta and turquoise-handled Colt .45. He had leather holsters with silver buckles and storage boxes with compartments so he could store his guns like jewellery. And of course he'd use them to blow apart his televisions: I remember a picture of his RCA Victor with a spider's web of broken glass and a clean bullet hole in the bottom right-hand corner. I blame the amphetamines but it's tricky reconciling the drug-addled Elvis with his younger innocence. I've had to pace myself through the second part of his biography because there's some sense that if I stop reading, I can delay the unfolding events.

A romantic might argue that Elvis was shooting the television because it had been pivotal in establishing his career—especially his stint on the *Johnny Carson Show*—and maybe he had regrets about fame. But this analysis implies a thoughtfulness that doesn't coincide with eyewitness accounts of his drug-hazed, temperamental, self-obsessed final years.

I try to imagine being in the room with him and a loaded firearm. In 1976, he broke up a Graceland recording session when he entered with a Thompson submachine gun and said he was going to blow up the speakers. He was joking around but the musicians disbanded quickly enough. If Sam had been there, I bet he would have moved on too.

People who support unrestricted access to guns don't anticipate being on the wrong end of one. Before I was born, Michael Cosgrove played Russian roulette with my mother's head. After the second empty click, Irene threw herself out the window. Punching through glass, she cut her hand badly and Serena remembers driving her to the hospital.

This story doesn't come up around the dinner table. I know the events from listening in—Serena and Irene whispering to each other—and the details are relegated to imagination and logic. Surely Michael had been drinking. Maybe he'd been arguing with my mother or playing 'risk'—another version of careening along the mountain pass or driving blindfolded. And then there's the question of whether Serena really could have driven a car at nine years of age. But regardless of whether that part of the story actually happened, it signals to me that my sister felt like she was taking care of my mother and this fact alone makes me unbearably sad. And then I think about Irene, sitting at the table, listening to the gun click quietly as my father pulled the trigger yet again.

HOW CAN YOU LOSE WHAT YOU NEVER HAD?

Scott and I travel north to Clarksdale, Mississippi, for the Sunflower Blues Festival. The blocks near town are manicured and clean, without frills. They have the same sensible feel as clothing in a second-hand store—aged but worth recycling. Further out, houses are deserted, with boarded-up windows and vacant doorways; even the abandoned architecture is regal, alluding to a former gothic elegance. Elvis first played in Clarksdale's City Auditorium on January 12, 1955, when the town had a bit more glamour.

The festival takes place in pubs and parks dotted around town—acoustic and electric blues, down-and-dirty to stripped-back-bare. At the day's end, the main gig is a rocking band that screams with electric guitar. Scott and I have a good vantage point on the grass, behind the dancing bodies. When the final encore fades, roadies descend onto the main stage as Scott and I wander through the thinning crowd. Sidestepping the garbage bins overfilled with plastic cups and aluminium cans, we're looking for Big Red's, a bar with a reputation for blues.

Two white officers are standing near the giant speakers with their arms crossed. In the dark, the park has the ambience of a seedy bar and the police don't look friendly.

'Excuse me, Big Red's?' Usually I hate asking directions, but the music has left me wide awake and buzzing, and I'm not ready for the night to be over.

'Big Red's? Haven't heard of it,' the closest one says.

The other turns to me, nudging an abandoned fold-out chair with his foot; someone's kicked the fabric out of it. 'You sure it's in this town?'

'Not really.' I get the distinct impression I should downplay our destination.

On the other side of the portable toilets, a teenage girl wearing too much orange lipstick is standing alone, snapping gum.

I make a beeline for her. 'Big Red's?'

She twists her mouth into a curious shape that adds too much emphasis to her leery mouth. 'Sorry.'

At the crosswalk, I ask a black man wearing a leather pilot's jacket. He stops and looks me over, surprised. He repeats it back to me and I nod.

'Two streets over and up. On the left.'

We weave away from the city centre, crossing against the lights. Just one block west, the street is shadowed except for an occasional flicker from the lights overhead. Broken windows reflect a scrawny moon.

I glance over my shoulder. 'I say we go back.'

A mewing cat walks by with bones jutting out of its fur and Scott taps my arm. 'Wait, listen.'

The only other sound is a car in front of us, ambling past, but after it's gone, I can hear what Scott's referring to: music is playing nearby—a lonely 12-bar that echoes like a soundtrack to our setting. It seems to be coming from an old shed across the street.

'I don't think there's anything over there,' I say. There's no sign marking a bar or nightclub, only an abandoned oil drum barbecue out front. The windows are covered with untreated wood, grey from neglect.

Scott watches the sagging exterior. 'Something's going on.'

'Well, if there is, I don't think we're invited.'

A couple strides up from behind us and crosses the street. Even in the faded light, her vivid turquoise dress glimmers. She swings with each step, her gait somewhere between walking and skipping. He's laughing with her. Stopping in front of the old shed, he bends down and grabs a handle from the ground, hefting a door upwards, and they descend into the belly of the shack. The camouflaged panel closes behind them.

'Big Red's.' Scott's voice is triumphant. 'Come on.' He's already across the street. 'Let's look. What's the worst that could happen?' he says. It's obvious my boyfriend didn't grow up in a country where citizens have the right to bear arms.

I let Scott's question hang in the air while he lifts the door, stepping down. Below us, a converted blues bar is filled with patrons. Everyone is black. I step back.

'You're so weird,' Scott whispers.

'I'm not weird, I'm respectful. They probably don't want to hang out with a pair of stupid, honky white people.'

A large man has begun walking towards us from the bar. He's wearing a white t-shirt that just covers his big belly, and his brown plastic sunglasses remind me of my grandmother. 'Can I help you?'

Scott grins. 'We're looking for Big Red.'

'You've found him.'

I'm about to start apologising—we didn't mean to interrupt, obviously we're in the wrong place—but Scott's already talking. 'We heard this was the only place in town worth visiting.'

'Well then, hello.' Big Red shakes Scott's hand and then mine. 'Where you from?' he asks.

'Australia. We're travelling to Memphis,' Scott asserts.

'You're getting close.'

Inside, the walls are covered in metallic gift-wrap wallpaper. Smoke has settled in the air over the two pool tables in the centre of the room. Holes have been punched into the ceiling—from a fistfight, maybe? I have the sudden, absurd image of grown men standing on chairs, swinging at each other.

A few small tables, all filled, have been set up on the left side of the room near a cosy stage. The bar—leaning to the right—has a few empty stools. Big Red gestures for us to sit down.

'Sorry. Nothing on tap.'

Unconcerned, Scott rests his forearms on the sticky bar. 'Whatever's going down.'

Big Red reaches into a hidden workbench built into the heart of the bar. It must hold coolers because the beer is cold. He empties two cans into glasses for us. I realise he's operating without a licence; the place feels like a speakeasy.

As soon as we sit, Big Red passes a long, thin tray to us. Scott peels back the aluminium foil and reaches in to grab a charred piece of pork. It seems the drum barbecue upstairs isn't abandoned. Scott gnaws on the meat while he grills Big Red: 'So who you think's going to win the Series?'

Next to me, a thin guy about sixty years old sits on a stool, arms curled before him and feet tucked onto the lower rung: it's like he's trying to keep within the line of the barstool. Turning only his head towards me, he introduces himself as Georgie and asks what I'm doing in Clarksdale.

'I'm busking my way to Graceland. I'm going to get there for the twenty-fifth anniversary of Elvis's death.'

Georgie offers a cigarette but I shake my head.

'He was such a sad man.' Georgie's voice holds a certain intimacy. Maybe he knew Elvis, I think. Or maybe Elvis's power as a singer and performer was that his audience felt like they knew him.

'Rich,' I say.

'Yeah, but he never recovered from his mother's death. Never. You could tell from the interviews—his life was spent chasing her memory. Parents pass on their legacies for good or bad.'

It takes a moment for me to respond—I'm thinking about Michael Cosgrove. 'You're not wrong.'

He laughs. 'Tell my wife that.'

'What's she doing tonight?'

'Don't know. Left me five years ago.' He watches his beer glass as though sheer will might fill it again.

As we pause, I realise there are two perspectives on Elvis. One held by those who were alive during his life and one held by those who weren't. People alive in the 1950s and '60s were naturally unaware of the fate that awaited him. His rise was unprecedented, glorious. Those of us who are younger can't help but view his successes through the ignominy of his death. If you know that Elvis died on the toilet, it's hard to understand the heroism of his life without framing it through that inglorious image. You can never see history with fresh eyes. You're tainted by knowing what will happen. And that has ramifications for me in trying to understand my family in retrospect.

The lights flicker and eventually I lean towards Georgie. 'You know who I wonder about? Lisa Marie.' In the biography, I'm rereading the section where Lisa Marie is born. Overall, there's surprisingly little about her in the book.

'She'd know legacy, all right.'

Surely she'll be at Graceland, I think, and I have a crazy image of the two of us, jamming together through her father's songs— Lisa Marie helping me with chord changes.

At the end of the bar, Scott's still talking to Big Red and he's got another big hunk of pork between his fingers.

I turn back to Georgie. 'Let me buy you a beer.'

Clarksdale is famous as the home of the Crossroads, the intersection where 1930s Delta blues legend Robert Johnson sold his soul to the Devil for the ability to play the guitar. In music folklore, it is the story of creation: as if getting that soul into your music depends on surrendering it absolutely and only a pact of the highest order will suffice. Robert Johnson died at the age of twenty-seven.

Scott and I march to the intersection where three blue and white guitars have been posted on top of a pole. It should be a junction of two dirt roads lost among rough cotton fields—I had imagined an abandoned farmhouse peering meekly from the distance—but the reality is an industrial stretch near the bus station. Streetlights sag over the road. Letters have fallen off the shop signs—EVERYTHING MUST BE –OLD! The crosswalk signals take so long to change I wonder if they're broken.

I first heard Robert Johnson's music at college. I'd taken the class 'Blues in American Culture', thinking it might explain my father. The homework entailed trekking across the snow-settled campus to the music library—a stone building with turrets—and listening to vinyl and cassette recordings of Robert Johnson, Bessie Smith and BB King. They had the power of the sun on an uncomfortably hot day—humidity hummed in their voices. In 'Cross Road Blues', I could hear Robert Johnson on his knees, begging for a ride; even his guitar sounded thirsty. At the time, I pictured him in this exact spot where I'm now standing, though the only consistency between that mind's-eye version and the one before me is the pounding heat.

In the music library that year, listening through insulated headphones to Robert Johnson, I decided to call Michael Cosgrove. I'd suffered a series of mild heartbreaks and was determined that the cause of them was related to our nonexistent parent–child relationship. Of course the fact that I was studying at a college that was seventy per cent women may have played a role in the lack of appropriate suitors but I wasn't going to let the obvious keep me from resolving this one. I called Irene for his phone number.

Sitting at a wooden desk in my dorm room, I waited as the line crackled between us. Eventually she sighed. 'If that's what you really want, Shady, he's living in Vancouver, Washington.'

She dialled information and called back with his number, her voice excited now, as though we could share any nuggets gleaned from this panning expedition.

With his number carefully written on a page in my journal, I waited until late the next morning to punch the numbers into the phone. When the connection was made, his answering machine message echoed back.

I cleared my throat. 'Hi. Um, it's Shady here. Shady Cosgrove. Maybe you don't want to talk to me, I don't know . . .' I was suddenly shy, the idea of calling felt ridiculous. 'But I'm going to leave my address. If you want to write me, feel free. Maybe that's a better way of doing this.'

I went to lunch at the campus dining hall, humming Robert Johnson's 'Hellhound on My Trail'. When I returned forty-five minutes later I thought my answering machine had broken. It was blinking out of control. Usually it'd flash once if I had a call but it was going nonstop, thirty-five or forty times in a row, so I unplugged it from the wall. When I reconnected it, the darting light resumed. Bewildered, I pressed play.

'Hi, Shady. This is your *father*. Yes. Your *father*. So nice to hear from you. It's been a few years. I called campus information for your number.' His voice faltered, slurred. The message cut out and another started—he'd been leaving messages for almost an hour.

The phone rang. I stared at it. My hand reached for the receiver. He was already talking on the other end when the headpiece reached my ear.

'Are you a real English major or a fake one? You'd better not be a pretentious asshole English major. Though I bet you are, going to Vassar. Here's the test—what's your favourite Shakespeare sonnet? If it's not 93, I refuse to acknowledge you as my daughter. DH Lawrence, what do you think of him? He's the best fucking writer ever.'

This is it? I thought. This is what I get after fifteen years? After waiting at the driveway and playing the piano, hoping he'd hear me? The guy was ranting on about *Lady Chatterley's Lover* and then changed tack, telling me that pretension should be a sin. He was serious—he'd written to the president and the pope but the fuckers hadn't gotten back to him. Imagine that.

He was still going. He hadn't stopped. He hadn't even noticed that I was there, that the answering machine hadn't picked up. He'd started in on my mother—what a bitch she was and how she was never good in bed. I didn't need Irene or Serena to tell me their versions of my father. I could see it for myself: the guy was a fucking lunatic.

I could have sat there listening to his stream-of-consciousness tirade but the stuff about Irene pissed me off. I didn't even think of the early violence or the fear; it was funny: that stuff, the big stuff, isn't what made me angry. I was angry about how many extra tiles my mother had to glaze so I could be sleeping in that dorm room. I thought about her fingers dabbing the paintbrush into the glaze and smoothing the liquid bubble along the bisque. And this guy, who'd never even helped out with child support, thought he could call me up and curse her?

My voice was firm. 'Don't talk about her like that.'

'Oh. You're there.'

'Yeah. I'm here.'

'Well, your mother's a fucking bitch.'

I hung up. Twenty seconds later, the phone rang.

'I'm sorry. I won't talk about your mother or your idiot sister.' Click.

After another twenty seconds: 'So you're at a Seven Sisters college. You must think that's pretty special.'

'I sure do. But if you say one more thing about Irene or Serena, I'll hang up this phone and change my number and you'll never hear from me again.'

'Okay.'

'Other than that, you can keep talking. I'll write down the crazy shit you say and turn you into a story.'

'That sounds good.'

I'd just started my first creative writing class. The teacher told us to write about what we knew and look for unusual experiences in our day-to-day life. We were supposed to record as much detail as possible so I reached into my backpack for a notebook.

I was never afraid during these phone calls. I never got the sense he was going to drive across the country and confront me. All up we spoke about twenty times over the course of two weeks. Michael was unstable, yes, and he clutched at his former influence (insulting Irene when he forgot himself), but these attempts at demonstrating authority only seemed absurd. From the way he kept pausing for breath, I imagined him overweight and smoking, and wasn't surprised to find out he was living in a caravan park.

In the end, though, it was all too strange—he'd call in the middle of the night, crying. Sometimes he knew he was going to die. Other times, he'd rant about how much he liked to fuck Bolivian women. When he told me he only liked to eat white food—white bread, white onions, white potatoes—it struck me this wasn't a game. This wasn't a round of get-to-know-your-crazy-father. This man used to make my mother guess what he wanted to eat for dinner and if she didn't guess correctly, he'd throw his plate against the wall.

I changed my number.

After Robert Johnson's 'Crossroads', Scott and I trudge back to central Clarksdale where the festival is finished. Our only company on the walk is a dog with a mangy leg—the place that was heaving with people is now deserted. Without the crowds, it feels like the town has grown overnight: streets have widened, doors are taller, the park is huge and desolate.

'Where is everyone?'

'Maybe the world's ended,' Scott says.

'Again? Salt Lake, Austin—you wouldn't think a country with three hundred million people could have so many abandoned cities.'

'The joys of white flight, I guess.'

The midday light forces me to squint through my sunglasses and sunburn is already itching along my arms. I fan myself but my fingers just push dry, hot air in my face.

Scott points up the road. 'That must have been the original bus station.'

The art deco building, constructed when brickwork itself was decoration, is being torn down. Red netting has been draped around the entrance but even that's sagging, fallen to the ground in places. Doorways and windows have been knocked out. The high ceilings and tall counter inside suggest a sense of class that's hard to reconcile with the fluorescent-lit hut that waits for us on the byway.

We keep walking and then, like the night before when we heard Big Red's music seeping through the dark, a faint sound pines along the street.

I stop in the middle of a deserted intersection. 'Do you hear that? A harmonica.' The instrument is lonely. 'Come on.' I motion for Scott to follow me and we start down another vacant road, but the sound begins to wane so I backtrack.

Our eyes can't help us. We have to follow our ears, listening for the aching notes, retracing our steps when the song fades.

'This way?'

'No, I think it's down here.'

We keep going until we're directly in front of it. A door leads into a gallery with dark brown floorboards. The brickwork is exposed, sanded back in areas. Paintings of blues saints—John Lee Hooker, Memphis Minnie, Howlin' Wolf—cover the walls in cartoon colours.

A guy with blond dreads and a beret that's been stretched into a beanie sits on a makeshift stage at the front of the room. He holds an instrument on his lap crafted from a cigar box and a pool cue; a wire strand has been fastened into place making it a single-string slide guitar. A harmonica is braced to his neck.

Deeper into the room, tables are covered with CDs, books, ceramic pieces, photographs, altars: we've discovered Cat Head, a blues, folk art and music haven.

Behind the counter, a man with intense brown eyes explains the gallery-cum-shop. 'We're trying to create a centre here that honours the blues. Encourage investors here in town—keep it alive.' It's a ferocious battle, I think, though the bright room seems sturdy enough to take on the abandoned street outside. I imagine the artworks and CDs marching out, spilling colour onto the concrete and filling the air with pounding bass lines.

'What brings you here?' he asks.

I explain my Elvis mission as Scott ducks off to browse the CDs.

'We've got a break coming up soon. Why don't you play?'

Ten minutes later, I plug my acoustic into the system and adjust the microphone. The speaker moans with feedback so I edge the volume down. Sitting forward on the chair, I balance the guitar on my right leg. My chest fills and 'Heartbreak Hotel' echoes through the speakers. It comes easily, the notes rippling from my fingers. Customers stop talking and turn towards the stage; even Scott watches me as though he's unsure of how the verses will slip into the chorus. There's a severity to the performance that reminds me of ritual: it's like the song itself knows we're getting close to Memphis.

A LITTLE LESS
CONVERSATION

Scott and I make a detour to pay tribute to the Grand Ole Opry in Nashville. It began as a radio broadcast in 1925 and is now an established force in country music. It's changed venues over the years, but the stage still has the same six-foot circle of oak—anyone performing now is playing right on the same spot as Ernest Tubb and Patsy Cline once did.

Elvis imagined this historic place when he was eleven years old, tuning the radio to its live broadcast every Saturday night. His whole family would gather around the radio—parents, cousins, sometimes even Grandma Minnie. I imagine his father staring wistfully at the ground and his mother peering at her son as they all sat, ears trained on the speakers.

Scott and I arrive before the Opry opens and stroll around its country legend walls, sharing the walkways with other music fans. It's a massive building that towers over the parking lot. The walls are built thick like those of a log cabin, and its doors are heavy and solid. It looks out of place next to the large parking lot and mega-sized mall.

Scott stops. 'You going to busk?'

'I don't know.' It's too historic but also too mundane—the Dairy Queen next door seems incongruous. Like Robert Johnson's industrial-stretch crossroads, I wonder: can anything stand up to the power of the strip mall?

My set-up seems to take longer than the actual playing and I feel ludicrous in front of a place that's hosted such legendary musicians. As I hurry through my set, I think about Elvis's first appearance at the Grand Ole Opry in 1954. It wasn't a glorious foreshadowing of his future success—he was only appearing because his manager at that time, Sam Phillips, had hounded the booking agent. In the introduction, the announcer forgot his name and after the performance, he only received polite applause. But there's still an excitement to this place—I picture Elvis backstage, gawking at the country stars and glancing nervously at his future—that kerbside concrete can't cover.

In central Nashville later that afternoon, Scott and I follow faded blue and white signs for the Country Music Hall of Fame until we're standing at Music Row, a street of country music production studios.

'It has to be here somewhere.'

'Who's going to ask?'

After six weeks of travelling, Scott and I are both tired of asking directions so we play Rock, Scissors, Paper. I win. Sighing, Scott scuffs towards a man on the corner who's facing the street, wearing a trench coat that's too small for him. The man doesn't notice him so Scott edges closer. He waits a long moment and then turns like he's facing into a windstorm, both feet planted on the ground, and I remember how shy my boyfriend is. Scott must say something I can't hear then because the stranger turns towards him suddenly, talking, and gesturing with both hands.

When Scott strolls back, he jerks his head down the hill. 'It's moved. Other side of town, where we came from.'

'I don't understand you.'

'What?'

'You'd have no trouble tackling that man on the footy field, would you?'

'Who?' Scott turns back to the crosswalk but Mr Trench Coat is already on the other side of the street.

'That man there, in the coat.'

'Too skinny. Wouldn't even make winger.'

'Yeah, but you could, couldn't you?'

'Easily.' As the lights change, the cars pull forward.

'But you didn't want to approach him on the street?'

Scott smiles sheepishly and we follow the traffic, walking. The city is a concrete valley easing down to the river.

After more than an hour of trekking back the way we came, we find it. A huge grey wall with unmistakeable lettering shields the building. Inside, it smells of new carpet and costs $15 per person to enter the exhibit—our entire budget for the night's accommodation. I dole the bills carefully out onto the counter and the cashier takes them without even looking up. I know Scott's thinking there must be some way we could sneak in.

'Just follow through the turnstile and you'll be escorted to the top floor,' the woman says.

At the elevator, an attendant checks our tickets.

Scott whispers in my ear, 'No way to get through here even if we did run the gauntlet.'

Near the end of the exhibits, after listening to headset recordings of country legend interviews and walking along the glassed display switchbacks towards the ground floor, we arrive at the Country Music Hall of Fame. It's all worth it—asking for directions, hiking across town, outlaying funds—because Elvis is one of the inductees. He smiles out from the plaque on the wall, his face embossed in gold and the signature ducktail carved into place. Elvis Presley, the one man to feature in all three Halls of Fame: Country, Rock-and-Roll and Gospel.

I'm standing in front of Elvis. 'You know, he played touch footy.'

Scott's beside me, staring at the King. 'Really?'

'Yeah. He had trouble with the team in high school but in the early days, his circle of friends, the Memphis Mafia, was all about football.'

'Good man. I knew there was purpose behind this trip.'

Scott and I are running out of time: we have to choose between Tupelo (Elvis's birthplace) and Holly Springs (home to fanatical Elvis devotee Paul MacLeod, who lives in a mansion modelled on Graceland). Both towns are south of Memphis along the Interstate 78. I've seen photos of Tupelo. There's a museum and a memorial garden—it's the place where annual Fan Appreciation Day takes place for Elvis comrades. But after lengthy consideration, I decide it's more important to meet Paul MacLeod—this is a man who's dedicated his life to Elvis. His house is a live-in memorial. Surely if anyone can explain the power of the King to me, it will be this man.

On the Greyhound, we're sitting over the back wheel and I'm thumbing through the guidebook. 'According to this, he lives with his son Elvis Aaron Presley MacLeod and accepts visitors all hours of the day and night.' The bus hiccups over another pothole, jerking the pages free from my fingers. I can't be bothered searching for my place. 'Do you think that's true?'

It's already dark outside. Scott's eyes are closed, his frame fully stretched out. I continue, talking to the glass window: 'Like if we turned up tonight, he'd drop whatever it is he's doing and give us a tour?'

'Sounds a little weird.'

'No, it sounds committed.' This man is the spiritual guide for Elvis pilgrims, I think. I can't wait to meet him.

The bus drops us off at a bypass gas station with sliding glass doors. Fluorescent lighting illuminates candy bars and sunglasses with a uranium glow. A stocky man with a comfortable belly is leaning on the counter, talking to the woman behind it.

'Excuse me, do you know how to get to Graceland Too?'

The man looks up at us. He's in his late forties and his dark skin is pocked with acne scars. 'It's ten-thirty at night.'

The woman's words sound like an extended sigh. 'Not a problem—that guy is awake and doing tours twenty-four hours a day.' Her terse hands rest on the countertop—she seems like the kind who'd rather be bustling around than marking time behind a register.

Her friend looks at our packs and then at us, summing us up in the same way. 'It's on the other side of town. Don't know if you can walk it.'

'We'll give it a go. We've come from Australia. This trip started in Seattle and we've been riding the Greyhound for the past two months. We're going to see Elvis on the twenty-fifth anniversary of his death.'

I can hear Scott groan next to me. It's not a loud sound but his body weight shifts and I know he'd be nudging me if we were standing any closer. When I'm tired or nervous, my compulsion is to overexplain.

The man smiles, reminding me of Scott for a moment in the way his whole face commits to the expression. 'That's quite a mission. Look, I can give you a lift. I'm not doing anything, just waiting for Darlene to get off work. The name's Joe.' He extends his hand and Scott steps forward. After introductions, we follow him out to the kerb where a gangster Cadillac is parked.

'You'll have to just hold your stuff on your lap because the trunk is broken. And the front door, too.'

Scott and I scramble into the back and Joe adjusts the side gear column, the car hopping to attention. It's a vehicle with canine loyalty—if Joe hangs on to it, I wouldn't be surprised to see it still on the road in ten years' time.

'What do you know about Graceland Too?' I ask.

'The guy who runs it . . . I don't think he's fully there.' Joe circles his forefinger near his ear. 'But he's not hurting anyone and it pulls in tourists. What else would Holly Springs offer?'

'According to the guidebook, a good bookstore.'

'Well, that's true.'

We drive along the town's backstreets. Even in the dark, it's obvious the houses are large and tidy and welcoming—the kind of place where grandparents live and younger cousins take turns running through lawn sprinklers during summer. When Joe pulls up in front of Graceland Too, it's different from the surrounding buildings. Tall and striking, yes. Convincing, even, as far as Graceland replicas go. But there's something about it that seems vaguely disposable. The porch lights are bright, eager.

'You sure you want me to drop you off? The Holly Inn's on the other side of town. That's probably the cheapest place to stay.'

My watch reads 11.05 pm. The truth is, I'm convinced the father–son proprietors Paul and Elvis MacLeod will welcome us. They'll understand our quest, and Scott and I won't be much bother—we have a tent. Surely there'll be a spot on the lawn for us.

'My vote's for the Holly Inn,' Scott says, but he's climbing out after me.

The bell clangs inside so loudly I wonder if it was installed for the hearing impaired, and the door opens immediately. It wouldn't surprise me if the stout man in front of us had been waiting on the other side. His grey hair is slicked up and his Elvis t-shirt is worn, the collar fraying. He must be the father: Paul MacLeod.

'Welcome to Graceland Too,' he says, carrying the last syllable for several counts.

'Is it too late?'

'Never. I do tours at all hours but it'll cost five dollars per person.'

I scrounge in our money pouch for the correct change and hand it to him. He puts the bills straight in his trouser pocket.

Scott and I unload our packs under an empty coat rack. We're only in the entrance foyer and already the walls are covered with photos, posters, album covers, book sleeves, and cardboard cut-outs: all of Elvis. Some are close-ups, others full-body replicas.

I thought my family was into Elvis because we sent each other velvet greeting cards and fridge magnets embossed with his image, but even our plastic Elvis clock—his swinging legs the pendulum, his hips the gateway for time—is placid compared to this man's efforts. It's the sheer volume of paraphernalia that's overwhelming.

Before we're out of the entrance hall, I've blurted out, 'I'm on a mission to Graceland.'

Paul MacLeod nods for me to continue and I explain our journey. As I'm talking he seems distracted and as soon as I pause, he darts into the conversation. 'But do you have any of his original recordings?'

'No. I'm playing my own versions. It's about honouring Elvis—'

'Well, I've got it all. Cups. Awards. Badges. Autographs. I have exclusive special editions, specially signed records that even Bill Clinton has tried to buy from me.' His voice is triumphant as he reaches up to steady his gelled-back ducktail. 'The former president offered me a mint but there's no way I'd sell it to him. Who's he trying to kid?'

I didn't realise there'd be a pecking order—and indeed, competition—among Elvis fans. Two months' busking was nothing really if I didn't have signed albums and awards. And a *real* Elvis fan would never have skipped LA or Tupelo. The song 'A Little Less Conversation' is going through my head and I realise my action is left wanting. I'm all talk and a little bit of busking, not even in the league of hardcore.

Paul speaks louder as we climb the stairs. 'Look at these photos. I've taken pictures of everyone who's ever been here. Not just tourists, but celebrities, models, musicians. Anyone who's been touched by the light of Elvis.' Indeed, he has large poster boards, dozens of them, with hundreds of individual photos pasted on them. Each photo was taken in the same place so there is a repetition to the images, almost like a Warhol piece, but the faces are all different: some stunned, others glowing.

'Here. Stand still for the camera.'

Scott puts his arm around me and we both smile.

Paul's finger presses down, the camera flashes. 'Not only that, but my son loves Elvis. Together we run the house now.'

Scott relaxes out of the pose. 'What happened to his mother?'

Paul tosses the camera in a large cardboard box three-quarters full of unprocessed rolls of 35mm film. 'She said it was her or Elvis so I had to show her the door.' He says this proudly, as though it's a badge of his devotion to the King and I'm wondering what Elvis would have thought of this guy.

Scott and Paul start discussing Elvis's interest in sport and I'm thinking about what it means that our faces have been captured for the Graceland Too montage—will part of us stay forever in this house?

A photographed impersonator stares out from the display. His sunglasses are too small and his lips too big: he's a young man playing an older Elvis. His cheekbones are sharp but I like this temporal fluidity—that impersonators can choose which era to represent. It's almost as if Elvis impersonators are committed to a sense of immortality. They offer the illusion that (a) Elvis has not died, and (b) the many phases of his life can coexist.

Paul MacLeod is not in costume but his hairstyle is in tribute to the King, the cockatoo swoop bobbing as he lists Elvis's favourite sports.

'I think Elvis should have played rugby league,' Scott is saying.

We still have another floor to explore so I inch up the stairs. For the last forty minutes of the three-hour tour, I eye my watch, wondering where we're going to sleep tonight. When Paul leads us back to the front door, I pick up my pack and Scott follows suit.

Paul rests his hand on the coat rack beside us like it's a fourth person in the room and he's checking to see if it's okay. 'Thank you for your company tonight.' Then his voice drops to a whisper. 'You know, I don't believe Elvis is dead.'

I hedge my bets—it doesn't seem like a good idea to disagree. 'I'm not sure I do either.'

But Paul starts nodding his head too vigorously. 'I've got a few friends, diehards. We've . . . got a plan. We're . . . going to dig up his grave. What do you bet there's nothing there?' He's started to speak with increasing pauses, as though some data malfunction has affected his brain.

Like impersonators, I realise, conspiracy theorists support the idea of Elvis as immortal, and popular culture seems obsessed with preserving him. If indeed he is an example of the American dream, rising from poverty to unprecedented success, perhaps his devotees are afraid of the symbolic meaning of his death. That is, that the American dream doesn't have a happy ending: success produces consumption and Elvis—both physically and materially—consumed himself to death.

Paul looks at Scott as though they might drive to Graceland together, tonight, and find out for certain if Elvis is buried in his meditation garden. The question is sealed: would I feel comfortable sleeping on this man's lawn? I don't think so.

'Goodnight,' Scott says.

Paul peers at him for a moment, his voice resigned. 'Oh, goodnight.'

Scott pulls the door closed firmly behind us like he's leaving a church too eager for his conversion.

I take a deep breath. 'Here we are. On the front steps of Graceland Too at two-thirty in the morning.' There's no use asking Elvis for help. My faith has been blunted after this domestic display. I've realised there are limits to my reverence.

About fifty metres away, car lights turn onto the street and soon a Land Rover pulls up, the back door opening as three young men pile out. They all wear baseball caps and smell of cheap American beer. The last one slams the door loudly behind him.

'He still awake?' the first one asks, jumping up the steps.

'Yeah, we just left.'

He rings the doorbell. Paul MacLeod answers the door with the same eerie promptness. 'Welcome to Graceland Too.'

'We're ready for the Elvis freak show.' The first guy beckons to the other two boys behind him, who shout out a fraternity chant.

'We've got passes,' the last one says.

It's a frat house pastime, I realise, to get drunk and come here for Graceland Too tours in the middle of the night. Suddenly, I feel incredibly tired and zero in on the girl in the passenger seat. She gives me a sober smile and I'm willing to bet she knows where the Holly Inn is.

'Climb on in,' she says, introducing herself as Meredith. Elvis has taken pity on us. Maybe it's the exhaustion but I have this sudden, crazy image of everyone who's helped us on this trip—even the people who just dropped change into my guitar case—all in the same room for one night with lots of beer: Meredith, Joe and Darlene, my uncle Brooks and his friends Dorothy and Jeff . . . Elvis would be howling out from the jukebox and Big Red would be helping Scott pour the drinks.

Elvis devotees aren't limited to the northern hemisphere. Irene and I were travelling through New Zealand in February 1995 during my summer break from university. My mother had been reluctant to drive on the left-hand side of the road so she was sitting in the passenger seat and reciting excerpts from the first volume of Elvis's biography as I shifted gear, our rental car winding along the one-lane roads. Irene had just finished reading the book and would crank her seat forward to be in my frame of vision. Outside, the South Island landscape kept contradicting itself—one stretch was all trees and mountains, and the next suddenly empty with fields.

Irene took turns marvelling at the view and searching through the pages. The large paperback had wide margins, as though the author had as much space and time as he needed. 'Get this, Shady. Elvis kept going back to Sun Studios. This book is about creativity. It's about commitment. Did you know that Elvis first recorded a song for his mother? He paid for that recording time; it was a gift.'

When she finally set down the biography and looked at the guidebook, she found reference to an Elvis museum, the enterprise of a passionate fan, and of course we had to stop. The museum had been converted from a garage, its walls layered in posters and photographs. Fifties bench seats and Cadillac chrome fittings complemented the bright colours. Elvis stared out from key rings, clocks, tables, mugs—the paraphernalia had been collected for decades and all of it was maintained in polished condition. The space lacked the chaos of Graceland Too—it was clean and well-lit, as though we'd stepped into an immaculate shrine. The owner was an attentive man in his fifties whose head nodded in tandem with my mother's as she exclaimed over the events of Elvis's life. Halfway through the tour, she ran back to the car to grab the book.

'Have you seen this?'

He shook his head.

She passed him the 600-page volume. 'It's his biography, the story of who Elvis is.'

He touched each page like an artisan, feeling the weight of the paper. 'I don't think this has been released here yet.'

My mother had carried it on the plane with her and beamed like she had brought the scriptures of Elvis to the colonial outposts.

'It's yours,' she said.

A few days later on our Antipodean adventure, Irene and I stopped at a rest area. In the middle of nowhere, on New Zealand's South Island, someone had created a shrine for the Virgin Mary. It was tucked away on the left-hand side of the road next to a small waterfall. Beneath the plastic Virgin—a postcard of Elvis.

At the time, it seemed a kooky prank played by someone with an ironic sense of humour. Now I wonder if it might have been in earnest. In New Zealand especially, the Elvis museum seemed a temple of honest worship. And out between the sheep stations and the mountains, the Virgin echoed that same sense of hope and loss.

BLUE HAWAII

As the bus coasts into Memphis on August 11, I watch the buildings like they can explain Elvis, but the city limit strip malls and low-lying brick houses are just as curious as I am: he's before their time, too.

I riffle through my bag for the ten-page anniversary program downloaded from the internet and hand it to Scott. 'You know, there's a baseball game on this afternoon.'

'Since when do you like baseball?'

My relatively recent conversion to Australian sports (rugby league especially) hasn't translated into a deeper engagement with American codes and it's Scott who fulfils my civic duty, watching the newspaper for reports on the Seattle Seahawks (gridiron) and Mariners (baseball), so one of us proves loyal to my city of birth.

'It's the Twenty-Fifth Anniversary of Elvis's Death Commemorative Baseball Game.' My tone implies the absurdity of it—maybe if Elvis were a sports hero, the event would make more sense—but Scott nods gravely: where he comes from, a sporting event is the biggest honour to bestow on a man. It's like Elvis is finally coming into perspective for him.

The renovated AutoZone Park is directly across the street from the bus station. It smells of fresh paint and grass. Red brick and steel offset each other in the courtyard and sun glints off the metal. I'm keeping one eye out for Lisa Marie—surely she's going to be here in Memphis for the occasion? And surely she's curious about the folk who have turned up to celebrate her father? She may not be into minor league baseball but Elvis is the drawcard here. I wonder what she'd make of this.

'Just so you know, the Memphis Redbirds are playing the Nashville Sounds,' Scott whispers to me as we pass through the turnstiles.

'So it's a local derby?' I understand that this matters in the way that it matters when the Cronulla Sharks play the St George Illawarra Dragons: hometown proximity increases the sporting stakes.

'It's Elvis Fan Appreciation Day. Get your free baseball,' a woman wearing a red cap shouts. Free baseballs for Elvis Fan Appreciation Day? A mob has gathered in front of a deep wooden box. Unable to control himself, Scott rushes over and holds both our ticket stubs out.

When he returns, Scott hands me one of the balls. If I needed any evidence that Elvis is connected to iconic American pastimes, this is it. The red lacing curves gently around the sphere. Inside one of the loops, there's a round photo—a mid-twenties Elvis smiles at the camera, one side of his mouth higher than the other. Behind him, a jumpsuited Elvis stands with his guitar.

We march past the barbecue stalls and ticketed seating areas to the grassy hill on the far side of the park. Every third person is wearing an Elvis shirt, many of which are long-sleeved and collared despite the heat. In front of us, a family plays Elvis trivia. The father has concentrating grey eyes even though he's the one asking the questions. 'In what year did Elvis perform the Aloha concert?'

His kids, maybe five and seven years old, have no idea.

'1989?'

'1960?'

'1925?'

He leans back, shaking his head, and they all crack up.

Propped back on my elbows, I'm equal parts stunned and compelled—baseballs, specialty shirts, trivia? And this is only the beginning of the Elvis celebrations—the real fanatics will be here on Thursday for the candlelight vigil. I scoot in next to Scott, who's staring at the field: a runner has just crossed home plate. As his foot plants, there's an eruption of noise around the stadium and Elvis starts blaring out of the speakers.

Our next official event is the Elvis fashion show at the Peabody Hotel. My first question is what, exactly, will it display—Elvis's clothing? Perhaps his Lansky suit jackets or the early black pants with pink stripes? In high school, Elvis had a style that provoked derision from his peers. When he grew his hair long and began to wear dress pants and bolero jackets to school events he was called names like 'Squirrel'. I wonder how much of that back story we're going to get from Elvis Presley Enterprises.

At twelve-thirty in the afternoon, the street outside is rowdy with car horns and vocal pedestrians. As soon as we step inside, the hotel's assured quiet is sudden and disarming. Tall ceilings and elaborate chandeliers imply a preference for formal wear, and a thick, sombre banister guards the stairs.

Scott waits in the doorway. 'Do you think we're in the right place?'

We pass the tearoom that's about half filled. Just beyond, guests are sitting in the lobby, watching live ducks wade through the centrepiece fountain. The Peabody is famous for this and the quacking mallards have the air of fussy Victorian gentlemen. I make my way to the registration desk that's designed as much to be formidable as elegant. When I'm finally to the front of the line, I ask somewhat sheepishly, 'The Elvis fashion show?'

'Upstairs, ma'am.' The young man doesn't laugh.

I want to repeat myself: the *Elvis* fashion show—have you ever heard of anything like it?—but he's asking the old woman behind me how he can be of assistance. My feet are planted. I want some sign to acknowledge the strange world waiting for me but the woman nudges me aside. Her hand is outstretched for a key.

The boy glances up and then stops, turning to face me, as though he's realised I might be a little slow. He enunciates his words more clearly. 'The Elvis fashion show is just upstairs. Follow that staircase.'

I nod meekly. 'Thanks.'

Scott follows as I scurry away and climb the steps two at a time. We've arrived twenty minutes before the show begins, which isn't early enough to secure good seats. Already, the room is packed. The closest vacant places are three-quarters of the way down the hall. We push past knees and handbags to the open spots.

He nudges me. 'I think I'm the only man in here.'

'I think we're the only ones under forty.'

'Apparently not.'

A five-year-old girl with white-blonde ringlets has followed us, inching along the aisle. She smoothes her skirt and points to the empty seat beside Scott. 'Is this taken?'

I've never heard a more polite English accent. I shake my head and she hoists herself up on the chair, her back straight and hands curled in her lap. No one is following her down the row—it seems the girl is by herself. After a moment, a woman sitting behind us leans forward.

'It's okay,' the taller but equally blonde version—clearly the little girl's mother—says. 'I'm just here.'

'Where are you from?' I ask the girl, making eye contact with her mother.

'England.'

'That's far away. Do you like Elvis?'

She sighs and presses a tiny hand against her heart. 'My whole family—we love Elvis. If I could meet one person living or dead, it would be Mr Elvis Presley.'

Scott's eyebrows lift: who on earth could have spawned this delicate, passionate creature? He turns around abruptly to check out the mother and my elbow lands in his side.

'I bet Elvis would have some interesting stories to tell,' I say.

'I'd listen to anything the King has to say,' she replies.

The mother bobs her head proudly in agreement.

'I would too. Do you have any other ambitions?' My voice sounds almost as formal and prim as the little girl's. Scott peers at me like aliens are taking over my body but he doesn't have to worry—I'm finding this as bizarre as he is.

The girl pats her head with slow grace, the gesture reminding me of Priscilla and her massive beehive. 'I'd like to find a boy who looks like Elvis.'

Is this kid for real? Before I can ask anything else, the lights dim and the crowd starts shrieking. There are at least a thousand people in attendance. It hits me that many of the women sitting around me were screaming in the crowds when Elvis performed. The volume is not forced, nothing is false about the anticipation that surrounds me, and it feels as though Elvis might appear again. Perhaps through his clothes, we will get a sense of this man who has become myth.

When the first model appears from behind the curtain, wearing an Elvis t-shirt, it's obvious I didn't understand the premise of the fashion show: it's an event to showcase the Elvis fashion line and all of the garments modelled are available for purchase at the Graceland complex. Men's silk shirts with Elvis's face painted across the front. 'Jailhouse Rock' pyjamas. Women's nightgowns. Each set is themed, coordinated with an Elvis soundtrack. Peering at all of the outfits, I search for something so kitsch it's cool, something with the delicate taste of my Shady Grove t-shirt, but it's all too overt, Elvis's face in oversized proportions and the writing garish. It's not the unconcealed commercialism that gets me, it's the cheap polyester.

Then, a young man with his hair gelled into a Paul MacLeod ducktail struts out wearing nothing except a pair of snug boxers, a new line of Elvis underwear. A girl in front of Scott shouts out and others join in with whistles and catcalls. The models remind me of strippers—Chippendales and Manpower have joined forces with the power of Elvis. I wonder if I should reach over and cover the English girl's eyes but she's now kneeling in her chair, yelling out in tandem with her mother, any trace of reserve dissipated. Sweat and sweet perfume permeate through the crowd, causing me to sneeze. A large woman on my left jostles me for a better view, stepping on my foot: a particularly well-endowed man has paused in the middle of the stage, running his finger along the band of his Y-fronts, and lusty screams envelop the crowd.

Scott stares at me, slack-jawed in mock amazement, and it's obvious the blame is falling squarely on my shoulders for this one.

'At least you can say this is a cultural experience,' I shout in his ear.

Sun Studios is a two-storey brick building wedged between a street and a laneway. A giant guitar hangs outside, over the door. It's a classy Gibson—the kind of instrument that Elvis's guitarist Scotty Moore used to play, an electric known for its rockabilly sound—and the famous yellow letters S-U-N seem humble near that giant guitar. It's such an iconic place I'm surprised by how ordinary the rest of the street is. It's like the surrounding buildings and empty parking lots don't realise what's in their midst.

When Scott and I arrive, the road has been closed off and a band is playing Polynesian music in honour of Elvis's 'Aloha from Hawaii' concert. Just below the stage, a line of hula dancers move with gentle arms and rocking hips. People in the audience wear frangipani leis and a couple carry ukuleles.

Many Elvis impersonators are bopping through the crowd, each one capturing the King at a different stage of life. Younger ones tend towards the casual—their outfit isn't an identity, it's an accessory. Older ones seem more committed and I can imagine them scouring second-hand stores in search of the perfect eagle belt buckle.

I've been wondering about professional impersonators, about what it means to be adored for being someone else. In Australia, Scott took me to an 'Elvis to the Max' show. When performer Max Pellicano began to hand out scarves Aloha-style, women ran to the front of the room, hands outstretched, reaching for the polyester nylon as though greatness could be gleaned from the sheer fabric. But part of the performance perplexed me: professional impersonators make their living *as someone else*. Fans are paying for artifice; all of the applause and catcalling is for the imitated icon. On stage, does 'Max' ever get the urge to assert himself so fans remember he's the performer, not Elvis?

At Sun Studios, a thirty-something Elvis impersonator with a thin face bops from photograph to photograph eagerly while fans take the opportunity to stand next to him. Scott sidles up like he's asking for an autograph. After introducing himself, he calls out, 'Come on, Shady,' and I pose too, on the cracked, grass-lined sidewalk. The man has a soft voice and makes no pretense of being Elvis as he speaks. We chat about the crowds and the weather like we're at a party and though we both know the host quite well we've just been introduced.

Inside, tours are running nonstop but I'm sidetracked in the gift store. This is the place Elvis used to visit each week for almost a year, talking to receptionist Marion Keisker, until Sam Phillips finally gave him a chance to record. It's since been renovated: the black counter is glossy and new, covered with postcards and trinkets. In front of it, red soda fountain stools offer a sense of the 1950s as though the current-day Sun Studios is trying to impersonate itself of fifty years ago. After all, Sam wasn't interested in chrome fixtures and checkerboard tiles when he discovered Elvis—he was struggling to keep his business together and open pathways for musicians. Now, people are shoving into line, signing up for studio tours, waiting on those vintage seats as Hawaiian music wafts in from the street. It's not the seats or even the recording space that interests me—it's this area in front of the ringing cash register, the actual physical space. *This* is where Elvis stood, waiting for his chance—I'm standing in the same spot as Elvis on the cusp of his career. Once he got beyond it, he had Sam listening as he belted out 'That's All Right', but when he was leaning against this counter, Elvis had nothing save faith and perseverance. Everyone who came out of Sun Studios had to wait here at some point—Carl Perkins, Johnny Cash, Roy Orbison. It looks like a normal benchtop, but it was the gate for them all.

Outside Sun Studios, I'm leaning against the building and listening to the Polynesian music. A couple of the ukulele players are barrel-chested men who should be lining up as forwards in rugby league. I'm surprised at how quickly their fingers move on the strings and realise I'm also thinking about my father.

Seattle's First Avenue was hazy. Michael Cosgrove and I were alone in the car, heading west towards the Fauntleroy ferry dock. I was turning five years old. The glowing streetlights stretched upwards in gigantic proportions—everything seemed oversized. He pressed the dash lighter and fished in his shirt pocket for a smoke. The cigarette hung from his lip, unlit, as we veered up onto the viaduct, his arms crossing over each other to turn the steering wheel.

'What do you want for your birthday, Shady?' Michael asked as the lighter popped out.

'A guitar.'

He pressed the glowing orange tip to the cigarette and inhaled deeply. Then, with a gust of smoke, 'A guitar, you sure?'

I nodded fervently. With a guitar, I could imagine my hands and arms growing to encircle the instrument. It would happen in my sleep—a gift curse. People would stare at me: a little girl with abnormally long arms, giant hands. But I would use the deformity to advantage. The metamorphosis would prove essential—I'd be a child prodigy, a guest on *The Muppet Show*.

He didn't come to Vashon for my birthday. I have no memories of him ever on the island so it was probably the following week that I saw him. Maybe we were in a park or in the front yard of his Tacoma house—where he lived before moving to Portland. The grass had been freshly mown but over near the road, the concrete glittered with broken glass. I wanted to step through it but Michael guided me along the sparkling perimeter to a picnic table.

'Wait here and don't look.' He strode back to the trunk of his car. My hands covered my eyes but I peeked through. Even though the gift was wrapped, the shape was unmistakeable: a miniature guitar.

'Are you looking?'

My fingers snapped together.

'Now. Open them.' Half his mouth rose in a smile. 'It's a ukulele. You can start with Hawaiian music.'

I nodded enthusiastically, plinking the strings. The sound was tinny, the notes hollow.

'What do you think?'

'I love it.' And I did, while he was wrapping his arms around me, manipulating my fingers into position. But as soon as he pulled away, I knew the instrument was too small. I'd never be able to transform without a proper guitar.

Outside Sun Studios, the hula dancers are streaming through the crowd, bestowing leis with tropical smiles. I sit down, leaning my back against the sun-warmed wall. My memories of Michael Cosgrove glow with a persistent warmth, but they don't match the man who created Michael Cosgrove Jr or shouted about Bolivian women on the phone, and I realise I have no idea who he is.

Another memory: I was three or four years old. Carrying my swimsuit, I walked bravely into the changing rooms while Mike stood behind me: 'I'll be right outside, waiting for you.'

The lights were bright, glinting off the micro-tiles and mirrors while chlorine steam wafted across the islands of lockers. Showers lined the far wall, occupied by laughing women with large voices. I pulled the straps of my Wonder Woman bathing suit over my small arms and carefully gathered my towel, trekking back to the pool.

I couldn't wait to climb the water slide. It was tall—a skyscraper of plastic that arced down and then kicked up at the bottom. No one else was near it: it was too big, even for adults. I gripped the handles and placed my foot on the bottom rung. Step by step, pulling my weight, creeping upwards. The ladder was slippery and it took careful negotiation to hoist my body up at the top. I sat, waiting. Cooling jets of water slid by my legs.

'Come on.' Mike was treading water below. His arms were outstretched, his palms facing towards me, proof he could be trusted. But I waited too long, biting my lip.

'Remember to blow out when you hit the water,' he called.

I had to separate my arms from my body, imagining they belonged to someone else and commanding them to push me off. They did and I flew down—speed, water, plastic. My heart was pounding. I hit the water with a rush and his arms wrapped around me, lifting me back to the surface—I was safe.

But this version of safety is infused with longing, pale and weightless as a silk scarf, and doesn't fit with our dinner table folklore. A chasm exists between memories I don't trust and stories I do—it's not that the memories are contrived but I wonder what else is lurking there, what else I can't remember.

After one summer meal with my family, I was talking about Michael Cosgrove and layers of memory. We were sitting outside on an unexpectedly balmy night for Vashon and I drilled into a new bottle of wine with strong, full twists. I'd heard the story before but my mouth formed the question anyway: 'What did Mike do the night I was crying?'

When I was a few months old, I came down with high fever seizures. Even out of the hospital, I kept crying like an alarm: high, piercing, insistent. Apparently, Michael didn't like the noise. He bundled me onto a balcony and threatened to throw me off. The only ledge I could think of at the north-end house was out the back, through the kitchen. I imagined the scene—the grass overgrown, the uneven door that would never quite close. Maybe he was yelling over my shrill voice, his arms outstretched, my baby blanket caught in the grip of his fist. Irene talked him back from that edge but this was the incident that triggered our departure. This was when we had to leave.

I waited for Jim's voice to cut across the table with a small sarcasm that would make us laugh, but he was watching the glass-blown candleholders. My mother looked at the clothesline like she was looking into the distance. 'It seemed you knew everything that was happening.'

Serena faced me squarely. 'He'd been drinking. And there was nothing quiet about you in those early months.'

'It was like you blamed everyone around you . . .' My mother turned so she was staring at me and a withdrawn quiet spread across the table. I looked down at her forearms resting by her glass. She was wearing a plastic kid's watch with mermaids on the band and it was like her small veined hands offered some understanding of our family future. Perhaps a palm reader could see where we were going and through that we could understand the past.

My younger siblings, Grace and Lucas, had long since excused themselves and it felt like Jim had receded from the table. It was just the three of us: Serena, Irene and me. It felt like it had only ever been the three of us.

ALL SHOOK UP

In Memphis, Scott and I are staying with generous friends of friends from Australia. On Sunday morning, we borrow their car and drive to Reverend Al Green's congregation that's renowned for its full gospel tabernacle. Al Green was a legendary seventies soul singer but I'm interested in the church in its own right as well as the connection between Elvis and black America. In Tupelo, Elvis and his family lived in a predominantly black neighbourhood and he'd walk by clubs, listening in on the Louis Jordan numbers. Years later, in Memphis, he'd sneak out of church with his girlfriend Dixie Locke and drive to the East Trigg black church, less than a mile away, where Reverend Brewster would preach and Queen C Anderson and the Brewsteraires would sing. I wonder what that was like.

At church, we follow mostly black parishioners into a wide hall where the pulpit stretches out like a stage. A drum kit is set up and a young man checks the leads to the bass and guitars. The crowd murmurs like it's waiting for a concert to start.

The service doesn't begin on time. After half an hour, another man—tall, solid, suited—paces onto the raised platform. He tells us the famous musician preacher has been held up at the airport and instead he will be leading us in prayer today. Then

he takes a deep breath and it feels as though the lights have
gone down.

'Hello, ladies and gentlemen. I hope you're well this morning
because I have a serious message for you. I want you to be wary
of temptation. And when the Devil comes to prey on you, shake
him out.'

His voice looms over us. He paces along the stage, stretching
his arms out. The people in the front call back: 'Shake him out.'
The white folk up the back are uncomfortably quiet.

'What was that?'

'Shake the Devil out.'

I chime in and Scott digs his elbow into my side. He's shy and I'm
the only white person who is talking back in an audible voice.

'What are you doing?' he whispers.

'It's the Devil. I don't want to take any chances.'

'What was that?' the preacher asks.

I call, 'Shake the Devil OUT.' I do feel conspicuous, but it seems
more conspicuous to enter someone's church and not participate:
spiritual voyeurism dressed up with the exoticism of race.

The reverend is now shouting: 'HOW you gonna shake the
Devil out, friends? HOW? Like this.' He extends his arms to the
side and begins to shake his hands with spirit fingers. Now his
whole arms are jittering and the rest of his body follows. He's up
on the platform, convulsing in front of us. People in the front
are mimicking him. Soon almost everyone in the room—white
and black—is shouting out and shaking. The reverend is impressed
with his effect. He's smiling, joyous. 'The Devil means you no
good. Shake him out.'

We're still shaking. In the fury of the moment, the preacher
starts moon-walking, gliding backwards across the stage. 'What
did I say?'

The crowd answers in one strong voice: 'Shake him out.' Only
Scott murmurs this quietly, mouthing the words. My voice is
loud, cathartic. I'm wondering if the Devil is another way to

consider the legacies of inheritance, a metaphor for shaking out the past.

The preacher pauses and we take this as our cue, sitting down while he reaches behind him for an electric guitar that's already plugged in. 'I'd like to call on my band here today to come and join me. Join me up here and we're going to raise our voices in song to shake the devil out.'

A young man climbs up behind the drum kit. Another picks up the bass.

'And I'd like to invite our choir.' A group of women, dressed more like back-up singers than choir members, lines up behind him.

'What are we going to do today?' he asks.

'We're going to sing about shaking the Devil out,' one of them calls back, igniting catcalls from the audience.

The bass line grooves along, the guitar answering back to the voice of the preacher. Feet pounding against the floorboards. Hands clapping. The song continues for twenty-five minutes.

When the service is finally over, we head back to the car. Scott looks over the roof as he unlocks the driver's door.

'Guess what I am?' His voice follows with the rhythm of a knock-knock joke and I have a sudden premonition of Scott as a father, telling bad dad jokes to our kids. 'I'm "All Shook Up".'

A few days after attending the church service, Scott and I celebrate our anniversary—exactly four years ago I was guzzling water in the Kembla Street kitchen and enjoying the whiskey spins, wondering if anything would transpire with Scott. Now we're pulling into the Graceland complex and parking our borrowed car. It should feel like we're close to our destination, but the famous house is still over half a kilometre away. We're about to navigate through the sprawling commercial spree of Elvis Presley Enterprises—retail outlets, restaurants, airplanes, car museums, hotels—but the first test is getting across the asphalt. The sun is ferocious and we're lost in a sea of glinting windscreens but the sturdy pilgrims streaming in are ready and we step into line with the marching faithful.

When we enter the ticket office lobby, it takes a moment for my eyes to adjust to the dimmed lighting. In front of us, a line stretches from the glass ticket booths—maybe twenty people are waiting, and this fills me with relief. I'd had visions of a queue zigzagging across the hall.

As we file between the markers, I spot an altar that's been erected for Elvis. It reminds me of the folk art in Clarksdale. Covered in photos, figurines and cards, the shrine is about two metres square. The gentle detail is immaculate, with lucky charms, handwritten lyrics and etched drawings of Elvis in his many phases. There's a timeless magic to the piece that doesn't compare to the gaudy Elvis underwear at the fashion show.

But it's not just Clarksdale, I realise: it reminds me of my mother. Over the years she's made a number of altars and shrines in honour of our family. One took up an entire table—with hand-built shelves and candleholders, it was a woodworked piece of art. Every available space was covered with photographs: her mother and father, all of us kids at different ages, Irene herself. In one corner, there was a picture of Irene at twenty, another of Serena at twenty, and then me at twenty—like that year was the entryway to life and there we all were, next to each other and waiting. Or maybe it just seemed like a gateway because that was the year I first arrived in Australia.

Irene's altars vary in scale. She gave me a portable one for that cross-Pacific trip that still sits in my hope chest in Wollongong. It's a rectangle about four inches by three inches.

'You need something to protect your journey when you travel,' she told me when we went out to dinner the night before my flight.

The altar is a small basket with sequins from our car, Ruby, shellacked on the outside. Two quotes have been glued onto the bright glitter: 'We seem to get what we expect out of life' and

'Something good will happen to you'. It's lined with fabric from my favourite shirt in eighth grade and the remnants of a skirt Irene sewed for me when I entered high school. 'Shady is loved' is written in silver ink on the inside of the lid. A woman holding a baby—an African symbol of the Virgin Mary—is pinned to the top. Two lockets with pictures of all our family members are attached to a bag of magic glitter, and a quartz crystal and ceramic pencil are also nestled inside.

It may seem like a funny distinction to make but our altars are spiritual in that they celebrate what is holy to us—the importance of family and creativity—but they're not necessarily religious. I think my mother's relationship to the Virgin Mary operates in the same way—the Madonna is a symbol of hope and strength that is particularly feminine and can be appreciated without going to church. In that spirit, the altar in front of me seems like a tribute to Elvis himself, not only his gospel leanings.

When I return, Scott is talking to the man before us in line. He's wearing a singlet that reveals a large tattoo of the King on his shoulder.

'That's a beauty, isn't it?' Scott is admiring the inked Elvis, who's wearing a tuxedo, legs akimbo. 'What kind of an accent is that you have?'

'Liverpool. And you?'

'Australia.'

Maybe it's thinking about spirituality but the two men shake hands and I'm reminded of the time Scott and I stumbled upon an Alcoholics Anonymous retreat out at Wombeyan Caves—it took us a little while to figure out why everyone was so open and friendly. When we did, I wondered at the connection between easy conversation and assumed common ground. There's a sense of that intimacy in Memphis—anyone who's made the trek must be a real enthusiast. And there's also relief: no one here will be making fun of us for appreciating Elvis.

Upon reaching the front of the line, Scott and I scamper to the open booth. The woman on the other side of the glass smiles patiently but her expression is tired and I'm thinking she's not an Elvis enthusiast.

'The next available tour of Graceland leaves in three and a half hours.'

'Three and a half hours? I thought this was the line.' After my moment with the Elvis altar, I'm surprised to be faced with anything as mundane as a queue. What did I expect, the power of Elvis to show us straight into his residence?

'They all think that. No, you line up over there.' She nods to a door behind me. 'Three and a half isn't too bad. Yesterday it was five. The mansion's across the street. Maybe two hundred and fifty metres up the driveway. You could walk it but we like to control the numbers so you have to take the shuttle bus.' She shrugs like she doesn't quite understand it herself. 'The wait will give you time to tour the shops. And the airplanes—would you like to purchase tickets for those?'

We haven't travelled all this way to miss out on the airplanes: I push my money forward.

Memorabilia shops line the road opposite the Graceland mansion. Racks are piled with key chains and magnets, clocks and posters, postcards and pens. Mannequins are in celebratory poses, showing off clothing from the Elvis fashion show. Granted we're seeing this place during one of its busiest times, but Elvis Presley Enterprises must be enjoying record profits—the lines are wrapping around the stores and people are fighting each other off in front of the sales racks. A woman walks by with her arms full of King coffee mugs and I wonder how many Elvis cups one kitchen can hold.

Because we're on budget, Scott and I each get to pick one piece of paraphernalia. Even though they're all owned by the same company, we scour each shop, checking prices and stock availability. Scott decides on a poster with an illustration of a carved Elvis statue surrounded by doves. I choose the CD of Junkie XL's recent remix of 'A Little Less Conversation' that's just made number one in Britain, moving Elvis past the Beatles for the highest number of chart-toppers.

We still have two hours. Scott and I visit the car museum and then the airplanes. When we reach the *Lisa Marie* aircraft, a woman with a massive bottom pushes me aside to climb the portable staircase, each foot plonking down on the steel steps with decided force. I'm tempted to tell her Elvis was known for his manners but Scott laughs at our slow climb, exaggerating as he shifts his weight up each step, and by the top I'm smiling. The *Lisa Marie* is a converted Convair 880 jet with an original passenger capacity of about a hundred. It originally cost $250,000 but after refurbishments the total was closer to $600,000. Though even I have to admit the interior doesn't have much retro flair—the wood panelled bed and shag pile carpet is firmly from the seventies, without any hint of contemporary irony.

'What next?' Scott asks. We have forty-five minutes.

The white rendered Heartbreak Hotel, with its neon red heart logo, sits just behind the Elvis compound. Bizarrely, it seems the accommodation is a romantic haven: couples roam hand-in-hand along the plush corridors.

A few floors up, the elevator stops. A kid in a fake satin vest and bow tie pushes a trolley in and I'm reminded of the crying bellhop from the hotel's namesake. I bet Elvis wasn't imagining this guy when he sang 'Heartbreak Hotel'—he has an eyebrow ring and angry front teeth.

'It must be crazy for you right now,' I say.

'You have no idea.'

'Anything you'd recommend?'

'Getting as far away from here as possible.' The door opens and he moves off.

The commercial spree that's hovering over the Graceland complex has me thinking—Elvis sang about aspirational America in his number 'Baby Let's Play House', but he also lived these ideals. In 1955, Sun Studios sold Elvis to RCA and manager Colonel Tom Parker handled the negotiations. At the time, it was the largest deal ever made for an artist. In the following decades, Elvis's commercial and cultural empires only grew and in 2005, twenty-eight years after his death, Elvis was still making money: Robert FX Sillerman, a billionaire media entrepreneur, paid Lisa Marie Presley $100 million for control of Elvis's name, likeness and image, and the Graceland visitor complex.

By all accounts, the Colonel was the driver of Elvis as a financial machine. He was ferociously committed to securing every possible penny for his singer. The manager came from a carnival background and devoted himself to obsessively plotting Elvis's career. He didn't simply represent Elvis, he merchandised him: there was always another place the King could be sold or another dollar that could be earned. Even when Elvis was overseas in the army, the Colonel was strategic with song releases and publicity, ensuring that his star was in the public eye during his whole two-year hiatus. For his part, Elvis felt the Colonel had made everything possible—that he was a good luck talisman and without him, the singer would fall into obscurity.

There's no question Elvis enjoyed his wealth. He was an avid consumer and his purchases were often linked with entertainment and distraction. He was famous for buying cars—both for himself and his friends. On a whim, he bought Triumph motorcycles for his entire gang. Then, horses. He soon had so many he needed a ranch so he bought Twinkletown Farm. Go-carts, guns, televisions, airplanes, a designer Greyhound for travelling (George Barris customised it for him: a retired D'Elegance coach, complete with sleeping quarters and portholes to emulate a 'luxury yacht' atmosphere). This consumerism isn't surprising, though Elvis's desire for commercial distraction seems at odds with his spiritual leanings at the Self-Realization Fellowship in California and, I think, connected to an inner boredom and restlessness. As Elvis said in an interview with the *Commercial Appeal*'s Jim Kingsley: 'There is a lot of difference in Christmases today and when we were growing up in East Tupelo. (But) honestly, I can't say these are any better. We are just in a better position to spend . . . Everything is so dreamy when you are young. After you grow up it kind of becomes—just real.'

My mother's friend Lucy may be right—perhaps the power of Elvis was driven by sex appeal. Certainly the Elvis fashion show supports her theory but I also see Elvis as a guinea pig: he was mass-marketed in the 1950s, a time when the United States was just beginning to develop its relationship with consumerism and television. The Colonel, driven by market interests, ensured Elvis Presley inundated American culture and Elvis benefited enormously from that, at least financially, but there was a 'realness' he couldn't escape, no matter how many things he purchased or how many pills he took.

Even with tickets, it's necessary to line up for the Graceland tour half an hour early and then we're grouped into departure times— here is the long procession I'd been expecting. The line concertinas back and forth in an open area built specially for this purpose. In front of me, two women stand with thrust hips and bored shoulders. As they talk, only their heads move, circling like aged birds of prey while their husbands fiddle with a new camera, stopping periodically to photograph their progression in the queue—though I suspect their subject is actually the large-breasted sorority girl on the other side of the rope.

The line creeps forward and a plump woman with a walkie-talkie hands us each a pair of headphones with a gruff gesture. 'Next.'

We step up and she shifts us into position in front of a painting of the Graceland gates.

'But we don't—'

'Doesn't matter. Smile, please.' She's murmuring into her headset as the camera clicks and we're pushed into an open minibus on the other side of the backdrop. As soon as every seat's filled, the door shunts closed with clockwork precision.

'Welcome to your tour of Graceland,' the driver says.

The woman who sold us tickets was right. We're carried about two hundred and fifty metres, literally across the street and up the driveway. The short trip seems excessive—after all, we could walk—but it does keep the front wall clear for those writing messages to the King. Scott and I climb out and we're there, directly in front of Graceland. The white columns are as forthright as the photos suggest but the exterior lacks the hubris I'd expected: the mansion is surprisingly modest. I step back to take a picture of the entryway and other tourists clamber in front of me for their shots. Every time I shift position for an isolated view of the house, someone moves in the way.

Graceland—an eighteen-room colonial revival-style mansion— was constructed in 1939, south of central Memphis. Elvis bought it in 1957 after his parents spotted it for sale and, according to decorator George Golden, he had two priorities when he moved in: a beautiful room for his mother and a soda fountain for his friends. These concerns strike me as adolescent—the fountain, especially—and there's an aura to the estate as if the place itself is trying to prove it's grown up.

Inside, I'm struck by the curtains and carpets. It's the combination—the carpets are ordinary and the curtains are majestic, covering whole walls. The sweeping folds of fabric imply a heraldry that seems lost on the fans streaming in. There are two consistent categories of people here: larger women with body odour and smaller men with Elvis tattoos. In all of my research, I never imagined hordes of flapping tourists arriving at ten-minute intervals, talking on cell phones and pushing into photos. It's the anniversary of his death: who did I think was going to turn up—Elvis intellectuals drinking chardonnay? I try to remember everyone here feels connected to Elvis, that my experience isn't a favoured one, but the pushy throng has turned the house into a carnival theme park.

Eager devotees peer upstairs, an area that's cordoned off. The carpeted stairs lead to the bathroom where Elvis died and security guards are stationed here in force. Of course I also imagine him slumped on the tiles but I'm glad we can't see it for ourselves; the fans have brought out a curiously protective urge in me to shield Elvis from their aggressive adoration. I overlook the fact that I too have paid an entry fee, that I am just as much a tourist.

In one of the first rooms on the right, three televisions denote the era—they're large boxes firmly from the mid-seventies. It's difficult to see these heavy sets as indicators of wealth and glamour: they just look obsolete. Their casings don't match the subtle charm of the furnishings and walls, soft yellows and dark blues. I press a button on my tour guide recording, trying to reconcile this space—and the stories of what happened here—with its palpable physicality.

In the trophy room, we wait for a family with three kids—all wearing stick-on sideburns—to trot past. Scott's grinning at the glassed-in display: he has over eighty sporting trophies himself and has made me swear to bury them with him if he dies first.

'They're for his music, Scott. Not sports.'

'A trophy's a trophy.'

Even though it's ridiculous, I feel territorial about Elvis, as though I'm the only one in this place who understands him. I read everything as an offence—people staring at each exhibit are taking too much time, those pushing past aren't taking enough. Even Scott's cheery mood seems like an affront. This is supposed to be the climactic hub of the journey—right here, in this house, I'm ready to be received. Paul Simon's song is pattering through my head and I'm waiting for a revelation that will shift everything into perspective—my passion for Elvis, my relationship with the States, my memories of Michael Cosgrove. Even if I've earnestly ignored it, this trek has hovered between the sacred and the ridiculous and I want a sign, a small assurance. Standing in front

of the white eagle jumpsuit, all mannequined and upright, I'm
waiting. But a large woman in a floral muu-muu stomps down
on my foot and I'm forced to continue on.

Plaques line the walls and gold albums gleam from glass cases
like museum artefacts. I'm most impressed with his book
collection—open pages reveal highlighted passages, circled words,
dog-eared pages. In front of the display, someone pushes me from
behind and it takes all my self-control not to shove back. I'm
squinting, trying to make out the title. I know his favourites
included Joseph Benner's *The Impersonal Life* and Paramahansa
Yogananda's *Autobiography of a Yogi*.

All along the tour, enlarged photographs of Elvis adorn the
walls. In one, he's looking up from a magazine in the barbershop,
a white cloth secured around his neck, eyebrows lifted in surprise,
forehead rumpled. He stares straight at the camera, straight at
me—who am I to be interrupting his haircut? In another, he's
leaning on the hood of a shiny white car with chrome detailing.
He's grabbing at the officer who's writing him a ticket but he's
looking at me. Everything else in the photograph—the brick
buildings and lit marquee—seems to fall away. Even when he's
posing next to his wife Priscilla, if he's looking at the camera, it's
like he's looking outside the photograph and I feel seen, as if Elvis
is seeing *me*. I'm not drawn to the ones where Elvis is looking
away; these don't hold the same power.

In my favourite, he's standing with his guitar, a strap holding
it high over his waist, but his hands are stuffed casually in his
pockets. He seems younger than he must have been, judging by
the sixties cut of his jacket, and he's laughing: somehow, I'm
included in the joke. Elvis and I are laughing at the world, laughing
at all these stupid tourists roaming along the roped pathway. I
have enough awareness to understand most people here probably
think Elvis is looking at them but I know they're wrong. He's
looking at me.

GRACELAND

Heather and Katherine arrive in Memphis that afternoon. They're friends from college who were on the fencing team with me but Heather, not fencing, is the central link. She's the kind of person who sends diligent emails and gift packages, the one who keeps track of what everyone's doing, the one who emailed me back in May, telling me I had to go to Graceland. She's also an Elvis fan.

Heather sped nonstop from Philadelphia to Baltimore where she joined Katherine. From there, the two drove the fourteen hours to Memphis in continuous shifts. We all look older: time is a circus mirror. Heather's brown hair is still stubbornly straight and Katherine's eyes are the same piercing blue, but both wear gold frames now and I can't remember the glasses they wore in college. When Heather laughs, I see her at age seventeen, a freshman running through épée drills in her fencing whites. Then she'll say something serious and I can imagine her at forty with kids. I'm not surprised that Katherine's older. She seemed too old for college even when we were there—like she was just biding her time, waiting to get out into the world while the rest of us were still figuring things out.

We're sitting in a diner drinking endless cups of coffee. Heather, Katherine and I huddle over the table, our accents bouncing off the plastic booth. Scott leans back with his feet in the aisle as though he's camped out on an airplane.

I hold up a plastic key ring. It has a photo of Scott and me standing in front of the fake Graceland gate. 'We felt the generosity of Elvis today.'

Heather scrunches up her shoulders and lets them drop loose. 'And?'

'He gave us a key ring.'

Just beyond the complex, after the Graceland tour, Scott and I had passed the display. Every photograph taken before the shuttle ride flashed up on a large television screen. In ours, my smile was thin, goofy, my long t-shirt unflattering. Scott was standing at an awkward angle that made his stomach seem huge—it was a bad photograph. Part of it was my vanity, part of it was my two tight fists, but I couldn't reconcile paying good money for a bad photograph taken in front of a two-dimensional backdrop. The thing was, that plastic key ring felt like an artefact, a piece of proof that we made it. After ten minutes of deliberation, the woman behind the counter pushed the key ring towards us, shaking her head. 'Just take it.'

Heather stretches her arm across the laminate and inspects the key ring. 'You know, there's not a lot of people our age who understand Elvis. There's a lot more to his music than people realise.' Her voice is even and it's hard for me to decipher her meaning. I can't tell if she's speaking with devout sincerity or having a laugh at Elvis's expense. She grins and it dawns on me she's doing both. I understand this inconsistency.

'You think?' Scott asks.

Heather continues: 'Yeah, of course there is. Take "Return to Sender". Is this a simple love song or something deeper?' She nods with all the conviction of a conspiracy theorist and I can't help giggling.

A waitress arrives carrying two pots of coffee and Scott downs his cup quickly for a value-for-money refill. I wait for her to leave. 'Like a message is encoded in the song?'

Heather nods.

Scott pipes up: 'Like don't trust the postal system.'

We pause, ignoring Scott, but try as I might, I can't come up with a deeper meaning to the song. 'What about "Baby Let's Play House". I reckon you could argue he's deconstructing notions of the nuclear family.'

'What do you mean?' Katherine asks.

'You know, like stable identities don't exist so the closest we can get to the nuclear family is through role-playing—let's "play" house?' I'm joking, sending up my attraction to Elvis. All of us sitting at the table are pilgrims for a mocked cultural icon. Our appreciation for the King defies rationality and good taste but it still exists and so our discussion is like ironic scaffolding—we're making fun of the obviously banal lyrics to hide the embarrassed devotion lurking beneath. Elvis was thoughtful but he wasn't an intellectual. Even if he had been, a few decades needed to pass before post-structural theory would be in vogue.

But whether I'm serious or not, my reference point here is the family: 'Baby Let's Play House'. It seems even when I'm joking, Elvis is connected to ideas of the familial—or its lack. Unable to sustain a nuclear family with Priscilla, Elvis was a talented, charismatic musician brought down by his addictions. And again I'm thinking of Michael Cosgrove: Elvis Presley is not the only one I'm romanticising.

Scott nudges me under the table. 'What do you think, Grove?'

My family terrain is about as stable as the empty cream containers that Heather is stacking along the edge of the table. I'm waiting for the teetering plastic tubs to collapse onto the pastel formica. 'Huh?'

'Ready for the bill?'

★

The final word from Elvis comes on August 15 when Scott and I join Heather and Katherine for the candlelight vigil. We were going to wait the rain out but in the end we don our parkas: the King waits for no one. Elvis Presley Boulevard is closed for the event—a queue zigzags back and forth in front of Graceland. Portable waist-high steel divides have been set up to corral us but still the line exceeds them. People carry national flags: Scotland, England, South Africa, New Zealand. In the midst of the foot traffic, a huge screen has been set up: Elvis in concert. The pixels are too big, the picture unclear, but it becomes the landmark—as the line moves, progress can be judged in relation to the display. Any departure for the facilities needs to be timed with the hairpin turns: duck under the rail, run to the toilet and return before the line's progressed too far.

The queue holds a certain sense of camaraderie. I recognise people from other events—the mother and daughter who sat near us at the Elvis fashion show are about ten metres ahead of us, holding hands. The impersonator who posed with me at Sun Studios scurries by and waves. When Scott returns from the restroom, he says he saw the grey-eyed father from the baseball game. Then there are religious devotees—the Christian clubs which have come to honour the King because of his gospel songs. And the country fans.

Heather smacks her lips. 'It's a wonder the gun lobbyists aren't represented.' I think of the bar in Natchez and the cousins who couldn't understand Australia.

After the novelty of being part of this eccentric group wears off, we're still four full bends away from the front gate. Scott steps back and forth to increase circulation. 'This is like watching grass grow.'

A short man in front of us jerks around at the blasphemy, the Elvis 'TCB' tattoo on his arm flexing, but after glancing up at Scott he must think better of defending Elvis because he turns back towards the gate.

'They take this stuff seriously,' Scott whispers to me.

'Be careful, I'm one of them.' I'm only partly joking and Scott nods, lifting an imaginary microphone to his mouth: 'It started on the Seattle pavement with a guitar—now look at her: she's growing sideburns.'

But even my enthusiasm has begun to wane when, three and a half hours later, we've only edged up to Graceland's front wall. The famous sandstone partition receives so many devoted messages that it's sandblasted clean each January to make way for the next year's onslaught of adoration. I like this temporality—words written over words written over words. The impermanence is probably a good thing as many of the notes lack basic spelling and grammar—'Your the King' is my favourite. Pilgrims ahead of us pass Scott a black marker and he signs his name on a clear corner before handing me the pen. The ink is running dry and anything that comes to mind seems inadequate. How can I summarise the past two months?

'What about "Seattle–Memphis 2002"?' Scott asks.

I write the words out, going over them with the blunted felt point. Next to me, a teenager has a smaller, newer pen. Her name is secure with strong, black ink: Alicia.

'Can I borrow that?'

She hands it to me and in a fit of madness I jot down 'Elvis, I love you', encircling the whole thing in a heart—not a small one, a big voluptuous one. Scott's shaking his head but I don't have time to retract it. The line's pushing us through the gates of Graceland.

The gates are famous for the two guitar-playing figures welded to the metal backdrop. Musical notes fill the space between them. Stepping across the threshold, I touch one of musicians—he's cold and slick. A woman hands us each a white candle and we take turns using the lighter, joining the string of flickering light. We still have to plod up the driveway and around to the meditation garden.

My legs are stiff from standing, my rain jacket pulled close in case the skies open up again. There is a delirium to the exhaustion, like the first time I stayed up all night. To my right, Heather is practising Elvis dance moves while Katherine claps her on. By the time we're halfway along the drive, it's almost one-thirty in the morning. The video screen is no longer visible but the Elvis numbers are now a quiet soundtrack for the procession—rock-and-roll lullabies. Beside us, the grounds are immaculately presented; the grass is lush and buoyant, the trees lean protectively overhead.

Heather and Scott are now bantering about sport in front of me and Katherine is talking about Elvis with a cute boy from Idaho. To our left, maybe thirty metres away—Graceland. Spotlights beam up from the ground, accentuating the entryway. The house seems more regal from this distance. No one is pushing for photographs; the view is entirely mine. I step off the driveway, away from the line. Leaves shift overhead in the slight breeze and the air smells new with rain. I'm just thinking that we made it, we finally made it, when a deep, honest voice resounds behind my shoulder: 'Shady. If you're drunk in Memphis and you need a place to stay, you can always crash on my lawn.'

I turn around, searching for the speaker. Directly behind me is empty space. A few metres away, a teenage couple have their arms around each other and a family lines up beyond them but neither group pays any attention to me. And it's not a stranger talking to me—I know the voice. It feels like it's from an early childhood memory but it's from the songs, the movies, the interviews: it's Elvis. Elvis is talking to me. I wait but nothing else follows.

I step back. 'Did you guys hear that?'

Scott and Heather look at me. 'What?'

I don't think it's a joke but I scan the crowd for hidden cameras. 'Elvis. Did you just hear him?'

In retrospect, maybe I should have kept quiet. It's enough to know it happened, I don't need anyone else to validate it. But I've already spoken and Scott and Heather are peering at me.

'What?'

'I just heard him. He just spoke to me.'

Heather watches me sceptically. 'What'd he say?'

You'd think if I was going to have a spiritual experience with the King it might have involved a message with a bit more meaning but I'm willing to take whatever I get. 'He told me I'm safe here. I can crash anytime.'

Scott wants details. 'At Graceland?'

'Around abouts.'

'What do you mean?'

'He said I could crash on his lawn.'

Heather clearly enunciates each syllable: 'Crash on his lawn?'

'If I was drunk.'

Again, her voice is precise and her American accent strong as she repeats my words.

'I didn't have any control over what he'd say.'

It doesn't take a sceptic to come up with an explanation. I was exhausted. Maybe I fell asleep for a brief moment and dreamed it. Maybe in my excitement, I overheard someone else and misconstrued the meaning. But right then I didn't really care: I heard Elvis and he told me I was safe.

Heather continues: 'What are his security guards going to say when you tell them you've been given an explicit invitation?'

In a moment of third-person perspective, I see Shady being escorted from Elvis Presley Boulevard. The camera pans out and she's carrying a sleeping bag. 'But, officers, Elvis told me, he told me I could stay.' It's a little too close to Las Vegas for my liking.

Scott tries to squeeze my waist. 'I think you're making it up.'

'Think whatever you want. Elvis had his own visions, you know.'

Heather nods. 'That's true. Outside Flagstaff—saw Jesus in a cloud.'

The line shifts forward and we follow the crowd through a corridor of signs and offerings set up along the driveway from the world's Elvis fan clubs—the American ones are separated by state, the international ones listed alphabetically. I forget to look for Australia until we're halfway along and I'm too tired to double back.

Through the gate, the graves—of Elvis, Gladys and Jesse—are piled with flowers and gifts, letters, jewellery, stuffed animals. The colours are bright and festive, despite the eerie solemnity of the occasion. Two women in front of me are crying and I notice that I'm crying, too. I guess any chance of anthropological objectivity was lost when I heard Elvis. Standing there, directly in front of his grave, I think suddenly and fiercely of Lisa Marie. What is she doing right now? Is she inside Graceland, peering out through the curtains, watching us pay our respects? Maybe she waits for the last pilgrim to leave and the gate to close, then walks barefoot along the covered walkway with her own offerings. Maybe she'll push the gifts aside and lie down, curved towards him like a baby, resting beside her father.

My fingers clench the artwork of the dancing woman, given to me that first day I was busking in Seattle. The photograph is creased but I lean down and place it on the pile.

At the bottom of the driveway, as we're leaving, Heather blows out her candle. Scott, Katherine and I follow suit. I glance at mine as the smoke trails away.

Scott looks at me. 'You know, that *is* a little weird.'

'What?'

Scott holds up his candle; it's not much more than a stub. The white wax has burned down. He gestures to mine: 'Almost new.'

My candle is at least three times taller than his. The wick is charred but the tall column hasn't burned.

'Did you blow it out at all? Earlier, I mean?'

'No, I've been with you the whole time.' A few clumsy drips mar the side but mine is indisputably bigger than Scott's.

At the bottom of the driveway, we take turns posing for photographs. My parka is like a plastic tent billowing around me, my hair slicked back with rain. Katherine snaps a picture of the three of us, then hands the camera to Heather.

'Here, let me get you guys,' Scott says. We get every combination and then a passing Elvis fan takes one of the four of us.

We go through the process again with Heather's camera. Only later, after Heather and Katherine have returned home and developed their pictures, we discover that in all of their shots taken that night, I'm surrounded by white light. Everyone else looks normal—the three of them, the strangers in the background— but my face is beaming through an effervescent aura.

The night after the vigil the Memphis Pyramid Arena has sold out for the first time ever and it's been done by a dead man. Heather and Katherine have already ordered their tickets online for the 25th Anniversary Elvis Concert but Scott and I thought we could get them in town. We're out of luck, no more are available.

'Elvis will see us in,' Scott says. 'After all, you're on such close terms with him.'

I play my repertoire down the street, about five hundred metres from the Pyramid. I'm beneath a concrete overpass where the road is blocked off. Empty lanes wait overhead but the roadworks have been abandoned. It's a good spot because it's right between a large parking lot and the arena—hundreds of Elvis fans have to walk past me.

'What if they ask for songs I don't know?'

Scott bends down, making sure my sign is angled properly. 'You'll be fine.'

He strides towards the venue to see if any tickets are being sold on the street and in the next hour I make my best earnings since Austin, with more than one five-dollar note appearing amid the change. It seems like a good sign but I glance at my watch: the show is just starting and Scott hasn't returned. A woman with a sparkling silver dress and stiletto heels clips by, urging her overweight husband to keep up. After them, the street is quiet.

It's a lonely night with everyone inside, rocking out to Elvis. I hum through 'Heartbreak Hotel' in honour of its writer, Mae

Axton, and then pack the guitar up and sit on the kerb, which is still warm from the afternoon sun.

Ten minutes later, Scott appears down the street, running towards me. The urgency means he got tickets and this bolts me up. I'm whooping and grabbing the guitar at the same time, then sprinting as fast as I can towards him.

'We're in the rafters, but we're in.'

Scott takes the guitar and we leg it to the Pyramid, checking the instrument at the front desk. Music is pounding inside but in our excitement we can't find the right entry gate. The corridors are wide and unending—we keep retracing our steps, staring at the markers above the doors. 'Where's section 232?'

Finally, we climb the right staircase and enter the dark arena. An usher with a pencil-thin flashlight shows us to our row. As we inch through the aisle to our seats, I glance down at the stage, trying to pinpoint the band members below. My foot catches on someone's handbag and I fall into Scott. The owner of the handbag doesn't notice: she's singing as loud as she can to 'Jailhouse Rock'. Onstage, members of Elvis's original bands are playing. There's a screen three storeys tall set up behind them, stretching to the top of the arena. It's showing film clips and movie excerpts. Every time the opening chords begin, there's another sweep of noise across the stadium. I try to focus both on the people onstage and the man, twenty times larger than life, singing to us from the screen.

Then Priscilla comes onstage wearing all white. Her image is enlarged into mega-pixel proportions on the screen behind her.

'I'd like to thank you all for honouring Elvis Presley. I know people are here from all over the world.'

Scott and I shout in agreement.

'I can't tell you how much it would mean to him to know that.'

She continues and the audience is silent, listening. I find myself staring at her, trying to merge the woman in front of me with all the photographs I've seen of her. I think how young she was when she met Elvis—fourteen years old, half my age.

'I'd like now to welcome Lisa Marie.'

Lisa Marie struts out onstage wearing a black suit. The paternal resemblance is eerie: there's no question she's her father's daughter. Her cheekbones rest at the same angle. Her eyes are catlike, hidden beneath a strong brow. But it's her mouth that resonates the most—her lips form the same sexy snarl. Lisa Marie has a handsome face.

'I'm going to play a song tonight about my father.'

We scream in support but she's nervous. She doesn't look straight at the crowd. It's as though she's pretending we aren't here—she's actually alone, in her bedroom.

'I know I'm crazy playing this to such a hard audience,' she says. We holler again, supportive, but she's right. She's taking a big risk: we're here for her father. We are the dedicated mass in the full throes of worship. The unconditional love we feel for him is the stuff of fanaticism. She could be eaten alive.

'But I thought if I could be understood anywhere . . .' Again, we scream. We do understand loving Elvis Presley, we do understand feeling grief at his death. But we don't understand having to grapple with him as a person, as a father. Who could possibly relate to having Elvis Presley as a dad? He was a man of godly and profane proportions—an entertainer who stirred millions and died on the toilet. He embodied it all: generosity and excess; insistent poverty and mad wealth; the luck of the famous and the curse of the mortal. I wonder at the woman-girl onstage below us—who on earth could possibly understand what she's been through?

Lisa Marie turns around like she's suddenly realised what she's done, where she is. I like her for the fear on her face—even if her song is appalling, I'm going to support her. I clap my hands together, cupping them slightly so they boom a deep, hearty applause.

'Everyone has their version of my father. Here's mine.'

She sings along with the words that flash up on the screen. The song 'Nobody Noticed It' lacks charisma. The melody isn't daring. The background music could be playing behind any top-40 radio hit but the story is clear like a window so clean you tap the glass to be sure it exists. The story of being Elvis's daughter, of losing him on August 16, 1977, when she was only nine years old. She'd had to piece together a version of her father from stories she'd been told. And now she's ready to claim her own story. It's not a defensive act or one of retribution, simply a matter of voice and perspective.

I start crying. At first they're quiet, seeping tears, but within a few seconds they're honking and convulsive. There's nothing attractive about the spectacle—my mouth is smeared with saliva; I can feel red blotches breaking out on my cheeks. When my sleeves are too damp from blowing my nose, Scott offers a corner of his shirt.

In a subsequent review of Lisa Marie's album *To Whom It May Concern*, Carly Carioli would report: 'She has lived the kind of life that invites armchair psychoanalysis: a life in which her father, and his absence, appear to have played a more profound role than any fiction writer would ever allow.' And I get that absence. I get how much of a presence it can be and in this moment with Lisa Marie onstage she becomes suddenly real—her father, her celebrity marriages to Michael Jackson and Nicolas Cage, her public support of Scientology—all of the details as flippant as the magazines I'd read them in. But here, in front of us, she is determined to live beyond her myth. Carioli goes on to say: 'For her part, Lisa Marie . . . is unwilling . . . to cede responsibility over her life to a ghost.' In some weird and wacky way, I understand—it's about responsibility, claiming your version of your life, and no one else can do this for you.

As I'm crying, Lisa Marie steps back and Priscilla takes the microphone: 'We have a treat for you tonight.' A white limousine enters from the back of the auditorium, pulling slowly along a red carpet to the stage.

'Do you think that's Elvis? Do you think he's come back?' I ask Scott, distracted for a moment from my snotty display. I've finished the biography—I was too young to remember his death in 1977 and reading those final chapters felt like I was watching him die, reading him to death. But the hall echoes with shrieks and clapping and catcalls, and the anticipation defies logic. Maybe he's sitting behind those tinted windows, watching us. Maybe all of those conspiracy theories were only conspiring with a truth— Elvis in Mexico, Elvis as a mechanic, Elvis in a retirement home. Everything about this journey has been worth it to be here in this exact moment where I really do believe it's possible that Elvis is still alive.

The door opens. The arena swells with noise.

And then suddenly, as though he'd leapt from the Cadillac to the stage, Elvis Presley appears on the large screen. The clips are taken directly from concert footage so it's like Elvis is really here in front of us.

My voice joins in, screaming. Scott watches me yelling and crying, and smiles towards the screen like he's sharing a joke with Mr Presley.

The gospel section separates the early and late Elvis numbers but my favourite songs are those from the '68 Comeback concert when he sings directly to the girls perched onstage. Elvis is in his early thirties: his chest is fit; his legs almost too thin; his face both charming and carnal, gleaming with sweat.

When the first image appears of Elvis in a jumpsuit, the crowd goes mad. During clips from the Aloha concert, I think of the father at the baseball game and his kids guessing the date of this performance—they're probably somewhere in this throng, watching. I'm still crying, now in relief: we've made it. Whatever I needed to do in Graceland, I'm doing it.

It's a concert that defies its three-hour lifespan. It seems impossible that the stage will be broken down, that basketball games could be played or wholesale carpet shows held in the same space. It really seems as if Elvis could live forever. This sense of magic is cemented when we hear the remixed version of 'A Little Less Conversation'. The song pulses from the stage, its video clip reminiscent of 'Jailhouse Rock'. My feet tap ferociously to the heavy bass line. In 2002, Elvis is still topping the charts.

After singing 'An American Trilogy', Elvis leaves the screen. The audience calls out, shouting, hoping for an encore. But the door to the limo opens and, after a moment, closes. The Cadillac backs out of the arena smoothly. When it disappears, a deep voice booms over the sound system: 'Elvis has left the building.'

★

We stand just to the left of the entrance that funnels people into the warm Tennessee night. Heather and Katherine had tickets towards the front of the stage—they'll be a while yet. My case is open, the Martin hanging around my chest by its strap, my fingers in position for 'Hound Dog'.

This is the last stop on our journey, my final performance. The Elvis fans push past me into the wet-hazed night with a force that's both exhilarating and anticlimactic. In the place where I thought it would matter most, I've lost any need to prove myself. Something about the concert, the release that came with crying, has freed me from Elvis and there's an independence to my playing, as if the only person listening is me.

Scott is standing beside me, staring out at the crowd. When he speaks, his voice is too casual, wafting towards the street. 'We're here in the States. It's really okay if you want to visit him.'

The air is steamy. People are singing and calling out, unworried by the increasing rain. I shift backwards, under the concrete awning, to protect my guitar. 'Who? Elvis?'

'Your father.'

'Michael Cosgrove?' Only in a family with three fathers would this clarification be necessary.

Scott nods and I realise he's been waiting since New Orleans to bring this up again. He steps in close. 'We have time, you know. We could track him down if you wanted.'

My right hand holds a pick—in my final hurrah, I've decided to shout the Big Mama Thornton number. I stare out at the starless night and think about Scott's question. When Irene and Mike first married, he didn't like her to have friends. So when Patty and Leonard came over for dinner, he climbed beneath the brightly patterned rug and rolled back and forth, moaning. It's an absurd image—one that almost makes me laugh until I think of how awkward my mother must have felt, her guests reaching for their coats while the casserole waited, untouched, in the oven.

About the same time, Mike used to wake Serena up in the middle of the night and sit her in front of the television to watch the nature channel. When the show was finished, he'd grill her on antelope eating patterns and punch her for wrong answers.

I've heard these stories but I have my own. It waits at the bottom of my memory chest, beneath the visions of driving trains and playing ukuleles. I've overlooked it—some part of me convinced it was irrelevant, unnecessary—but since Scott and I landed at the Portland bus station, I've remembered more of that night at Mike's townhouse when we were playing musical instruments. Something must have happened—maybe Serena had tried to call Irene, maybe I'd refused to eat my dinner—because my sister rushed me into the bathroom and locked the door. I remember our father's weight punching against the plywood, his voice slamming insults. Serena was sitting on the ledge of the bathtub, holding me, and I stared at the dark brown shower tiles, praying he wouldn't break through the door, knowing even at four years old that the bathroom is the most dangerous room in a house because of its hard ceramic edges.

I don't need to visit him—my reckoning has already happened, I realise. On this journey, I may have been drawing parallels between my father and the King, but Michael Cosgrove is not Elvis, even if his middle name is King. Michael is a coin with two sides: father and monster. I keep flipping it in hopes of seeing the presidential face but it doesn't exist without the monster on the back, grinning through the silver. And absence isn't so bad.

The absence of Michael Cosgrove led to the presence of my strong
bonds with Irene and Serena; it led to my stepfathers Garry and
Jim. The absence of America opened the space for Australia. It's
not always ideal but absence is never alone.

I start in on 'Hound Dog'.

★

The morning after the anniversary concert is moist with heat
when we arrive for the five-kilometre Elvis Fun Run. Hundreds
of runners are milling around, all wearing the same commemorative
t-shirt that came free with registration.

We wait in a parking lot off Elvis Presley Boulevard. The
earnest festivity of the night before has been replaced by an
energetic countdown: forty minutes until the race starts, thirty
minutes, twenty minutes . . . Runners pose in flamingo stances,
stretching their quadriceps. Others are drinking coffee out of
jumbo-sized mugs or eating free doughnuts.

'You ready?' Scott motions towards the starting area in front
of Graceland. We're lined up when the gun sounds, cracking
through the air. The crowd builds forward momentum but we're
all slow, wading through the muggy air. An Elvis impersonator
next to me wipes the sweat off his forehead and fans the neck of
his jumpsuit.

My walkman is turned up as loud as it can go, the first
number—'That's All Right'. My feet keep time with Bill's bopping
bass line. I want to dance along the street, shifting my hips and
jumping up when Elvis reaches crescendo but the heat is debilitat-
ing and I didn't get much sleep after the concert. The music seems
to be sweating into my ears. My feet plod faithfully, staying on
Scott's tail for the first kilometre until he pulls ahead.

The second kilometre is the hardest—the thrill of running
with Elvis fans has worn off and most of the race is still ahead.
Elvis's neighbours are lined up on the street, passing out glasses
of water and spraying down eager runners with hoses. I press stop

on my walkman—some of the houses have Elvis songs belting from the windows to urge us along.

After the emotional night at the concert, it's like I'm undergoing a physical equivalent, each step bringing me closer to some corporeal revelation, one that will only become apparent in the future—in five months' time, Michael King Cosgrove will die at the age of fifty-nine. According to police reports, he was changing a tyre by the side of the freeway and suffered a heart attack.

My grief will surprise me, and I'll imagine him pulling to the side of the road—a road we'd driven along on that first stint from Seattle to Portland. It's a stormy night. Maybe he throws off his seatbelt and clambers out quickly—the outside air wet, the jack under the rim, his large hands turning the handle. I can see the red Toyota pick-up lifting slowly from the ground, levitating. The rain slows but the spray whips up from cars and buses rushing past.

No one stopped to help him. It's this detail that seems the saddest. It makes me think of the bus driver in Las Vegas who talked about whether we were a generous country and the importance of little kindnesses. It makes me wonder what the United States has become. I may have written brash short stories that celebrated his death but I would never wish a lonely street on anyone.

I don't regret my decision not to visit Michael Cosgrove; there would have been too much hope and expectation on my part. Maybe that's the power of parents: despite everything, we still hope they want us. And whatever I might have gleaned from seeing him wouldn't be worth ransoming Shady, aged seven, waiting at the end of the driveway.

On our last night in Memphis, Scott and I borrow our hosts' four-door sedan and veer south. My hand grips the Paul Simon mix tape and slides it into the mouth of the cassette player, pressing rewind.

On the I-240 highway, Scott flicks the indicator on, shifting into the right-hand lane that feeds onto Elvis Presley Boulevard. It's raining gently. This is our last trip to the complex: we'll be boarding an early flight the next morning to San Francisco for Amy's wedding and then we'll spend a few months on Vashon. After that, our tickets will take us back to Australia.

I've been thinking about returning to Australia and what exactly that means. As most immigrants can testify, 'home' is a surprisingly complicated word for one syllable. Australia is my conscious home, the place I choose, the place that makes the most sense to me, but the United States will always be my homeland. One can't exist without the other. Living in Australia has influenced my understanding of the States, and yet I couldn't have ended up in Australia without following the path that led me there, the path that started on Vashon with Irene and Serena. This pilgrimage has shown me where I'm from—my country, my family—and I feel a quiet resolve because of that. Living in Australia, I'll miss Irene and Serena, and that tenderness will always feel a bit like heartbreak. But every time the clouds are low on the horizon, threatening to rain, the air will remind me of Vashon and they won't seem so far away.

The light industrial strip out to the great mansion is now familiar. Houses are quaint, built right on the street before it grew so many lanes.

Scott shifts gear. 'Almost there.'

The tape stops rewinding and a button pops up; the front speakers hum as the tape leads in. When we pull past the front gates, the percussive introduction is still playing and this frustrates me. I want Paul Simon's lyrics yelling through the car, the 'Graceland' reprise as a soundtrack—this is our drive-by closing shot—but a large truck is bearing down on us and there's no space to pull over. A couple of scattered devotees stand at the wall, scrawling messages for the King in the dim streetlight. The famous gates are closed—the wire figures holding their instruments in a triumphant display—but without the throngs of people, the sidewalk seems forlorn. Someone has dismantled the large screen and steel dividers.

We've already passed the estate. My head is craning back for last glimpses when the vocals cut in.

Scott slows down. 'Turn around?'

Before I have a chance to reply, he pulls into a petrol station.

This time, no one is behind us so we inch along the street in second gear. The house isn't visible but the grounds are illuminated, the trees welcoming in the focused light. Scott slows for a pedestrian crossing the street and the mansion is already behind us. I twist around, peering through the back window. 'Again?'

Scott smiles dutifully and turns left at the next intersection. The song is still playing, building to the climax, when my boyfriend starts in. His voice is loud and unabashed and off-key. I join him and we're both belting out the chorus, singing with all the air our lungs can muster about poor boys and pilgrims who are journeying to Graceland.

I'm watching Scott. His head's moving back and forth to the music and I understand how lucky I am. I'm not driving with an imagined ideal in Truth or Consequences or sitting next to a man wearing a blindfold. Somehow, by the grace of God, I've managed to escape my family legacies. My left foot is propped on the front dash, tapping in time to the powerful underbeat, and when Scott trails off, I call out even louder: 'I've a reason to believe . . .'

After we pass the iconic residence for a third time, Scott pulls up onto the sidewalk; there's a gap in the traffic—he's poised for a U-turn. If I needed to, we could drive back and forth in front of this mansion all night.

'It's okay—we've been received,' I tell Scott, and he eases onto the road.

AUTHOR'S NOTE

I've referred to notes taken along the journey and double-checked this manuscript with friends and family who were also witness to the events described. Because this trip was reconstructed after the fact, there may be details that don't coincide (and sometimes our versions differed), however every effort has been made to ensure an accurate and truthful representation. Sometimes memory has not coincided with verifiable fact—for instance newspaper accounts (complete with photographs) detail Lisa Marie as wearing white and Priscilla as wearing black at the 25th Anniversary Concert. Despite this, I clearly remember Lisa Marie in black and Priscilla in white—as does Heather—and represented it accordingly. With discrepancies such as this, I've tried to be as truthful to my memory as the integrity of the story would allow.

Sometimes I've made discoveries that impacted the very way I considered this journey. For instance, on December 9, 2005— more than three years after the trip had taken place—I called the Greyhound Operations Supervisor Gary Hahn to enquire about the Portland bus terminal, our first stop on the journey. It turned out the terminal I thought I remembered—the one that was pivotal in triggering memories of Michael Cosgrove—was not actually constructed until 1985, well after the events I remembered took place. It's certainly possible some of the items from the original bus station were shifted into the new one and these might have triggered my memory (indeed, Gary thought there could have been similar black plastic chairs with coin-operated televisions, and the Greyhound logo was reminiscent of the old one). But this discrepancy makes me wonder if I subconsciously 'remembered' the bus station as a way to remember my father. Weirdly, though, I could accurately describe the toilet stalls and sinks before stepping foot in the bathroom.

And finally, some names—especially those of people I met while travelling but could not contact for permission—have been changed for reasons of privacy.

Quoted material

Pages vii, 6–7 and 237: Paul Simon's 'Graceland'. Copyright © 1986 Paul
Simon. Lyrics used by permission of the publisher: Paul Simon
Music.

Page 8: The Alex Gregory cartoon 'Graceland Tours Ironic/Non-ironic',
originally published in *The New Yorker* (25 December 2000), can
be viewed at www.cartoonbank.com.

Page 41: Peter Guralnick. 1994. *Last Train to Memphis*. Abacus:
London, p. 121. © Peter Guralnick 1994. Extract from *Last Train
to Memphis* reprinted by kind permission of Little, Brown Book
Group.

Pages 104 and 126–7: Peter Guralnick. 1999. *Careless Love*. Abacus:
London, pp. xii and 195. © Peter Guralnick 1998. Extracts from
Careless Love reprinted by kind permission of Little, Brown Book
Group.

 Last Train to Memphis and *Careless Love* were of inestimable
use to me in writing this book. If you're interested in more
information on Elvis's life, I cannot recommend them enough.

Pages 126–7: Thank you to Larry Geller for his permission to relay the
story of Elvis's spiritual vision in Arizona. For further information
on Elvis's spiritual life and the vision briefly described here, see
Larry Geller. 2008. *Leaves of Elvis' Garden*, Bell Rock Publishing:
Beverly Hills.

Page 158: Kays Gary in 'Elvis Defends Low-Down Style', *Charlotte Observer*, 27 June 1956. Excerpt reprinted with permission from the *Charlotte Observer.* Copyright owned by the *Charlotte Observer*.

Page 162: *Memphis World*, 23 June 1956 and 6 July 1957, cited in Peter Guralnick, *Last Train to Memphis*, p. 370.

Pages 214–15: Jim Kingsley, 'Christmas to Elvis Means "Just Home"', *Memphis Commercial Appeal Mid-South Magazine*, 25 December 1966. Excerpt reprinted with permission. Copyright owned by the *Memphis Commerical Appeal Mid-South Magazine.*

Page 230: Excerpts from Carly Carioli's 'Royal Flush' reprinted with permission from the Boston Phoenix Inc. US Copyright belongs to the Boston Phoenix Inc. See http://www.bostonphoenix.com/boston/music/top/documents/03001017.htm.

Other references

Daniel Cavicchi. 2000. 'Seeing Elvis' in *American Quarterly*. Vol. 52, no. 4.

For references on Australian migration, view: http://www.abs.gov.au/ausstats/abs@.nsf/0/126fb11985123abdca2569ee0015d893?OpenDocument and http://www.abs.gov.au/websitedbs/D3110122.NSF/0/9F0F35D8A83A0AD2CA256D4A00016A56?Open.

For references on Australians and firearms, view the Australian Government's Trends and Issues in Crime and Criminal Justice web page: http://www.aic.gov.au/publications/tandi2/tandi269t.html.

For references on Americans and firearms, view the *Harvard University Gazette*'s web page: http://www.hno.harvard.edu/gazette/2000/09.28/firearms.html.

Chapter song titles

'A Little Less Conversation'. Performed by Elvis Presley, released in 1968. Written by Billy Strange and Mac Davis.

'All Shook Up'. Performed by Elvis Presley, released in 1957. Written by Otis Blackwell and Elvis Presley.

'America the Beautiful'. Performed by Elvis Presley, released in 1977. Words by Katharine Lee Bates, music composed by Samuel A Ward.

'Blue Hawaii'. Performed by Elvis Presley on the *Blue Hawaii* soundtrack, released in 1961. Written by Leo Robin and Ralph Rainger.

'Graceland'. Performed by Paul Simon, released in 1986. Written by Paul Simon.

'Guitar Man'. Performed by Elvis Presley, released in 1968. Written by Jerry Reed.

'Heartbreak Hotel'. Performed by Elvis Presley, released in 1956. Written by Mae Boren Axton, Thomas Durden, and Elvis Presley.

'How Can You Lose What You Never Had?' Performed by Elvis Presley on the *Clambake* soundtrack, released in 1967. Written by Ben Weisman and Sid Wayne.

'Lady Madonna'. Performed by Elvis Presley on the *Walk a Mile in My Shoes—70s Masters* CD Boxed Set, released in 1995. Written by John Lennon and Paul McCartney.

'Little Sister'. Performed by Elvis Presley, released in 1961. Written by Doc Pomus and Mort Shuman.

'Long Lonely Highway'. Performed by Elvis Presley, released in 1965. Written by Doc Pomus and Mort Shuman.

'Memories'. Performed by Elvis Presley, released in 1969. Written by Billy Strange and Mac Davis.

'Suppose'. Performed by Elvis Presley on the *Speedway* soundtrack, released in 1968. Written by George Goehring and Sylvia Dee.

'Suspicious Minds'. Performed by Elvis Presley, released in 1969. Written by Mark James.

'That's All Right'. Performed by Elvis Presley, released in 1954. Written by Arthur Crudup.

'Viva Las Vegas'. Performed by Elvis Presley, released in 1964. Written by Doc Pomus and Mort Shuman.

'(You're the) Devil in Disguise'. Performed by Elvis Presley, released in 1963. Written by Bernie Baum, Bill Giant and Florence Kaye.

SPECIAL THANKS

Thank you to everyone who provided hospitality or guidance on this journey. Sometimes this took the form of offering a floor to sleep on. Other times it involved a willingness to dive into (sometimes unsavoury) aspects of our family history. And back in Australia, it involved support during the writing process. Thank you.

Scott, Irene, Serena, Jim, Garry, Grace, Lucas, Brooks, Carolyn, the Bazleys, Amy and Jesse Pearson, Daniel, Aimee, Lockett Allbritton (and her parents Karla and Joe), Ben and the Mountain Shop, Vanessa Badham, Dorothy, Jeff, Shirley, Guy, Celia, Jo Curtis Lester, Wendell, John, Susie, Billy, Edith, Sam and Jenny Compton, Heather, Kristin, Linda Meyns, Wes Chung, Stephanie Snell Caine, Tamryn Bennett, Bridget Price, Sally Evans, Lisa Sewell, Yasmin Tadditch, Adrienne Foster, Emily De Jonge, Libby, John Purvis, Chrissy Howe, Colin Dray, Robert Peet, Tom Wayman, Jill Jones, Tony Macris, John Scott, Alan Wearne, Nick Hartgerink, Anne Cawsey and Peter Guralnick.

Thanks to Annette Barlow, Catherine Milne, Clara Finlay, Dominic Rolfe, Josh Durham and Jo Jarrah, at Allen & Unwin, and Lyn Tranter, my agent, for their faith and guidance. Thank you to Vogel's for their support of young Australian writers.

Thanks for support from the School of Journalism and Creative Writing at the University of Wollongong and the Humanities Research Centre at the Australian National University.

Thank you, too, to Irene's Tiles at www.irenes-tiles.com.

Also, thanks to Andy and Molly, who visited me in Australia and generously shared their recollections of Michael Cosgrove. For structural reasons, I have not detailed these conversations but they were invaluable to me throughout the writing process.

And musically: Paul Simon, Mark Knopfler, Ani Difranco and, of course, Elvis Presley.